English Tense and Aspect in Halliday's Systemic Functional Grammar

Discussions in Functional Approaches to Language

Series Editors: Christopher Butler, Honorary Professor, University of Wales, Swansea; Robin P. Fawcett, Emeritus Professor, Cardiff University

Editorial Board: John Bateman (University of Bremen); Joan Bybee (University of New Mexico); Huang Guowen (Sun Yat-sen University); Lachlan Mackenzie (Free University of Amsterdam); Jim Martin (University of Sydney); Jan Nuyts (University of Antwerp); Mick Short (Lancaster University); Anna Siewierska (Lancaster University); Anne-Marie Simon Vandenbergen (Ghent University); Michael Stubbs (University of Trier); Gordon Tucker (Cardiff University); Robert van Valin (University of New York at Buffalo)

The books in this series are addressed to university teachers, researchers and postgraduate students of linguistics as well as bright undergraduate readers. The books are short (normally 150–200 pages) and readable but scholarly. They are all published in paperback, so ensuring a flow of lively books on central topics in functional linguistics that are within the financial reach of the intended readership.

The purpose of the series is to meet the need for a forum for discussing theoretical issues in functional approaches to language that are too large for publication in journal article form. It also welcomes descriptions of areas of language that are too large for journal publication – and works that combine both theory and description. While the series complements *Advances in Cognitive Linguistics* (also an Equinox series), it welcomes works that are both functional and oriented to the cognitive aspects of language use.

Books in this series therefore typically present and evaluate new work in theory or description or both. But they may also offer a critique of one or more previously published works of these types. In all cases, however, authors are expected to survey the relevant alternative approaches, and to say which they see as the most promising one, and why. Books in this series therefore always give reasons for preferring one position to another rather than simply describing a position – as in all good discussions.

Published:

The Development of Scientific Writing: Linguistic Features and Historical Context, David Banks

Forthcoming:

Alternative Architectures for Systemic Functional Linguistics: How do we Choose?, Robin P. Fawcett

Process Types and Participant Roles in the English Clause: A New Systemic Functional Approach, Amy Neale

The Structure of Modern Irish: A Functional Account, Brian Nolan

English Tense and Aspect in Halliday's Systemic Functional Grammar

A Critical Appraisal and an Alternative

Carl Bache

LONDON   OAKVILLE

Published by Equinox Publishing Ltd.
UK: Unit 6, The Village, 101 Amies St., London SW11 2JW
USA: DBBC, 28 Main Street, Oakville, CT 06779
www.equinoxpub.com

First published 2008

British Library Cataloguing-in-Publication Data
A catalogue record for this book is available from the British Library.

ISBN-13   978 1 84553 351 9   (hardback)
           978 1 84553 354 0   (paperback)

Library of Congress Cataloging-in-Publication Data
Bache, Carl, 1953-
   English tense and aspect in Halliday's systemic functional grammar : a critical appraisal and an alternative / Carl Bache.
      p. cm. — (Discussions in functional approaches to language)
   Includes bibliographical references and index.
   ISBN-13: 978-1-84553-351-9 (hb)
   ISBN-13: 978-1-84553-354-0 (pb)
1. Functionalism (Linguistics) 2. Halliday, M. A. K. (Michael Alexander Kirkwood), 1925-3. English language—Verb. I. Title.
   P147.B33 2008
   425'.6—dc22
                       2007048639

Typeset by S.J.I. Service, New Delhi
Printed and bound in Great Britain by Lightning Source UK Ltd, Milton Keynes, and Lightning Source Inc., La Vergne, TN

Contents

Preface

In 1998, while enjoying a research stay in Australia, I was invited by Jim Martin to give a talk on my work on tense and aspect in English at a Friday afternoon SFL seminar at Sydney University. At the time I knew only too well that Michael Halliday and Christian Matthiessen reject the adequacy and usefulness of operating with categories like aspect and action, in addition to tense, in the description of the traditional tense forms in English. But having put a lot of energy into constructing a model carefully sorting out the choice relations of finite English verb forms in terms of not only tense but also aspect and action (cf. e.g. Bache 1985 and 1997), I was rather hoping on that sunny Friday afternoon to be able to convince my audience (especially Christian, who was kind enough to attend the seminar) that it was high time to revise the standard SFL approach to tense, as put forth in Michael's *An Introduction to Functional Grammar* and supported by Christian in a number of publications. I failed miserably. I delivered my paper with what I thought was my usual gusto, and I was quite confident that my arguments had made an impression, but in the discussion afterwards it became abundantly clear that I was on a different planet, or spoke an entirely different language. I simply had not made sense to my distinguished audience. Imagine my humiliation: having spent most of my academic career on paradigmatic relations, I could not even get through to an audience of systemicists! On the spot I made a resolve: one day I would make them see the light.

A few years later, after a tedious period with many administrative chores, I tried again, this time at the ISFC in Lucknow. Michael was there, as always gracing the conference with his presence, and he listened to my (perhaps too) carefully studied rhetoric and took plenty of notes while I produced some really strong arguments against his recursive tense model (I remember being slightly worried at the keen scratching of his pen against the conference pad). I even plucked up the courage to suggest that the standard SFL tense description suffered from one or two disturbingly formalist features and that the model needed functional tuning. Again I was quite pleased with my own performance. Surely this time I had managed to raise more than an occasional eyebrow! However, in the ensuing brief 'discussion' time I again experienced a sense of displacement and utter failure. In the nicest possible way Michael told me he thought I was wrong and that I must have misunderstood his tense description. Unfortunately there was no time to go into details, and I didn't get a chance to respond to his very general remarks. Time was up and no one else was invited by the chair to comment on my paper or ask questions. Afterwards Michael and I had lunch together, sharing some fond memories and talking pleasantly about other things. In my misery, caused equally by the disappearance of my suitcase en route to India and my only too obvious lack of academic success at the conference, I was approached by Robin Fawcett, who always has a keen eye for dissidents. He suggested a new strategy: why didn't I work a bit on those arguments of mine and write a small book on the subject for his new Equinox series *Discussions in Functional Approaches to Language*? Well, to cut a long story short: here it is!

So this book is my third and most thorough attempt to reach out to the SFL community at large with my suggestions for a functional tuning of the SFL description of English tense and aspect. The enterprise would not have been possible without Michael's and Christian's remarkable achievements over the last decades. I remain for ever grateful to them, not only for our friendship, but for everything they have done for functional linguistics, and not least for providing a tense description worth improving. I am grateful also to Robin for inviting me to contribute to the series and for introducing me to the wonders of Cardiff School grammar. My sincere thanks also to Janet Joyce from Equinox Publishing, Chris Butler, who is the co-editor of the series, and my two anonymous referees for relevant criticism of the manuscript and for useful suggestions.

A number of friends and colleagues have been extremely helpful at various stages in the preparation of the manuscript, either by reading draft chapters or by discussing central issues with me, or both: Thomas Hestbæk Andersen, Steven Breunig, Niels Davidsen-Nielsen, Peter Harder, Kim Ebensgaard Jensen, Fritz Larsen, Steffen Nordahl Lund, Cindie Aaen Maagaard, Uwe Helm Petersen, Sonja Poulsen, Flemming Smedegaard, as well as numerous members of the national grammar network in Denmark. I owe a special debt of gratitude to Nina Nørgaard, who has offered detailed comments on several versions of the manuscript. They all deserve credit for any merit my book may have while I naturally remain responsible for any weaknesses.

Thanks are also due to the University of Southern Denmark and the Institute of Language and Communication for letting me carry out the major part of my project on English tense and aspect in systemic functional grammar. Although dark clouds are gathering on the horizon, my university has not yet given in completely to the commercialisation of research and the fierce restrictions on academic freedom introduced by the Danish government.

I am much indebted to Philip and Janet Bell, Phil Staines and Penny Rosier, Jim Martin and Sue Hood, Peter Collins, and Chihiro Kinoshita Thomsen, for making my research visit to Sydney in 2006 both beneficial and pleasurable. I also wish to thank the University of New South Wales, especially the School of Modern Language Studies and the Linguistics Department, for providing me with the opportunity to carry out my research in Sydney as a visiting professor. I am particularly grateful to the Carlsberg Foundation for generously supporting this phase of the project.

I have sorely missed the feedback I would have received from my parents if they had been alive. This is my first book without their loving support.

Finally I wish to thank my wonderful wife Hanne and our family for always being there for me and for helping me create a perfect balance between work and other pleasures. What would life be like without our two grandsons Adrian and Villads! This book is dedicated to them.

Carl Bache

1 Introduction

This book offers a critical examination of the standard description of tense and aspect in Halliday's Systemic Functional Linguistics (SFL) and suggests a new approach to these categories within a systemic functional framework. While SFL is developing very rapidly in its applications and in a number of theoretical derivations, many of Halliday's basic assumptions, as well as many of his descriptive tools and conventions, have remained largely the same for the last 25 years or so. There are really only minor revisions and alterations of the grammatical foundation in the second and third editions of Halliday's original (1985a) contribution to linguistics *An Introduction to Functional Grammar* (henceforth simply *IFG*, cf. Halliday (1994a) and Halliday and Matthiessen (2004)). Halliday's 'Sydney' version of SFL, as put forth in *IFG*, is thus in effect one of the most unchanging, intellectually conservative models on the modern linguistic scene, and while it is quite possibly this feature that accounts for its continuing success when it comes to applications to a number of important fields (such as education, literature, art, cultural studies, business communication, computer science, speech pathology, etc.), the curious reluctance among its main proponents to deal with possible weaknesses, problems and inconsistencies in its grammatical foundation may isolate the central theory intellectually and, in a worst-case scenario, eventually cause its grammar component to dwindle into relative insignificance. Perish the thought! Halliday's great work deserves a much better fate. A linguistic paradigm – a term which is most aptly used in connection with SFL – will survive and thrive only if its proponents continually seek to assess their own basic assumptions and descriptive apparatus in a thorough and critical manner. Criticism must come from within – a good example is here the 'Cardiff' version of SFL, cf. e.g. Fawcett (2000a) – or from scholars like myself who are genuinely sympathetic to Halliday's framework but who happen to be sceptical of some of the specifics. Linguists working within other paradigms are unlikely to provide the necessary input to the development and sophistication of SFL, and if they try, they probably will not receive much attention. Regrettably, interscholarly communication has its obvious limitations across different schools of linguistic thought. So the SFL community has a responsibility to save its standard grammar from scholarly inertia and stagnation and should welcome all endeavours to revitalise it. This is the more important because, as we shall see, the Sydney grammar is influenced by a number of disturbingly formalist features from the 1960s and 1970s and has not quite managed to live up to its own very explicitly formulated functionalist ambitions in all descriptive areas.

But why bother? Why not simply move on to other, more dynamic functional and cognitive theories of grammar? Well, because Halliday's version of SFL is not only one of the most comprehensive and detailed functional approaches to language, but it has developed a large number of useful applications, and it is based on some really sound principles and descriptive practices. I am here thinking especially of its focus on language usage and on whole texts (written as well as spoken), its broad conception of semantics (described in terms of metafunctional diversity), its recognition of the strong interrelationship between language and context (described in terms of register variables, genres and ideology), its insistence on the significance of grammatical systems in the analysis of language as purposeful behaviour (systems such as TRANSITIVITY, MOOD, THEME), and not least, the fact that it assigns a strong and explicit role to paradigmatic relations in language. In my view, SFL is most certainly a theory worth improving!

In this book I hope to be able to make a contribution to the much needed amendment and 'functional tuning' of the grammatical basis of SFL.[1] More specifically I want to subject Halliday's description of tense and aspect in *IFG* to a critical examination with a view to making this particular part of the grammar more adequate. Chapter 2 offers a detailed presentation of Halliday's categories of tense and aspect, and Chapter 3 is devoted to a critical scrutiny of his tense description with respect to both its theoretical implications and its empirical foundation. In Chapter 4, I describe various sources of inspiration and take my point of departure in the Cardiff school approach to tense and aspect, which differs significantly from Halliday's model in *IFG*, yet clearly conforms to systemic functional criteria more generally. In Chapters 5 and 6, I propose a new systemic functional description of tense and aspect and apply it to a broad range of data, including examples of tense usage in narration.

But let me first give you a brief outline of the central topic of this book: Halliday's approach of the tense category in English. Throughout this book I shall refer to this approach as 'the *IFG* approach' or 'the *IFG* model' even if some of the early descriptions actually precede the first edition of *IFG* (cf. Halliday 1976c and Matthiessen 1983, 1984). In the *IFG* model, tense in English is an **ideational** resource for construing time; more specifically, it belongs to the **logical** subtype of ideational meaning. Halliday and Matthiessen further hold that English tense is a basic, three-way system at **group rank**, providing a choice between 'past', 'present' and 'future', as in the following finite clauses, respectively:

(1a) Joan <u>won</u> the competition.

(1b) Nefertiti <u>believes</u> in justice.

(1c) Sandra <u>will leave</u> tomorrow.

The basic system of past, present and future is assumed to be **recursive**, thus allowing the speaker or writer, henceforth 'the **Performer**',[2] to make additional choices from the same system in order to derive more complex tense forms. The verbal groups in (2a) through (2d) below are hence viewed as the result of two or more choices from this basic system rather than as combinations of tense and other categories, such as aspect and phase (which many linguists outside SFL operate with in their descriptions of progressive and perfect forms):

(2a) This week Gerald <u>is singing</u> in the local church.

(2b) My brother <u>will be working</u> with her.

(2c) Dad <u>had been going to see</u> her for quite some time.

(2d) They <u>will have been going to have taken</u> a holiday.

According to the recursive interpretation of tense in the *IFG* model, the verbal groups in these examples are realisations of the following choice combinations: in (2a) 'present' has been selected twice, in (2b) both 'future' and 'present' have been selected once, in (2c) 'past' has been selected twice and 'future' once, and in (2d) both 'future' and 'past' have been selected twice (for this last example, see Halliday 1976c: 154). Below I shall return to the question of how the individual tense values are realised formally in the recursive cycle, as envisaged by Halliday and Matthiessen.

Halliday and Matthiessen consider the aspect category to be necessary or relevant only in descriptions where tense is viewed as a nonrecursive two-way system at word rank – a position they find untenable and misguided in the case of English tense. Instead Halliday employs the terms 'aspect', 'perfective' and 'imperfective' in the description of the distinction between the infinitive and the present participle. Thus, the underlined verbs in the following constructions are regarded as perfective:

(3a) He seems <u>to like</u> her.

(3b) Bob began <u>to cry</u>.

(3c) The first person <u>to speak</u> after the break was Sandra.

(3d) Jane saw Nigel <u>leave</u> the building.

(3e) <u>To reach</u> the monument, continue straight ahead.

By contrast, the underlined verbs in the following examples are held to be imperfective:

(4a) Henry kept <u>laughing</u>.

(4b) He stopped <u>smoking</u> cigars.

(4c) The first person <u>speaking</u> after the break was Sandra.

(4d) Jane saw Nigel <u>leaving</u> the building.

(4e) <u>Reaching</u> the monument, continue straight ahead.

(For discussion of some of these examples, see Halliday 1994a: 241, 278–282).

My reason for taking a fresh look at this description of tense and aspect is that I detect a possible discrepancy between Halliday and Matthiessen's very sound general functionalist intentions and the actual model they propose for English tense. Unlike most other current linguistic theories, SFL recognises the overriding importance of paradigmatic relations, or 'choice relations' in language (cf. e.g. Halliday 1976a, 1976b, 1994a), and I consider that absolutely vital in any attempt to offer a descriptively and explanatorily adequate account of English tense. As Matthiessen (1984: 9) says: 'I will concentrate on one aspect of systemic grammar: the paradigmatic organisation of grammar which comes from a *functional* view of grammar as a *resource* for achievement of higher-level purposes' (emphasis in original); and a bit further on he adds: 'When we see language as a resource, we are interested in the possibilities the resource gives a speaker in communication and the primary representation of these possibilities is the paradigmatic organisation' (1984: 9). These statements strike me as very sound and reasonable indeed, but having worked with the paradigmatics of verbal categories in English for many years myself, within a fairly eclectic post-Hjelmslevian era in Danish linguistics, I find it both puzzling and intriguing to see that Halliday and his closest associates arrive at results that are very different from mine. Although their description of tense and aspect in English is certainly attractive in some respects, it seems to me that it suffers from a number of weaknesses from a functional linguistic point of view. In fact, I am going to suggest that maybe Halliday and Matthiessen do not take the choice relations involved quite seriously enough. This, however, should not lead to a total rejection of SFL or any of its fundamental principles. On the contrary, I hope that the observations, arguments and analyses offered in this book may pave the way for a more adequate description of English tense within a systemic functional framework.

Notes

1. By talking of 'functional tuning' I want to indicate that I consider most of my suggestions in this book to be an attempt to *strengthen* the systemic functional orientation of the desciption of tense. In fact, I shall suggest that Halliday and Matthiessen do not take paradigmatic relations quite seriously enough.
2. In this book I use the Cardiff grammar convention of referring collectively to speakers and writers as **Performers** and to hearers and readers as **Addressees**, cf. e.g. Chapter 3 of Fawcett (2008).

2 An introduction to the *IFG* model of tense

2.1. Tense in English

As already indicated, Halliday and Matthiessen view tense in English as an ideational, more specifically logical, resource at group rank which is realised by means of either a single choice or a recursively generated series of choices from a basic tripartite system of tenses comprising 'past', 'present' and 'future'. They emphasise the following points in their presentation of this tense model:

(A) Choice relations

The notion of 'choice' is essential to an understanding of how tense works in English. In his early computationally inspired writings on tense, Matthiessen (1983, 1984) formalised this notion in terms of a 'chooser' mechanism in addition to the characteristic SFL system networks:

> Each choice point in the grammar (system, [...]) is assigned a choice mechanism, a so-called chooser (or choice expert). The chooser knows how to select among the alternatives of the choice point. It obtains the relevant information by presenting inquiries to the parts of the text generation system where conceptual information resides, for instance the knowledge base and text plans. We will call these other parts the environment of the grammar and its choosers [...] (1983: 375)

The various system networks proposed for English tense are relatively simple (for an example, see Figure 2.1) and leave implicit the precise operations of the chooser mechanism. However, whether or not the chooser concept is explicitly present in the formal apparatus, the point of the description is to show that any tensed construction in English is the realisation of one or more choices among paradigmatically related items. As pointed out in the Introduction, in a functional grammar it is obviously important to discuss the nature of the tense choices made in any given text: to arrive at a fully adequate description of the semantics of a tense it is essential to consider the Performer's motivation for choosing that particular tense instead of other options.

(B) The primary tense system in SFL

The primary tense system proposed by Halliday and Matthiessen is a fairly simple one, as we have seen. It is part of the MOOD system, it has **indicative** as its entry condition (cf. Figure 2.1, taken from Matthiessen 1983: 377), and it specifies the three options 'past', 'present' and 'future', all definable in terms of a bare 'precedence' relation between two time variables (Matthiessen 1983: 385):

'past': T_x precedes T_y $(T_x < T_y)$
'present': T_x neither precedes nor follows T_y $(T_x = T_y)$
'future': T_x follows T_y $(T_x > T_y)$

The subscripts $_x$ and $_y$ are conveniently replaced by numerals when the variables are reduplicated in a recursive process. In the final analysis, the time variables get specified as T_s (time of speech), T_r (relevance time) and T_e (event time), depending on the choices made. For example, if the Performer chooses only once from the system, as in the case of a simple 'past' (*She walked across the street*), T_s is assigned to T_y, and both T_r and T_e are assigned to T_x. If the Performer chooses a 'past in past' (see Subsection C below), T_r and T_e are differentiated as two different past times $(T_e < T_r < T_s)$: *She had already*

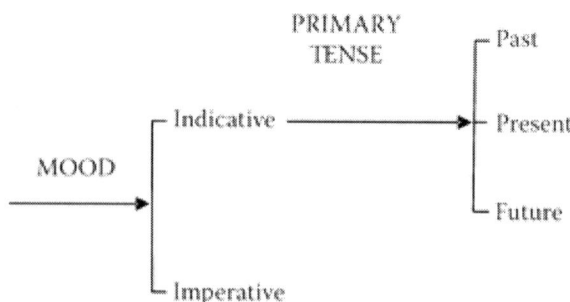

Figure 2.1: The basic *IFG* tense system.

walked across the street. The model is here greatly inspired by Reichenbach's work on tense logic (see Reichenbach 1947).

Note that the future tense is considered a primary tense along with the present and the past tense, and all three options are equipollently defined. Halliday and Matthiessen do not accept the frequent reduction in other tense descriptions of the traditional, Latin-inspired tense category (comprising e.g. 'present', 'future', 'imperfect', 'perfect' and 'pluperfect') to just two primary tenses (e.g. 'past' and 'present', or 'past' and 'nonpast', or even 'remote' and 'nonremote'), for discussion of this point, see Matthiessen (1996: 432ff). This reduction of course paves the way for categories like aspect and phase in the description of the verbal group (for discussion see Subsection D and Section 2.2 below).

(C) Recursion

In the *IFG* model complex tenses are viewed as realisations of repeated choices from the primary tense system. In other words, the system is **recursive**. As Matthiessen (1996: 438f) says:

> The point of Halliday's model is that English tense allows us to expand the first choice; it allows us to choose again: in addition to the primary tense selection, we can make a secondary one, realised by one of the auxiliaries *have -en* (past), *be -ing* (present), and *be going to* (future; also *be about to*). [...] Halliday's further point is that we can choose again, and again, and again.

This means that a progressive construction, such as *was singing*, is considered to be the realisation of a primary tense choice of 'past' (*-ed*) and a secondary tense choice of 'present' (BE *-ing*). Similarly, what is traditionally referred to as the past perfect, e.g. *had taken*, is considered to be the realisation of both a primary and a secondary tense choice of 'past' (*-ed* and HAVE *-en*, respectively). An example involving a future would be *was going to walk*, where the primary tense is 'past' and the secondary tense is 'future'. Halliday suggests that tensed constructions are named according to the choices but in a backwards fashion, beginning with the last choice: thus *was singing* is called a 'present in past' and *was going to walk* is called a 'future in past'. A more complex construction like *was going to have been taking* realises four choices and is an instance of a 'present in past in future in past' (cf. Halliday 1976c: 153f). A simplified version of Matthiessen's systemic representation of the recursive tense category is offered in Figure 2.2 (taken from Matthiessen 1996: 438).

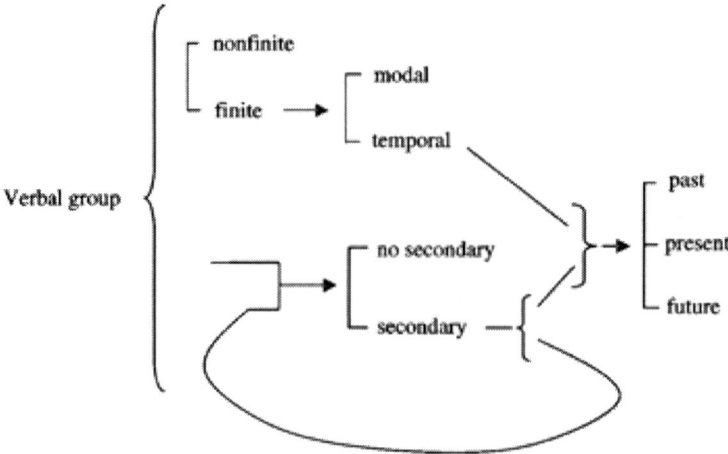

Figure 2.2: Matthiessen's recursive tense system.

Despite the principle of recursion in the English tense system, the number of possible tenses is restricted to 36 active forms by means of certain 'combinatory restrictions', or 'stop rules'. There are three stop rules: (1) ' "Present" can occur only at the outer ends of the series (as first and/or final choice)', (2) 'except at a and b [the realisations of the first and second choice, respectively], the same tense cannot be selected twice consecutively', and (3) '"future" can occur only once other than at a' (Halliday 1976c: 155). The recursive nature of the tense category has a number of important implications, cf. characteristics D and E below.

(D) Group rank

According to Halliday and Matthiessen, tense in English is located at group rank rather than at word rank to reflect the fact that the relevant values are not just realised morphologically but involve the organisation of the verbal group as a whole. Halliday and Matthiessen are thus critical of the tendency in most other linguistic descriptions to reduce tense to a two-member system, e.g. a past/nonpast distinction, and to explain the many complex verbal constructions as combinations of tense with other categories, such as aspect and phase. As we shall see later, in the Cardiff grammar the verbal group is rejected as a class of unit (Fawcett 2000a,b), and this has important consequences for the analysis of both simple and complex tenses.

(E) Univariate structure and the logical metafunction

Not only is tense located at group level in the *IFG* model, it is realised in terms of a number of interdependencies in the verbal group. Unlike the nominal group, which is said to have a **multivariate** structure, i.e. a structure with elements carrying distinct functions and properties (such as e.g. determination, quantification and modification), the verbal group is assumed to have a **univariate** structure, i.e. a structure which exhibits the recurrence of the same fundamental function and a building up of a set of interdependent relations of the same kind (cf. Halliday 1994a: 193). The realisation of tense in the verbal group is thus **serial** rather than simply linear. Semantically, the implication of this is that each new choice of precedence relation in a recursive process is based on the time established by the immediately preceding choice. This functional interdependence has lexicogrammatical repercussions in that the form of each verb in the group is determined by its relationship to the preceding one. For example, in a verbal group like *will have been dancing* (which is an instance of the 'present in past in future'), the temporal meanings are realised in this way: primary 'future' by *will* + infinitive, secondary 'past' by HAVE + past participle (V-*en*), and secondary 'present' by BE + present participle (V-*ing*). The realisations of these three choices are tightly interwoven in that *will* must be followed by an infinitive of *have*, which is followed by a past participle of *be*, which in turn is followed by a present participle of the lexical verb, DANCE, cf. Figure 2.3 (for a similar representation, see Halliday 1976c: 157).

The univariate, serial structure of tense resulting from recursive choices of values in the basic system of past, present and future is a natural consequence of tense being a resource for specifying temporal precedence relations within **the logical metafunction** (cf. Halliday 1994a: 198: '[...] it is the

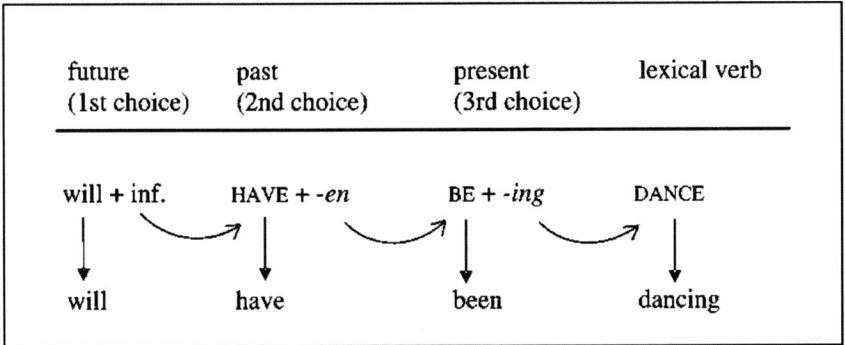

future	past	present	lexical verb
(1st choice)	(2nd choice)	(3rd choice)	
will + inf.	HAVE + -*en*	BE + -*ing*	DANCE
will	have	been	dancing

Figure 2.3: The serial model of tense – from a formal perspective.

logical structure that embodies the single most important semantic feature of the English verb, its recursive tense system [...]'). At the same time it is important to recognise the fact that language has other ways of expressing time, notably within the experiential metafunction (cf. e.g. through circumstantials like *yesterday / a few days later / before he arrived / in 1998 /* etc.), for a discussion of the metafunctional diversity in connection with the expression of time, see Matthiessen (1996: 445–472).

(F) Data

Halliday and Matthiessen naturally want their description of English tense to be empirically well-founded and thus deal explicitly with both written and spontaneous, unselfconscious spoken language. As a result, their data include kinds of examples often ignored by other tense theorists, such as:

> had been going to have been taking
> will have been going to be being tested
> must have been going to have finished
> is going to have been being discussed

(for discussion of these constructions and, indeed, of the inclusion of rather rare examples, see Halliday (1976c: 143–145)). In Section 3.6 below, I shall discuss the problem of observational adequacy and the empirical basis for the *IFG* tense category.

(G) realisation of tense

Halliday and Matthiessen recognise the following tense markers, i.e. lexicogrammatical realisations of the tense choices made by the Performer:

(a)   the morphological -*ed* suffix, which marks primary past;

(b)   morphological -Ø (or third-person -*s*), which marks primary present;

(c)   *will* + infinitive, which marks primary future;

(d)   HAVE + past participle (V-*en*), which marks secondary past ('past in');

(e)   BE + present participle (V-*ing*), which marks secondary present ('present in');

(f)   BE *going to* + infinitive, which marks secondary future ('future in');

(g)   BE *about to* + infinitive, which is an alternative secondary future with modal implications.

Note that the first three markers are realisations of primary tense and the others are realisations of secondary tense ('secondary' being used to refer to both secondary and subsequent choices in the recursive process). There are two important points to make in connection with this list of tense markers. First, Matthiessen (1996: 474ff) argues that word-rank auxiliary *will* has two realisations at group rank which can be kept distinct: a modal one and a temporal one. It is this separation of temporal *will* and modal *will* which makes the primary tripartite tense system possible in the *IFG* approach to tense. The distinction between *will* and *would* is fully relevant only at word rank (not group rank) since, according to Matthiessen (1996: 476), 'would can only be temporal if it is projected (*I will come : he said he would come*)'. The second point to make in connection with the SFL markers of tense is that BE *going to* and BE *about to* are recognised as genuine, central tense markers in connection with recursion. However, partly for convenience and partly because of the modal associations of BE *about to*, Halliday and Matthiessen mostly operate only with BE *going to* as the standard secondary future. In most other descriptions of tense, both these periphrastic forms are considered more peripheral.

(H) System I: 36 finite tenses

With the stop rules specified in Subsection C and realisations listed in Subsection G above, Halliday's recursive tense system in English generates the following 36 finite tense forms of the verb TAKE (cf. Halliday 1994a: 202f):

Tense name	Example
1. past	*took*
2. present	*takes*
3. future	*will take*
4. past in past	*had taken*
5. past in present	*has taken*
6. past in future	*will have taken*
7. present in past	*was taking*
8. present in present	*is taking*
9. present in future	*will be taking*
10. future in past	*was going to take*
11. future in present	*is going to take*
12. future in future	*will be going to take*

13. past in future in past	*was going to have taken*
14. past in future in present	*is going to have taken*
15. past in future in future	*will be going to have taken*
16. present in past in past	*had been taking*
17. present in past in present	*has been taking*
18. present in past in future	*will have been taking*
19. present in future in past	*was going to be taking*
20. present in future in present	*is going to be taking*
21. present in future in future	*will be going to be taking*
22. future in past in past	*had been going to take*
23. future in past in present	*has been going to take*
24. future in past in future	*will have been going to take*
25. past in future in past in past	*had been going to have taken*
26. past in future in past in present	*has been going to have taken*
27. past in future in past in future	*will have been going to have taken*
28. present in past in future in past	*was going to have been taking*
29. present in past in future in present	*is going to have been taking*
30. present in past in future in future	*will be going to have been taking*
31. present in future in past in past	*had been going to be taking*
32. present in future in past in present	*has been going to be taking*
33. present in future in past in future	*will have been going to be taking*
34. present in past in future in past in past	*had been going to have been taking*
35. present in past in future in past in present	*has been going to have been taking*
36. present in past in future in past in future	*will have been going to have been taking*

In Halliday's description of the tense category in English, these 36 finite constructions belong to the so-called 'System I' (cf. Halliday 1994a: 200). As we shall see below, there are two other relevant systems.

(I) System II: 24 finite tenses in projected clauses

In the *IFG* tense model, there is a separate tense system referred to as 'System II'. This is a subset of System I, comprising 24 tense forms found after a past projection (such as *They said* ... and *She thought* ...) (cf. Halliday 1994a: 200ff). As Halliday (1994a: 201) notes, there is in past projection a neutralisation of past tenses: *took* (past), *has/have taken* (past in present) and *had taken* (past in past) may all be projected as past in past:

> They <u>took</u> the key
> They <u>have taken</u> the key   ⎫   She claimed that they <u>had taken</u> the key
> They <u>had taken</u> the key   ⎭

Since there is neutralisation of pastness in six such 'triads' (as Halliday calls them) from System I, System II contains 12 tenses fewer that System I, i.e. the following 24, according to Halliday's specification (though he does not actually list them): [1]

Tense name	Example
2. present	*takes*
3. future	*will take*
4. past in past	*had taken*
6. past in future	*will have taken*
8. present in present	*is taking*
9. present in future	*will be taking*
11. future in present	*is going to take*
12. future in future	*will be going to take*
14. past in future in present	*is going to have taken*
15. past in future in future	*will be going to have taken*
16. present in past in past	*had been taking*
18. present in past in future	*will have been taking*
20. present in future in present	*is going to be taking*
21. present in future in future	*will be going to be taking*
22. future in past in past	*had been going to take*
24. future in past in future	*will have been going to take*
25. past in future in past in past	*had been going to have taken*
27. past in future in past in future	*will have been going to have taken*
29. present in past in future in present	*is going to have been taking*
30. present in past in future in future	*will be going to have been taking*
31. present in future in past in past	*had been going to be taking*
33. present in future in past in future	*will have been going to be taking*
34. present in past in future in past in past	*had been going to have been taking*
36. present in past in future in past in future	*will have been going to have been taking*

When offered as a list, System II seems like a fairly heterogeneous set of forms, and it is unclear why Halliday wants to operate with this system at all. I am not going to discuss possible arguments for or against System II at this point, but merely note that the criterion offered for inclusion seems insufficient, or rather inconsistently applied. First of all, the neutralisation between past, past in present and past in past is not obligatory in normal usage:

They <u>took</u> the key → She claimed that they <u>took</u> the key

Thus, the past should still be a member of System II (because it is found after past projection). Another reason why the past should be a member is that it is often used after a past projection of a present linguistic representation:

I <u>am</u> very happy for Jim → She said she <u>was</u> very happy for Jim

As Halliday (1994a: 261) himself notes, the past, while not obligatory, is the unmarked choice in many contexts (an exception being clauses stating a general proposition, as in *They said they close at weekends*).

Another immediate problem with System II, which will be taken up at a later point, is that Halliday apparently excludes *would*, which in standard English is a neutral, unmarked choice in past projection of primary future *will* constructions:

There <u>will be</u> another meeting soon

→ The dean said there <u>would be</u> another meeting soon

The status of both *will* and *would* will be considered more closely in Chapter 5.

(J) System III: nonfinite tenses

One significant implication of the concept of tense proposed by Halliday is that not only finite but also nonfinite verbal groups are described as **tensed**.[2] This is a natural consequence of viewing tense in terms of bare precedence relations rather than genuine deixis. Thus, for example, *to see* ('perfective') and *hopping* ('imperfective') are (nonfinite) examples of the basic nonfinite 'present'[3] tense (distinguished in terms of aspect, see Section 2.2 below), *to have seen* (perfective) and *having hopped* (imperfective) are nonfinite 'past' tense forms, and *to have been swimming* (perfective) and *having been hopping* (imperfective) are nonfinite 'present in past' forms (for comments on the first two pairs of forms, see Halliday 1976c: 137). For each of these nonfinite tenses there are not just two aspectual variants (a perfective and an imperfective) but also a 'modal tense', i.e. a bare infinitive following a modal finite: e.g. *can take* (modal perfective base form), *can have taken* (modal perfective 'past') and *can have been taking* (modal imperfective 'present in past'). In fact, Halliday 1994a operates explicitly with a separate tense system for nonfinite/modalised forms, the so-called 'System III', which comprises 12 tenses (cf. 1994a: 200ff), each with aspectual and modal variants.[4]

The inventory of System III is determined partly by the neutralisation of past forms similar to that in System II, partly by a parallel neutralisation of future forms (Halliday and Matthiessen 2004: 344): the nonfinite future *be going to take* corresponds not only to the finite 'future' *will take* but also the finite 'future in present' *is going to take* and the finite 'future in future' *will be going to take*. The result of this additional neutralisation is a further reduction of tenses to the following 12 (each with aspectual and modal variants, cf. Halliday 1994a: 202f):[5]

Tense	Example
1. (none)	*to take, taking; can take*
2. past	*to have, having; can have + taken*
3. present	*to be, being; can be + taking*
4. future	*to be, being; can be + going to take*
5. past in future	*to be, being; can be + going to have taken*
6. present in past	*to have, having; can have + been taking*
7. present in future	*to be, being; can be + going to be taking*
8. future in past	*to have, having; can have + been going to take*
9. past in future in past	*to have, having; can have + been going to have taken*
10. present in past in future	*to be, being; can be + going to have been taking*
11. present in future in past	*to have, having; can have + been going to be taking*
12. present in past in future in past	*to have, having; can have + been going to have been taking*

Among the 12 nonfinite tenses (and aspectual and modal variants thereof) there are some rather unusual constructions, like e.g. the imperfective 'present' *being taking*, the imperfective 'future in present' *being going to take*, the imperfective 'past in future' *being going to have taken*, and the perfective 'present in past in future in past' *to have been going to have been taking*.

General evaluation

The *IFG* approach to tense in English, as characterised above, has a number of attractive features. The most important of these, I think, is that the model very explicitly incorporates the paradigmatic, systemic dimension of language, and thus stresses the notion of choice. This is a huge advantage over most other accounts of this category: if we want to arrive at a genuine understanding of how the tense category works in English, it is obviously important to examine the native speaker's motivation for choosing a particular tense in any given case. Another attractive feature is the attention Halliday and Matthiessen pay to tense as a coherent serial system, in which choices and realisations in complex tenses are represented as clearly interdependent. A third feature of Halliday and Matthiessen's model which I am sure will appeal to many is that it is really very simple, yet powerful: by positing a basic tripartite system and allowing repeated choices of values from this system, the model is capable of generating a large number of verbal groups with distinct temporal meanings. By adding a small number of stop rules, the system is properly constrained so as to cope with exactly 36 active constructions which pose a serious challenge to any description of tense in English. In their application of this rather elegant description, Halliday and Matthiessen consider a large variety of both written and spoken data. At first sight it would thus appear that they reach a high degree of observational adequacy and descriptive finesse. Finally, Halliday's terms for the 36 different active constructions are pedagogically attractive – despite their complexity in the case of extended recursion – because they reflect the functional choices involved in each construction in a principled way and are therefore easy to manage.

2.2   Aspect and phase

There is no standard approach to aspect and phase in SFL. In fact, on the whole systemicists have failed to take a consistent stand on this important, if controversial, issue. One possible reason for this is that Halliday's tense model and his views on aspect were formulated before aspect was recognised by Comrie and others as an important general linguistic category (cf. Comrie's 1976 Cambridge University Press introduction) rather than 'just' an exotic language-specific morphological category in Slavonic and Semitic languages (for a discussion of the aspect tradition and of the question of aspect in English, see Bache 1985).

As we saw in Section 2.1 above, Halliday and Matthiessen do not consider aspect to be important or necessary in the description of finite tensed verbal groups in English. Their view is that aspect and phase are categories employed by linguists who make the grave mistake of *reducing* the traditional, Latin-inspired tense system to two members and therefore need other categories to fill the gap in the description of verbal groups. In such descriptions, complex verb forms are viewed as the result of combining tense with aspect and/or phase. More specifically, the perfect and the pluperfect are often considered a combination of tense and phase (or of all three categories), while the progressive forms are considered a combination of tense and aspect (or of all three categories). What Halliday and Matthiessen do is the opposite: they *extend* the traditional system to include all sorts of complex constructions under the heading of tense and therefore feel they can do perfectly well without aspect and phase. One way of describing the difference between linguists who recognise the relevance of aspect and phase, on the one hand, and *IFG* systemicists on the other, is to say that while the former operate with aspect and phase, the latter operate with recursion of the basic tense system. The difference is not trivial. In Halliday and Matthiessen's view, linguists who favour the reduced model of tense fail to recognise all the important characteristics of tense in English highlighted by the *IFG* approach. Thus in most reductionist models it seems that:

- tense is located at *word rank* rather than at group rank, and the descriptive focus is on morphological realisation;

- verbal groups are assigned a *multivariate structure* rather than a univariate structure (tense, phase and aspect being regarded as specific components serving distinct functions);

- the *future* is not recognised as a genuine tense (but rather as a modality);

- tense is most often treated as an *experiential resource* rather than a logical one (and the same applies to aspect and phase); occasionally it is given a modal interpretation instead of an experiential one, in which case it can be classified as an *interpersonal resource*;

- the structure of the verbal group is considered to be simply *linear* rather than genuinely serial;

- in short: *the recursive nature of tense is ignored.*

It is important to note that Halliday and Matthiessen's account of tense applies specifically to English. They do not claim that their model has universal validity. Quite on the contrary, Matthiessen explicitly states that there may be important categorial differences between languages:

> The English system of TENSE is one particular way of locating time.
> The tense systems of other languages may be more or less similar to the
> English system – there are types of tense system that are quite different.
> Moreover, tense is not a universal system; many languages do not
> construe time through tense but use another type of system, aspect.
> And languages often have mixed systems, embodying both tense and
> aspect. (1991: 23; capitals in original)

This means that in principle other languages can make use of both tense and aspect – especially if they are realised as experiential categories – or of aspect alone, or of aspect as the dominant category, or of neither of them. In this connection Caffarel's (1992) paper on tense in French is illuminating. Caffarel is strongly committed to the SFL cause and readily accepts most, if not all, of Halliday and Matthiessen's views on tense. At the same time she notes a slight difference between tense in English and tense in French:

> Languages construe time either experientially, logically or both. French
> tense rests within the logical metafunction, at the frontier of the
> experiential. But whereas English tense is clearly logical, French tense
> has only logical tendencies. [...] Within the grammar, French tense is
> located at group rank not at word rank. Descriptions of French tense

> based on a word-rank interpretation treat tense as an experiential
> component next to aspect. (Caffarel 1992: 387–388)

The impression one gets when reading this is that although French tense is
located at group rank within the logical metafunction like English tense, it is
much closer to expressing experiential meaning, i.e. to the kind of meaning
which can be supplemented by the aspect category. This impression is confirmed a bit later in Caffarel's paper when she says:

> French has five primary tense options: three pasts, one present and one
> future. The three pasts, the **simple past**, the **compound past** and the
> **past imperfect** are interpreted here as identical in terms of their
> temporal meaning but different as to their uses and semantic valeurs.
> The past imperfect, in addition to expressing precedence in relation to a
> reference time that is the speech time encodes also an aspectual
> meaning embodied in the term 'imperfect'. This past tense, specific to
> French, presents the events from an internal perspective, that is, as seen
> from within. (1992: 389–390; emphasis in original)

Caffarel elaborates on the difference between the three past forms in French
in this way:

> The simple past and the compound past or imperfect oppose each
> other in terms of topicality, [topical] versus [nontopical] whilst the
> imperfect and the compound past oppose each other in terms of
> perspective, [internal] versus [external]. That is, the use of the imperfect
> presents the event as seen from within in contrast to the external
> perspective. (1992: 402)

The difference between the imperfect and the compound past is thus described in terms obviously reminiscent of Comrie's widely accepted definitions of aspect, perfectivity and imperfectivity (Comrie 1976; for discussion
of Comrie's definitions, see Bache 1997: 257ff; 2002: 92ff).

Halliday himself uses the terms 'aspect', 'perfective' and 'imperfective' in
a somewhat different way, viz. to characterise the difference in the nonfinite
subsystem of verbal groups between infinitives (with or without *to*) and
present participles (including what used to be referred to as 'gerunds' in
traditional grammar, i.e. *-ing* forms with a nominal function). According to
Halliday, the infinitive is perfective while the present participle is imperfective. The past participle is basically neutral (and may in fact sometimes
neutralise the distinction between perfective and imperfective, as in *I saw it
(be/being) done*), but it 'usually stands for the perfective', cf. Halliday (1994a:
278). Halliday's aspect category applies to a variety of constructions including first of all dependent nonfinite clauses or verbal groups, as in:

(1a) <u>Reaching</u> the monument, continue straight ahead.

(1b) <u>To reach</u> the monument, continue straight ahead.

(2a) the first person <u>leaving</u>

(2b) the first person <u>to leave</u>

(3a) We saw her <u>climbing</u> the wall.

(3b) We saw her <u>climb</u> the wall.

As Halliday notes in connection with his presentation of the first two of these pairs of examples:

> The meaning of the two aspects is very fluid and indeterminate; in the most general terms, the imperfective means act in progress, actual, present, ongoing, steady state or (dependent) proposition, while the perfective means goal to be attained, potential, future, starting and stopping, change of state or (dependent) proposal. Sometimes the distinction is quite clear, as in [(1a) and (1b)] above; sometimes it is very tenuous, as between [(2a) and (2b) above]. (Halliday 1994a: 241)

But Halliday's aspect category also applies to nonfinite dependent groups in what he refers to as hypotactic verbal group complexes. Here are some examples of what Halliday calls perfective: *seems <u>to know</u>, starts <u>to win</u>, begins <u>to work</u>, try <u>to relax</u>, decides <u>to write</u>, would like <u>to paint</u>, managed <u>to open</u>,* etc. We also find perfective infinitives without *to*, as in *She helped him <u>wash</u> the dishes* and *I saw her <u>leave</u>.* By contrast, the following are classified as imperfective: *turns out <u>knowing</u>, ends up <u>winning</u>, keeps <u>working</u>, try <u>relaxing</u>, gets down to <u>writing</u>, likes <u>painting</u>, succeeded in <u>opening</u>,* etc. In these examples, both the perfective and the imperfective expand the verbal group hypotactically and always have dependent status. In connection with such verb group complexes, Halliday argues that the perfective (i.e. the infinitive) basically expresses something 'unreal', and the imperfective (i.e. the *-ing* form) basically expresses something 'real', but he emphasises that the distinction varies from case to case:

> The general principle is that the perfective is 'unreal' and the imperfective is 'real'; they may be opposed in any one of a number of contrasts, as future to present, appearance to reality, starting off to going on, goal to means, intention to action, or proposal to proposition; and sometimes the difference between them is minimal. (Halliday 1994a: 278)

The perfective or imperfective expansion of verbal group complexes may serve to *elaborate* a process or to *extend* it. In cases of elaboration Halliday speaks of **phase**, either time-phase or reality-phase, and in cases of extension, he speaks of **conation**. I am not going to go into detail with these different types of expansion, but will simply note a few interesting points.

First of all, while Matthiessen (1983, 1996) speaks of phase as a category employed for the description of perfect forms by linguists who favour the reductionist model of tense, or as a category which may be relevant in the description of perfect or perfect-like forms in other languages, Halliday speaks of phase as a more generally relevant concept which comprises two major types: (1) **reality-phase**, which concerns expressions involving the contrast between what is 'apparent' and what is 'realised', as in *seems to be* versus *turns out to be* (which both include perfective infinitives); (2) **time-phase**, which has split into two types: [A] one which has evolved into tense (the BE + -ing form with secondary 'present' ('present in') meaning and the BE *to* form with a modalised secondary 'future meaning', as in *he is to see her tomorrow*); and [B] one which has 'remained as a category of phase' (Halliday 1994a: 279), and which expresses actional meanings like 'inception', 'duration' and 'conclusion' (or 'termination'), as in e.g. *begin to sing, start swimming, kept talking, go on thinking, stopped smoking, ceases to believe*, etc. As these examples show, the middle phase is expressed by means of a dependent imperfective, and the initial and final phases are expressed by either a dependent perfective or a dependent imperfective (cf. Halliday 1994a: 279–280).

Second, though Halliday and Matthiessen clearly oppose the introduction of aspect and phase as supplementary categories to tense in the description of the finite verbal group (cf. Section 2.1 above), both aspect and phase are recognised as relevant lower-level components, not only in the description of (finite or nonfinite) verbal group complexes, but also in the finite secondary tense system. Thus, as we have seen, in progressive forms like *is singing, had been swimming, will have been working*, etc. the secondary 'present' is realised by a form of BE plus the imperfective present participle. And, as Halliday (1994a: 279) notes, the modalised form BE *to* followed by the perfective infinitive (as in *she was to see him the next day*) originated in the time-phase system as a secondary 'future'. We can also assume that the infinitive following the current secondary 'future' BE *going to* is to be regarded as perfective, though Halliday is nowhere very explicit about this.

Finally, it is important to note that even though aspect and phase are accommodated in the description of nonfinite verbal groups, these categories are considered to be strictly independent of the tense category. Halliday (1976c: 137) says: 'Both *to see* and *hopping* are present tense; the corresponding past would be *to have seen* and *having hopped*. The choice of tense is thus independent of aspect.' One implication of this strict separation of tense and aspect is that meanings related to aspect (and recognised as such by Caffarel (1992)) are not to be regarded as aspectual if they happen to be expressed by finite verbal groups. Halliday recognises the distinction between the a-example and the b-example in the following pair as one of aspect:

(4a) I saw her <u>leave</u> the building.

(4b) I saw her <u>leaving</u> the building.

The infinitive *leave* in (4a) is perfective and the present participle *leaving* in (4b) is imperfective. It is in such pairs of examples that Halliday's notion of aspect is closest to the more widespread understanding of the aspect category in other branches of modern linguistics. But, significantly, he does not recognise the aspect category at work in the corresponding finite pairs of examples:

(5a) She <u>left</u> the building.

(5b) She <u>was leaving</u> the building.

Although the present participle in (5b) is imperfective by itself, in Halliday's sense, the actual choice of the so-called 'present in past' (or past progressive in more traditional terminology) is not an aspectual choice but the combined result of two temporal choices: a primary choice of 'past' and a secondary one of 'present'.

General evaluation

Halliday's approach to verbal groups has many virtues, not only in relation to tense, as noted in Section 2.1, but also in relation to the specific characteristics of nonfinite verbal groups. Halliday throws a lot of new light on the many descriptively challenging uses of nonfinite verbal groups, especially in hypotactic group complexes, and he recruits interesting specific categories for their description. His approach is characterised by a high degree of consistency: it is easy to identify and refer to tense forms because there is a one-to-one correspondence between each tense marker and the functionally defined systemic choice(s) of tense value. Similarly, there is in his account a pedagogically convenient one-to-one correspondence between infinitives and perfectivity as well as between present participles (including gerunds) and imperfectivity: whenever we come across an infinitive (with or without *to*) it is perfective, and whenever we come across an V-*ing* form it is imperfective. However, as we shall see in Chapter 3 below, we pay a high price for this convenience.

Notes

1. The tense numbers from System I have been retained.
2. Note that the incorporation of nonfinite constructions in the tense category is not reflected by Matthiessen's system network, cf. Figure 1.2 above.
3. Halliday (1976c: 137) calls 'to see' and 'hopping' *present* tenses, but Halliday (1994a: 202) and Halliday and Matthiessen (2004: 340) seem to consider them basic, label-less nonfinite tenses: in the relevant slot in the column for tense names they merely write '(none)', reserving the term 'present' for the nonfinite equivalent of the finite present in past/present/future, e.g. *to be taking*.
4. Table 6(11) in Halliday and Matthiessen (2004: 340f), which offers an overview and exemplification of nonfinite tenses, is full of mistakes (probably typos): at least 15 in the column containing nonfinite examples and one in the column containing finite ones. The problem seems primarily to be the use of HAVE instead of BE in the following nonfinite tenses: the 'present', the 'future in present', the 'past in future', the 'present in future', the 'present in past in future' and the 'present in past in future in past'. The corresponding Table 6(7) in Halliday (1994a: 202f) seems to be correct.
5. Halliday's roman numbers for System III have been retained.

3 Problems with the *IFG* approach to tense

3.1 *IFG* tense: a functional category?

In this chapter of the book I am going to look once again at the characteristic features of Halliday and Matthiessen's approach to tense, aspect and phase, although this time much more critically. I shall raise a number of important questions, but there is one issue in particular which requires close attention and that is the assumed recursive feature of the basic tripartite tense system. It is from this feature that most of the other assumed characteristics of tense in English are said to be derived in the *IFG* approach: its status as a logical resource, its application at group rank and its serial, univariate structure within the group. But it is also a feature which has certain more general implications for the nature of the relationship between form and function, and for the nature of choice in language.

Before delving into some of the finer details, I would like to pose a very general question: just how *functionalist* in nature is Halliday and Matthiessen's approach to tense in English? Their description is obviously *meant* to be a genuinely functional one, a natural component within the systemic functional framework, as we know it. Matthiessen (1984) repeat-edly stresses both the functional and the conceptual nature of tense choice. He speaks of 'the purposeful control of tense selection' (1984: 1) and 'the general concern with making choices in the grammar in conformity with a purpose for communicating' (1984: 135), and he characterises his chooser as 'a procedure that consists of steps that ascertain conceptual distinctions and make grammatical choices according to the conceptual distinctions' (1984: 1). Despite these very reasonable and indeed both descriptively and explana-torily adequate goals, I must say that on first reading Halliday and Matthiessen's descriptions of tense, I was more than once struck by what seemed to me an uncharacteristically formal twist in their handling of the subject matter, not only with respect to the priority they sometimes give to the formal properties of the categories involved but also with respect to the kind of formalisation and jargon they use.

An example of this is Halliday's distinction between perfective and imperfective, which, on critical reflection, seems to be a purely formal distinction between infinitives and present participles devoid of a consistent functional differentiation: all infinitives are perfective and all present participles are imperfective, and the meanings associated with these forms are extremely variable and elusive. In other words, the terms 'perfective' and 'imperfective' would appear simply to be metalinguistic alternatives to the traditional terms 'infinitive' and 'present participle'. When Halliday speaks of this distinction, it is as if he takes his point of departure not in function or meaning, as we would expect, but in form alone: like many traditional grammarians (often criticised for their *form-to-meaning* analyses) he simply lists various meanings of the two forms and notes that the distinction is often very blurred and imperceptible.

Another example has to do with the metalanguage employed more generally for the description of tense and the theoretical orientation reflected by this metalanguage. In my view, as functional grammarians we should avoid construing a world of machines and automatic procedures (even if our descriptions are based on, or related to, computational projects, such as the Penman project and its Nigel component). Instead we should give *Performers* (i.e. speakers and writers), the choices *they make*, and the *texts* that they *create* our undivided descriptive attention. Rather than concentrating narrowly on **recursion**, **stop rules**, **chooser devices** and **text generation** and other technical details in relation to establishing the **inventory** of system networks, we should emphasise *the human factor* in tense choice, i.e. the Performer's communicative intention. It may perhaps seem a bit unfair to criticise some of the early systemic functional work on tense in this way, especially because it appeared in contexts which invited formal procedures and terminology, but the problem is that the description did not change as it grew into the *IFG* model and was aimed at a much broader functional linguistic community.

My most revealing example of the formal nature of Matthiessen and Halliday's approach to English tense is the assumed recursive feature of the tense system and the resulting serial nature of complex tense forms – the very essence of English tense, according to their description. To regard complex forms and constructions as the result of repeated 'operations' on a basic system was one of the cornerstones of early Transformational Grammar. Recursion was Chomsky's strongest argument against positivist and behaviourist trends in psychology and linguistics, and it was a very convincing formal example of human linguistic creativity (which he defined in terms of the ideal native speaker's competence, i.e. her tacit knowledge of how to construct (or 'generate'), through finite means, an infinite number of grammatical sentences, many never spoken or heard before). However, early transformational grammarians, including Chomsky, soon realised that their transformations (some of which operated recursively) were far too strong and powerful: the transformational component had to be properly constrained in order to avoid massive automatic overgeneration, i.e. generation of an infinite number of ungrammatical and unacceptable strings (cf. e.g. Chomsky 1957, 1965, 1968, 1986; Radford 1981). Halliday and Matthiessen's **stop rules** are clearly reminiscent of such transformational constraints: they serve exactly the same purpose, viz. to avoid generation of impossible tense constructions. The stop rules reduce the number of tenses in System I from infinite to 36 forms which are considered more or less relevant options to discuss in connection with tense in English. The serial nature of the permitted complex tense forms, which resulted from the recursive choices, according to Halliday and Matthiessen, was recognised in a formal way already in some of the earliest works on Transformational Grammar and led to the formulation of the famous 'affix-hopping' transformation (in fact, Figure 2.3 might serve as an informal representation of this transformation), cf. e.g. Huddleston (1976: 73ff).

By raising these issues I do not to want to criticise Halliday and Matthiessen unfairly – Halliday's respect for Chomsky in the early days of Transformational Grammar (cf. Halliday (1976b), entitled 'Deep Grammar: system as semantic choice') is both understandable and justified. My aim is rather to pave the way for a discussion of English tense in more genuinely functionalist terms. If we consider the fact that Halliday's approach to tense was formulated in the 1960s and 1970s, the heyday of Generative Linguistics and its pervasive, and I might add, in many ways unfortunate dominance of the linguistic scene, the real surprise is not how formal Halliday's description of tense is, but how much he actually managed to *depart from mainstream formal linguistics* by insisting on the integration of semantics and pragmatics in his grammar, and on taking paradigmatic relations seriously – areas where Generative Linguistics failed miserably or simply had no descriptive ambitions. Thus, what I am trying to do by pointing to some influence from formal linguistics on the *IFG* model of tense is not to mock the model or its founding father. Quite on the contrary, I want to suggest that there may be room for certain adjustments and developments of the model and for strengthening its accommodation of the functional properties of tense in English.

Put more generally, I am going to show that the *IFG* model of tense in English is not fully adequate, either descriptively or explanatorily, in any functional linguistic sense. In other words, I shall argue that this description does not bring out the genuine functional nature of tense choice. In Sections 3.2 to 3.5 below I deal with four specific problems in order to substantiate this argument. Finally in Section 3.6, I shall try to determine how well the model reflects actual tense usage in English and discuss certain limitations of the model with respect to observational adequacy.

3.2   How are the choices ordered?

Although Halliday and Matthiessen are very explicit in their description of complex forms as the product of a series of *ordered choices*, the actual ordering of the choices involved is unclear. The impression one gets when reading some of Halliday and Matthiessen's less technical descriptions of how the recursive system works is that the order of choices is completely straightforward: the Performer *first* chooses from the basic tripartite system of 'past', 'present' and 'future', *then* she may or may not choose *again* from the same system. If the Performer chooses a secondary tense, *then* there is the possibility of a third choice, and so on. As Halliday says, after having noted the existence of a large number of tense forms in English:

> When the speaker chooses a certain tense, he is not making a sudden selection all at once from this huge inventory; he is choosing from a very small set of possibilities, namely 'past', 'present' or 'future', and he will more often than not make this selection only once with each verbal group. *But it is open to him to make a second choice from the same set*: the verbal group may be both 'past' and 'present' at the same time; and *then a third choice, and so on.* [....] In analysing these forms therefore, and in suggesting coding for them, we need to reflect this patterning and to avoid suggesting that the choice of a simple 'present' form of a verbal group is like, say, choosing a number between one and fifty. *It is more like choosing a number between one and three, and then going on to decide whether or not you are going to do so a second time.* (1976c: 147f, emphasis supplied)

Matthiessen wholeheartedly subscribes to this account. He says: 'After selecting a primary tense, the next step is to decide whether to have secondary tense or not' (1983: 109; see also 1983: 24ff and 1996: 438f). However, if we look more closely at the system network he actually proposes as a formalisation of the theory (see Matthiessen 1996: 438; offered as Figure 2.2 in Section 2.1 above), the sequence of choices seems to be somewhat different: in this network the choice between 'secondary' and 'no secondary' is posited as simultaneous with the choice between 'finite' and 'nonfinite', which implies that it actually *precedes* the initial choice of 'past', 'present' or 'future'. As Matthiessen (1996: 437) notes, '[...] there are two simultaneous systems [...], FINITENESS ("finite/nonfinite") and TENSE RECURSION ("secondary/no secondary")'. It follows from this that the Performer must decide whether or not she wants to re-enter the tense system before she enters it the first time. If we go back to Matthiessen's (1983) account to examine the corresponding system network in his Figure 3-1 on p. 381, we find that the choice between 'secondary' and 'no secondary' is presented as simultaneous with the choice between 'modal' and 'temporal'. Here, too, it seems that the Performer's decision to re-enter the system has to be made before her first choice of 'past', 'present' or 'future'. This is very confusing in the light of the informal accounts above of the sequence of the choices the Performer makes. Even if one allows for a blurred ordering of choices, it is not at all clear how the recursive cycle gets up and running in Matthiessen's system network.

In Matthiessen's early (1983, 1984) work on tense (but not in his later 1996 contribution), there is a more detailed description of the tense chooser mechanism, and here we get a more precise explanation of the order of choices. According to this description, choosing a tense in fact involves *two kinds of choice*, each formalised as a chooser located at a choice point in the system network. The two choosers are both repeated in a recursive process. Matthiessen defines them in this way: the first chooser has to do with 'the reasoning that leads to a selection of the appropriate type of tense (*past*, vs. *present* vs. *future*)' and the other one has to do with 'the reasoning that establishes whether to have a higher order tense or not (*secondary* vs *no secondary*)' (Matthiessen 1984: 26; emphasis in original). The two choosers collaborate to establish *the chain of times between the moment of communication* (T_s) and *the event time* (T_e). The way it works is this: if the first choice of tense type completes the chain, i.e. directly links an event time to the moment of communication, then 'no secondary' is chosen. If the first choice of tense type does *not* complete the chain but 'merely' establishes a relevance time (T_r) in a more complex relation, *and if* this more complex relation is to be expressed explicitly, then 'secondary' is chosen and we get a loop back to the first chooser. This process continues until the chain is completed (see also Matthiessen 1984: 109ff). In other words, choosing a tense does not involve only one kind of (potentially repeated) choice but is more complex, involving two different, systemically and temporally distinct choice situations, which are both repeated in connection with recursion.

However, like the informal accounts of the sequence of tense choices quoted above, Matthiessen's more technical specification of the timing of the chooser operations is at odds with the system networks he himself proposes. It would have been more consistent with the actual chooser operations if Matthiessen had constructed the system network in such a way that the second chooser (i.e. the choice of 'secondary' or 'no secondary') had *followed* the first chooser (i.e. the choice of 'past', 'present' or 'future') rather than *preceded* it. Moreover, even if we ignore the details of Matthiessen's system network, his account of the interaction between the two choosers is implausible from a cognitive and functional point of view: it is simply *not* the case that the Performer first chooses a precedence relation between two abstract time variables, then checks to see if this relation fulfils her communicative goal in terms of speech time, event time and relevance time, and if not, chooses one more precedence relation, and then checks again, and so forth.

Maybe a solution for Halliday and Matthiessen, if they want to save their model, would be to draw a distinction between 'decision to choose' and 'actual choice': thus, perhaps the function of the initial choice of 'secondary' could be said to *license a later actual choice*, to be made after the primary tense choice (correspondingly, the choice of 'no secondary' could be said to license the exclusive choice of primary 'past', 'present' or 'future'). This would be an attractive interpretation from a cognitive and functional point of view: the Performer's *intention* to express something which involves a complex temporal relation probably precedes (or possibly coincides with, but hardly follows) the first choice of 'past', 'present' or 'future'. In other words, the actual choices of temporal values are strictly ordered, one after the other, but the decision to make use of such recursion is made at an earlier stage, not only before the actual choice of secondary tense but before entering the system the very first time. However, this is not how Halliday and Matthiessen have presented the choice situations involved.

3.3   What is it we choose when we choose?

It is not at all clear what exactly is at stake at each choice in the recursive tense model. Do the values and contrasts of the system remain constant in the recursive process? Halliday and Matthiessen very explicitly state that choices are made repeatedly from the *same* set, and thus involve the same contrasting values. Matthiessen's (1996) system network is here more accurate than his 1983 one in that the choice of 'temporal' and the choice of 'secondary' lead to one and the same tripartite system of 'past', 'present' and 'future' (although the entry conditions of course differ). But what does it mean to say that the Performer can choose several times from the same set? If the entry condition varies (in that the *past systemic history* is necessarily different for each choice, whether primary or secondary), does that not affect the nature of the choice and the Performer's motivation for choosing a specific value? For example, is the value 'past' as a primary tense exactly the same value as 'past' as a secondary tense? Are the contrasts involved exactly the same? The impression one gets is that Halliday and Matthiessen intend the system to remain stable in the process of recursion.[1] As we shall see, things are not that simple. There are at least two related issues involved in this discussion: the first issue concerns the *principle* of recursion, i.e. sequential choices from the *same* system, and the second issue concerns the *actual* values of the system. In this section, I shall comment on both issues, but a specific problem in connection with the value 'present' will receive more exclusive attention in Section 3.4 below. I shall deal with Halliday and Matthiessen separately because their accounts differ somewhat with respect to the explicitness with which the tenses are defined. While Halliday focuses on the very general principles of the tense category, as he envisages it (cf. Halliday 1976c, 1994a), Matthiessen explicitly operates with **precedence relations, chooser mechanisms** and **time variables** (cf. Matthiessen 1983, 1984, 1996).

Let me begin my argument by commenting on Halliday's general account. If we assume that language is purposeful behaviour – a fairly uncontroversial assumption in SFL – and that there is therefore a close relationship between the *communicative effect* of an expression and *the Performer's communicative motivation and intentions*, it is very difficult to support the view that the tripartite tense system remains the same in a process of recursion, and that the primary tense values are therefore the same as the secondary values. What is more, if the Performer chooses only once from the system, that choice will *in effect* assign a temporal location to the process, whereas if the Performer chooses twice, so that the first choice is followed by another, the first choice will simply define some other relevant time and leave the temporal location of the process unspecified. In other words, not even the primary values remain stable from time to time. From both a cognitive and a functional point of view it is reasonable to assume that the Performer, when first choosing from the system, is keenly aware of the moment of communication, the absolute or relative time of the process that she is going to refer to, and any other relevant times. We can also assume that her tense choices are motivated by a desire to construe and relate these times according to her communicative needs. For example; she will choose 'past' once, and only once, if she is aware of a relevant time prior to the moment of speaking and wants to present a process as located at that time. She will choose 'past' twice if she is aware of a relevant past time and wants to present a process explicitly as located prior to that time. Consider the following pair of examples:

(1a) Lorna <u>left</u> at noon.

(1b) Lorna <u>had</u> already <u>left</u> at noon.

Example (1a) is the realisation of a single choice of 'past', while example (1b) is the realisation of choosing 'past' twice, as both a primary and a secondary tense.[2] The effect of choosing 'past' in (1a) is to construe the process of 'leaving' as located at a past time ('noon') relative to the moment of communication, whereas the effect of the same choice in (1b) is simply to relate a relevant past time to the moment of communication. So from the point of view of the effect of choosing 'past' on first entering the tense system, the two examples differ: choosing primary 'past' as one's only choice is different from choosing primary 'past' as the first choice, to be followed by another choice. We may conclude that the Performer's precise motivation for choosing 'past' on first entering the system depends on whether or not the system is going to be re-entered or not. What is more, in the series of choices in (1b), the effect of choosing 'past' the first time is different from the effect of choosing it the second time: the first choice relates a relevant past time to the moment of communication while the second choice construes the process as located at a time prior to that relevant past time. Choosing 'past' the second time thus clearly means something other than choosing 'past' the first time. Its overall function is different, and again we can assume that the Performer's motivation for choosing it is different.

It might be objected that in both examples the time of the process is construed as prior to the moment of communication, and maybe this is a result of the Performer's choice of primary past. But such an argument overlooks the fact that there are examples (as noted also by Matthiessen 1983: 391) where the time of the process defined by a secondary tense choice *potentially* differs from the time of the process expressed by a corresponding construction with only a primary tense. Consider the following examples:

(2)   Schmeichel <u>was going to leave</u> Manchester United.

(3)   They <u>will have received</u> the report by noon tomorrow.

In both these examples, the temporal location of the process is strictly unspecified in relation to the moment of communication: in (2) the 'leaving' may or may not have taken place at the moment of communication; and similarly in (3), the 'receiving' may or may not have taken place already. In other words, though the primary choice in (2) is 'past', the time of the process is potentially future, and though the primary choice in (3) is 'future', the time of the process is potentially past. All we know is that in (2) the process – if undertaken at all – is future in relation to the relevant past time, and that in (3) the process is past in relation to the relevant future time. This means that the primary choice of 'past' in (2) is obviously very differently motivated than the primary choice of 'past' in the corresponding *Schmeichel left Manchester United*, which clearly construes the process as past relative to the moment of communication. Similarly, the choice of primary 'future' in (3) is obviously very differently motivated than the choice of primary 'future' in the corresponding *They will receive the report by noon tomorrow.*

If the system of 'past', 'present' and 'future' had been completely stable in the recursive process, we would have expected the formal realisation of each value to be the same, or at least reasonably similar, in a grammar which emphasises the naturalness of the relationship between lexicogrammar and semantics (after all, 'reduplication' is a well-known linguistic phenomenon in other languages). But, as we have seen, this is not the case either. Primary 'present' is realised morphologically by the suffix Ø/-s, while secondary 'present' is realized periphrastically by BE V-*ing*. Primary 'past' is realized morphologically by the suffix -*ed*, while secondary 'past' is realised periphrastically by HAVE V-*en*. Primary 'future' is realized by *will* + infinitive, while secondary 'future' is realized by BE *going to* + infinitive. In each case there is a radical difference in formal realisation. In a functional approach to language we expect subscription to the no-synonymy principle: a difference of form implies a difference of meaning and function. It is not unreasonable, therefore, to assume that the very different formal realisations of secondary tenses reflect very different meanings and functions.

One could of course argue that recursion as a principle involves increasing complexity, and that it is therefore only natural that lexicogrammatical expressions should reflect such complexity. But this argument does not solve the problem: to what extent can we say that the system remains the same during the accumulation of function and form in the recursive process? In fact, I would venture to ask the question whether recursion understood as the (potentially multiple) repetition of exactly the same operation is at all compatible with the principles of functional grammar.

Before passing definite judgement on this issue, however, we need to examine Matthiessen's more explicit account of tense choices. Matthiessen defines the options of the system ('past', 'present' and 'future') *minimally* in terms of mere precedence relations between two time variables: 'past' ($T_x <$ T_y), 'present' ($T_x = T_y$) and 'future' ($T_x > T_y$). When the options are defined minimally in this way, it is of course much easier to argue that they remain exactly the same throughout recursion. However, such a descriptive strategy leaves the specification of T_s, T_e and T_r unaccounted for in the system network itself and thus threatens to make both the deictic nature of tense and the actual temporal location of the process rather peripheral in connection with the tense system. Matthiessen's solution to this problem is to set up the two **choosers** mentioned in Section 3.3. As will be recalled, the first chooser selects an appropriate type of tense ('past', 'present' or 'future') and the second chooser decides whether or not to go on to choose a secondary tense. This decision depends on whether or not the process so far has established the chain of times between the moment of communication (T_s) and the event time (T_e). If the recursive cycle is initiated, this will serve to express a more indirect link between these two times, with one or more relevance times (T_r) entering the chain, serving as 'stepping stones' for new relations in between T_s and T_e. The second chooser thus ensures the central relevance of T_s, T_r and T_e for the tense category as a whole.

However, Matthiessen's more explicit account of the tense system and the recursive process, as well as his ingenious approach to the problem of defining the tense values, does not actually solve the problems that I pointed out in connection with Halliday's more general account. Even if the minimally defined values of the tripartite system could be shown to remain exactly the same in terms of precedence relations, choosing just one value from the system (a primary tense) differs from choosing the same value as the first value in a recursive cycle if we take the *overall choice motivation* and *communicative effect* into consideration. The second chooser takes care of that by assigning T_e to different time variables. And if the same value is chosen as a primary and a secondary tense in a recursive cycle within the same construction, the effect of each choice is here clearly different, too. Again this is taken care of by the second chooser. Matthiessen's more explicit account just makes the problem more transparent. Thus, in the two examples discussed in connection with Halliday's account (repeated here for convenience):

(1a) Lorna <u>left</u> at noon.

(1b) Lorna <u>had</u> already <u>left</u> at noon.

the single choice of 'past' in the a-example will lead to the assignment of T_e to the first T_r established in relation to T_s (i.e. $T_e = T_r$ in the following chain: $T_e = T_r < T_s$), whereas the first choice of 'past' in the b-example will simply establish a past T_r as a basis for a new time relation to be specified by the second choice of 'past' (locating T_e as prior to T_r, which results in the following chain: $T_e < T_r < T_s$). Given that the overall effect is different, I think it is reasonable to assume a functional difference, i.e. a difference in the Performer's motivation for choosing.

As mentioned in Section 3.2, Matthiessen's chooser-incorporated system implies that the Performer *first* chooses a mere precedence relation, *then* decides if this relation assigns a temporal location to the process, and, if it does not, *finally* goes on to choose enough precedence relations to establish the desired chain of times. This is, I think, highly implausible from both a functional and a cognitive point of view: we would expect the Performer to be keenly aware of T_s, an absolute or relative T_e and other contextually relevant times when first choosing from the system, and we would expect her choices to be motivated by a desire to relate these times according to her communicative needs. She does not first choose minimally defined precedence relations and then afterwards associate them with more specific, contextually defined times.

We can conclude that a choice of option in the *IFG* tense system is always made *in the context of previous choices (i.e. relevant systemic history) and with a view to subsequent choices.* Each choice situation in a recursive process is therefore different, and each value is different (even if is nominally 'the same' as a previous choice), not only in terms of overall communicative effect but also in terms of Performer motivation. We have moreover found that the precise functional nature of the *initial* choice of *a particular option* depends on whether or not it is the only choice. In a functional grammar, where we want to characterise choice relations as part of purposeful linguistic behaviour, it makes little or no sense to operate with a mechanical repetition of choices from the 'same' system. As Matthiessen (1984: 19) himself proclaims: 'We are concerned with the semantics of choosing tense here, rather than the mechanics (tactics) of expressing tense selections structurally.'

3.4 Primary versus secondary 'present' – just a slight difference?

In the preceding section we found that *in principle* the choice of value in a recursive process can never be exactly the same, even if nominally the same. In this section I shall show that in the case of 'present' there is, in addition, a much more substantial difference between choosing this tense the first time and choosing it at a later point in the recursive process. The evidence for this is not new: in fact, both Halliday and Matthiessen provide relevant details and examples for this discussion. But I think some of their data challenge rather than support their description, especially the idea of recursion.

Before I begin it is only fair to mention that Matthiessen (1984) *does* recognise a 'slight difference' between primary 'present' and secondary 'present'. As he says: 'it is useful to keep the chooser of PrimaryTense [*sic*] separate from that of SecondaryTenseType [*sic*], since – although the basic principles are the same – they differ in some details' (Matthiessen 1984: 27). Thus while the value for primary 'present' is specified as simultaneous ('T_x neither precedes nor follows T_y'), the value for secondary 'present' is not just 'simultaneity' but more specifically 'inclusion', i.e. T_y includes T_x:

> Simultaneity [...] allows for several possible temporal relations between two times: They may overlap, one may include the other, or they may be perfectly coextensive. However, inclusion [...] is a more specific choice condition for secondary *present*, since it excludes all but one of these various further specifications of 'neither precedes nor follows'. (Matthiessen 1984: 30, see also p. 113; emphasis in original)

In other words, secondary 'present' is a specific version of 'neither precedes nor follows' and thus fully compatible with this value. As we shall see, Matthiessen's interpretation of the close relationship between primary and secondary 'present' is not unproblematic.

Choosing 'present' once, and once only, yields examples like the following (for discussion of the uses of the simple present in English, see Matthiessen 1983: 393ff, Bache 1985: 228–242, 258–280; and Bache 2000: 127–128):

(1)   Nefertiti <u>believes</u> in justice.

(2)   Her new sculpture <u>stands</u> in the middle of the square.

(3)   Oil <u>floats</u> on water.

(4)   The sun <u>rises</u> in the east.

(5)   Joan <u>is</u> in London.

(6)   Jack <u>walks</u> to work.

(7)   He <u>speaks</u> seven languages.

(8)   There <u>is</u> someone in there.

The simple present is used primarily to describe mental or physical **states**, **habits**, **abilities** or **characteristics** of the subject (in SFL terminology: primarily 'mental', 'existential' and 'relational' processes). Verbs with a clear potential to express 'material' processes (dynamic activity or action such as RISE and WALK in the examples above), or 'verbal' processes (such as SPEAK in (7)) tend to express habits, ability or characteristics of the subject when used in the simple present. More generally we can say that dynamic processes as such are not usually expressed by the simple present form. Obvious exceptions to this generalisation are texts found in special, well-defined contexts, such as narration, dramatic accounts of past events (the 'historical present'), commentaries of present processes witnessed (sports, ceremonies), demonstrations, exclamations and performatives (cf. Bache 2000: 128, 141):

(9)   The two little girls go with him, then slip out of their shoes. Paul takes off his shoes and socks, rolls up his trousers like an elderly tripper at the seaside. (narration: FET 245)[3]

(10) We proceeded along the main road. Then suddenly this chap comes up to us and starts to laugh. (historical present)

(11) Wright passes the ball to Bergkamp. (commentary)

(12) I now remove the moss and top up the pot with compost. (demonstration)

(13) Here comes the bride! (exclamation)

(14) I promise to be back by ten. (performative)

Except for such well-defined cases, present action or activity requires the present progressive ('present in present'):

(15a) No, I'm afraid she can't see you before lunch, she is working hard to finish her TWS report.

(15b) *No, I'm afraid she can't see you before lunch, she works hard to finish her TWS report.

(16a) Look! She is already packing her suitcase.

(16b) *Look! She already packs her suitcase.

This means that in pairs of examples like the following:

(17a) She speaks like a real professional.

(17b) She is speaking like a real professional.

(18a) He sings in the local church.

(18b) He is singing in the local church.

the most immediate interpretation is that the 'present' a-examples describe habits or characteristics of the subject while the 'present in present' b-examples describe ongoing activity in the present (or temporally limited present habits as in e.g. *This week he is singing in the local church*). The reason why (15b) and (16b) are unacceptable, unlike (17a) and (18a), is that the meaning expressed by the rest of the sentence or the context specifically requires situational reference to an ongoing activity in the present.

As all these examples show, there are two characteristics of 'present' as the only temporal choice: (a) it typically relates some process (in the SFL sense) to the present; and (b) the process is non-dynamic (a physical or mental state, a relation, a habit, an ability, a characteristic of the subject) and is in fact normally *incompatible* with *simultaneous* dynamic actions and activities. If we want to refer to actions and activities taking place simultaneously in the present we normally have to use the 'present in present', i.e. we have to select 'present' twice. The second 'present' thus *ensures* a dynamic reading of the process. In addition it presents such an action or activity with an internal focus, i.e. as something in progress.

In the past, secondary 'present' has a very similar effect. It presents an action or activity with internal situational focus, as something in progress:

(19)   Linus <u>was doing</u> the dishes when the phone rang.

(20)   The sad memory of his betrayal <u>was</u> gradually <u>coming</u> back to her.

But here the *contrast* between simple and progressive forms is different because the simple past, unlike the simple present, is fully compatible with actions and activities. Thus, examples like:

(17c)   She <u>spoke</u> like a real professional.

(18c)   He <u>sang</u> in the local church.

are vague or ambiguous between a dynamic and a stative reading. The simple past in (17c) may refer to a process on a single occasion (e.g. *At the meeting yesterday she spoke like a real professional*) or to a past characteristic of the subject (e.g. *As a young woman she spoke* [= *used to speak*] *like a real professional*). In (18c) the simple past may refer to a single guest performance (*When Pavarotti visited Llantwit Major last Tuesday, he sang in the local church*) or to a habit (*As a teenager he sang* [= *used to sing*] *in the local church*). The division of labour between progressive and non-progressive forms is thus somewhat different in the past: since both forms are compatible with dynamic actions and activities, the focus of the progressive form is more exclusively on the 'ongoingness' of the process. The simple past, unlike the simple present can represent a specific dynamic process with an external, holistic focus, i.e. as a complete fact.

We can conclude the following from our discussion of 'present':

(a)   primary 'present' is strongly associated with the experiential meanings of mental, existential and relational processes (mental and physical states, habituality, ability and characteristics of the subject) and is in fact typically incompatible with simultaneous present material processes (dynamic actions and activities);

(b)   conversely, secondary 'present' is strongly associated with material processes and in fact typically incompatible with mental, existential and relational processes;

(c)   secondary 'present' in the present is different from secondary 'present' in the past because the division of labour between the competing forms is different and this obviously affects the paradigmatics involved.

In other words, the difference between primary and secondary present is not just a minor one of specialisation, as Matthiessen has it, but one which has strong experiential repercussions obviously affecting choice relations. More generally, the distinction between progressive and nonprogressive forms in English is clearly in need of a much more fine-grained analysis than the one offered by Halliday and Matthiessen.

3.5   What contrasts and choice relations should be reflected by system networks?

In this section I shall examine the notion of choice more closely in connection with the recursive process. As we have seen, the recursive model operates with only one kind of choice in the tense system, that between 'past', 'present' and 'future'. To derive the large number of complex forms in the inventory of English tenses, the Performer repeats that choice recursively. In the preceding sections I have argued that the system (and hence the kind of choice it offers the Performer) changes significantly in the process of recursion: the effect of the initial choice is in principle different from the effect of later choices (even if nominally the same), the effect of the initial choice in fact depends on whether or not it is followed by later choices, and in the specific case of 'present', the initial choice differs radically from later choices of 'present' in terms of experiential implications and compatibility with simultaneous dynamic processes. Given differences in effect, we assume differences in Performer motivation, and we would expect such functionality to be reflected directly in the system network. In this section I shall argue that even if the functional variation noted so far is condoned within the *IFG* tense model, the recursive system does not capture all the relevant lexicogrammatical and semantic contrasts. The Performer often finds herself in a situation where the relevant options to choose are simply not those provided by the system network.

What are the relevant choices in connection with the tense category in English? Well, as Halliday (1976c: 147f) notes, the Performer hardly chooses one form directly out of a large, unmanageable number of different options. The choice must be much more limited to make sense. In a similar vein Matthiessen (1984: 104) argues (quoting Kirsner and Thompson 1976) that: 'to fully explain the use of a given signal and its meaning, we must consider the *semantic* oppositions: the *other* options, the *other* signals and *their* meanings also available to the speaker' (emphasis in original). Put somewhat differently, in a functional approach that highlights language as a meaning-making phenomenon, we expect there to be choices between lexicogrammatical forms which share some general semantic domain – a category concept – but which profile this domain differently (for a lengthy discussion of the nature of choice in language and of categories and form-meaning relationships, see Bache 1997: 103–198 and Bache 2002). This formulation ought not to be controversial or problematical in an SFL context. Thus, in principle we may characterize the primary tense choice in the recursive model by saying that 'past', 'present' and 'future' *share* the general category concept of 'time structured in terms of precedence relations' but that they *differ* with respect to the precise nature of the precedence relation expressed. The choice between them, as characterised by Matthiessen, is not in fact a completely inappropriate one because it is a choice between different ways of realising a particular linguistically relevant function. In that sense it is a choice between *minimally distinct options*: 'past', 'present' and 'future' differ in only one respect, viz. the actual profiling of the general tense concept or function (but within the context of that function, the three options are of course maximally distinct). Interestingly, Matthiessen (1984: 9) explicitly refers to the tripartite tense system as a 'minimal paradigm'. We would not want to operate with a model positing a direct choice between e.g.

(1a) Everyone <u>believes</u> his dramatic account of the events.

(1b) His dramatic account of the events <u>was believed</u> by everyone.

In this 'pair' of examples, the contrast between the simple present in (1a) and the past passive in (1b) is too complex because it involves not only primary tense ('present' versus 'past') but also voice ('active' versus 'passive'). The choice of 'present' in (1a) should be seen in the more limited choice context of the competing constructions in:

(1c) Everyone <u>believed</u> his dramatic account of the events.

(1d) Everyone <u>will believe</u> his dramatic account of the events.

And the choice of 'passive' in (1b) should be seen in the more limited choice context of the competing active construction in (1c).

The choice relations involved in examples (1a) – (1d) reveal that the simple past form in (1c) fuses the realisation of two different choices: the choice of 'past' in the tense system (where it contrasts with (1a) and (1d)) and the choice of 'active' in the voice system (where it contrasts with (1b)). An exhaustive description of the simple past in (1c) thus involves (at least) two different categories. I refer to such forms as **non-monadic**: a non-monadic form or construction is a multifunctional one which requires description in terms of two or more semantic domains.[4] Needless to say, in a larger corpus of examples, it would be easy to demonstrate that the verb forms in (1a), (1b) and (1d) are equally non-monadic in this sense. Furthermore, it seems not unreasonable to assume that non-monadic forms and constructions are the result of more complex choice relations than monadic forms and constructions (for further discussion, see Section 4.4.6 below).

Summing up so far, we can conclude the following: (a) choices should be described in terms of minimally distinct options (i.e. options which share one, and only one, general concept or function, but which differ with respect to the specific profiling of that concept or function); (b) lexicogrammatical constructions are often (always?) non-monadic in the sense that they require description in terms of more than one categorial choice; a particular construction may thus enter minimal pairs with different contrasting constructions. For the description of the multiple contrasts expressed by non-monadic forms, we need a repertoire of different metalinguistic categories (such as e.g. tense and voice) as a basis for an account of the complex choice relations involved.

Turning now to the choices reflected by the recursive *IFG* model, we find that it sometimes assumes some reasonably plausible choice situations, such as e.g. the initial choice of primary tense exemplified in examples (1a), (1c) and (1d). In other cases, however, it assumes some rather more curious choice situations. Matthiessen (1984: 117ff) is aware of certain limitations of the SFL model and suggests that we consider other 'competitors' than the main ones reflected by the recursive tripartite system, thus in effect *extending* the relevant tense paradigm. He suggests the following principle for the extension (1984: 117):

Principle of potential tense competitors For any tense, there is a potential competitor for specifying the location of T_e with respect to T_s that can be arrived at by subtracting one of the tense choices.

Thus, for example, a 'past in present' (e.g. *has left*) competes with both the simple 'past' (*left*) and the simple 'present' (*leaves*) in addition to its systemically more natural secondary tense competitors 'present in present' (*is leaving*) and the 'future in present' (*is going to leave*), which both share the primary tense choice of 'present' but differ with respect to secondary tense choice.

However, this attempt to cope with the immediate limitations of the *IFG* tense category runs into severe difficulties because it ranks in a counterintuitive fashion the various choice relations created by the non-monadicness of tense forms. It is reasonable to expect the basic recursive tripartite system to reflect the most obvious, most immediate choice options (competitors) within the tense category, and to treat the choice options provided by the extended paradigm principle as somehow secondary. However, in some cases the most obvious choice relations are not the ones specified by the basic system, and conversely, some rather doubtful choice relations are in fact represented as the central ones by the system. This becomes clear if we take the functional notion of minimal contrast into consideration.

Here is a set of examples which are defined as a central, immediately relevant choice relation by the *IFG* model but which in actual fact display a rather doubtful choice relation:

(2a)   Joan <u>had won</u> the competition.

(2b)   Joan <u>was winning</u> the competition.

(2c)   Joan <u>was going to win</u> the competition.

The verbal groups exemplify a 'past in past', a 'present in past' and a 'future in past', respectively. In other words, in all three cases the primary tense is 'past'. After the initial choice of 'past', the Performer goes on to choose a 'past in' in (2a), a 'present in' in (2b) and 'future in' in (2c). The examples thus show the most immediate contrasts after the initial choice of 'past'. It is only if we extend the paradigm that we can legitimately view the three examples as choice-related to e.g. *Joan won the competition* (with a simple 'past' form). And even if we extend the paradigm according to Matthiessen's principle, (2a) is never choice-related to e.g. *Joan has won the competition*, and (2b) is never choice-related to e.g. *Joan is winning the competition* – despite the fact that there is a sense in which such pairs have a clear potential for being minimally distinct.

What is the effect of choosing (and hence the Performer's most likely motivation for choosing) *had won* in (2a) instead of *was winning* in (2b) or *was going to win* in (2c)? If we were completely faithful to the *IFG* model we would probably say that (2a) construes the process as located prior to some past relevance time rather than as simultaneous with it or as posterior to it. However, there is much more to these constructions than simple precedence relations. The differences between them are much more complex. In (2a) and (2b), but not necessarily (2c), the event time is prior to the moment of communication ($T_e < T_s$: this means that part of the Performer's motivation for choosing (2a) and (2b), but not (2c), is to locate the process in the past. In (2c), unlike (2a) and (2b), the truth conditions are such that we cannot be sure that the competition actually took place, or will take place: at the moment of communication it may have been cancelled or it is yet to take place but may be cancelled. All we know is that if it takes place it will do so after some past relevance time ($T_e > T_r < T_s$). In fact, these factors may well motivate the Performer to say something like (2c) (e.g. *Surely the only reason they called off the competition was that they knew she was going to win it*).

In addition to a difference in terms of the precise precedence relation between a past relevance time and a past event time, examples (2a) and (2b) exhibit another contrast: that between *completion* (the actual winning of the competition) in (2a) and *progression directed towards completion* (the attempt to win the competition) in (2b). This contrast is of an experiential nature, concerning the exact nature of the process construed. The two examples are thus truth-conditionally and propositionally distinct: while in (2a) 'she' has clearly won the competition, in (2b) 'she' may or may not win the competition. *She was winning the competition* does not necessarily imply *She had won the competition* or even *She won the competition*.

We can thus conclude that examples (2a), (2b) and (2c) are *not* minimally distinct. In addition to the bare precedence relations expressed, they differ with respect to the location of the process relative to the moment of communication and in terms of precise experiential meaning. This means that the choice situation involved is a rather doubtful one: having already chosen 'past' as the primary tense, the Performer is never likely to consider secondary 'past', 'present' and 'future' to be genuinely competing, minimally distinct options. They are simply not genuine competitors.

The final problem that I would like to call attention to in connection with choice relations is that certain important minimal pairs of forms or constructions are not presented as directly opposed choice options in the *IFG* model but are relegated to the extended paradigm. Consider the following examples:

(3a) They <u>walked</u> along the beach, arm in arm.

(3b) They <u>were walking</u> along the beach, arm in arm.

(4a) Roger <u>swam</u> across the river.

(4b) Roger <u>was swimming</u> across the river.

(5a) The door <u>slammed</u> behind me.

(5b) The door <u>was slamming</u> behind me.

In the a-examples we have simple 'past' tense forms, in the b-examples 'present in past' tense forms. These variant constructions are in much closer competition than the 'past in past', 'present in past' and 'future in past' in (2a) to (2c). We do not have to look far to find appropriate contexts for examples (3a,b) to (5a,b), in which the event time is past relative to the moment of communication in both the a-examples and the b-examples: the Performer wants to say something about a past process, and in both cases the process is tagged on to some particular past relevance time. The difference between the two variants is one of 'situational focus': in the a-examples the process is presented with an external focus, as a complete whole, whereas in the b-examples the process is presented with an internal focus, as something in progress. Sometimes, as in (3a,b), the difference is experientially neutral and seems to be of a purely textual kind: the two sentences are simply slightly different ways of saying exactly the same thing. Thus, if it is true to say that *They walked along the beach, arm in arm*, then it is also true to say that at some point *They were walking along the beach, arm in arm*, and vice versa. The meaning of the a-example implies the meaning of the b-example, and the meaning of the b-example implies the meaning of the a-example. Now, this is a genuinely minimal pair, and the choice between them should be explicitly reflected by our systemic network apparatus, rather than by some extended paradigm.

In other cases, such as (4a,b) and (5a,b), the difference is not just one of textual, presentational meaning but, in addition, one of experiential meaning. Though *swam* and *slammed* construe the process referred to with an external focus like *walked*, and though *was swimming* and *was slamming* construe the process with an internal focus like *was walking*, the two simple past forms are associated also with completion and punctuality, respectively, and the two progressive forms are associated also with activity directed towards completion and iteration, respectively. Note here that *Roger was swimming across the river* does not imply that *Roger swam across the river*, and *The door slammed behind me* does not imply *The door was slamming behind me*. In a number of publications (Bache 1985, 1997, 2000), I have shown that the various actional meanings associated with progressive and nonprogressive forms can be seen as systematically related to the minimal difference shown in examples like (3a,b), i.e. to variation in textual meaning. The choice relation between the past progressive and the simple past, unlike the one between the past perfect, past progressive and past future, can be described in terms of a minimal semantic opposition and its functional derivations across metafunctions.

This kind of pattern in choice relations is not exceptional. Something very similar applies to the distinction between the simple present and the simple past. Consider the following examples:

(6a) Nefertiti <u>believes</u> in justice.

(6b) Nefertiti <u>believed</u> in justice.

(7a) She <u>speaks</u> like a real professional.

(7b) She <u>spoke</u> like a real professional.

In (6a,b), the simple present and the simple past differ only with respect to the temporal location of the mental process referred to (as present or past in relation to the moment of communication), and thus constitute minimally distinct options like the past progressive and the simple past in (3a,b). As noted in Section 3.5 above, in (7a,b) we find the same distinction between present and past location of the process referred to, but the two constructions have different actional (experiential) implications: the most immediate reading of (7a) is that it describes a present characteristic of the subject (or an ability, or a habit), whereas (7b) is ambiguous, describing either a past characteristic of the subject (*As a young woman she spoke like a real profession*) or something which took place on a particular occasion (*In her address to the board members last night, she spoke like a real professional*).

What is important to realise in our search for minimal pairs or sets of constructions is that the contrast involved is potentially minimal and may serve as a basis for more distinct systematic uses of the constructions involved. In this sense, *IFG*'s collection of primary 'past', 'present' and 'future' may qualify as a minimal set, but the collection of secondary 'past', 'present' and 'future' (in combination with e.g. 'past') does not. Progressive and nonprogressive forms enter minimal pairs but this is not directly reflected by the *IFG* model. An analysis of perfect forms would show something similar: that important choice relations are relegated to the extended paradigm and thus not directly reflected by the *IFG* tense system (for discussion of minimal pairs in connection with perfect forms, see Bache 1985: 176–207; 1997: 151–173).

3.6   Is the *IFG* model observationally adequate?

I turn now to an entirely different problem which needs careful attention in my critical examination of the *IFG* approach to tense in English: the problem of observational adequacy in a functional grammar. To what extent does Halliday and Matthiessen's model accommodate the relevant data, and how do we determine what the relevant data are? The **meaning potential** of the English tense system, as reflected by the central tripartite system in conjunction with recursion and stop rules, has always been a central descriptive concern for Halliday. But how does one strike the right balance between mapping this 'meaning potential' and characterising **actual usage**, which is a central concern for any functional grammarian? As shown in Section 2.1 above, the recursive *IFG* model generates 36 finite tense forms in Halliday's System I. Some of these tenses are perfectly common: e.g. 'past' *took*, 'future' *will take* and 'present in past in past' *had been taking*. Others, especially the more complex ones, are infrequent and may occasionally strike even native speakers of English as somewhat unusual, e.g.:

> has been going to be playing
> > (a 'present in future in past in present')

> will have been going to have laughed
> > (a 'past in future in past in future')

> had been going to have been taking
> > (a 'present in past in future in past in past')

> will have been going to have been singing
> > (a 'present in past in future in past in future')

The inclusion of such rather unusual examples is quite deliberate on Halliday's part (cf. 1976c: 145ff, 2004: 19; see also Halliday and James 1993). He offers three points in support of including them in his model. First of all, he says, it is important that one's description should cope not only with written language but also with spontaneous, unselfconscious spoken language, and it is in this mode that we find the more unusual examples. He notes that especially the combination of two consecutive nonfinite forms of BE (*been being*) and the 'future in future' (*will be going to* + infinitive) are rare, and that native speakers may well find them odd if their attention is drawn to them. Nevertheless, such examples are recorded in informal conversation, he claims, and they should be taken seriously because it is in this mode that 'the essential nature of language, its semogenic or meaning-creating potential, is most clearly revealed' (2004: 25).

Halliday's second point in support of paying attention to rare examples in his description of tense is that they are only rare because the contexts in which they appropriately occur are rare, not because they are odd or inappropriate as such. When these forms are needed in a particular context, they are in fact readily available to the Performer, he argues, and should therefore be regarded as a natural language resource worthy of descriptive attention.

Halliday's final point in connection with rare tenses is that they are not formally independent but naturally integrated in the tense system. He notes that they are 'built up out of very simple resources' (1976c: 145) and that, more specifically, they are the result of tense choices being made more than once in the basic recursive tense system. This means that they are not directly contrasted with the more frequently occurring simple tense forms but with other, equally complex forms in a recursive cycle. In other words, we are left to infer that their inclusion in the tense description is not a violation of the principle of descriptive simplicity often invoked in linguistics but comes almost 'for free', as a natural extension of the basic system.

I agree with Halliday that it is important to consider spontaneous and unselfconscious spoken language, and that there is a sense in which such data should have priority in any analysis of the meaning potential of language. I also agree with him that all data, spoken or written, should be considered in relation to the context in which they were produced, and that it is only to be expected that contextual factors may determine the relative frequency of forms and constructions. But I do not subscribe to the claim that there is anything particularly natural or inherently economical about a description involving recursion and stop rules.

When considering the frequency of forms and constructions there is always a danger that rare instances get ignored, especially if they occur only (or primarily) in spoken language. Halliday is right to raise this issue. However, there are at least two factors that need to be addressed when we decide to take a closer look at less usual forms and constructions in spontaneous, unselfconscious spoken language. The first is that there is always a tenuous dividing line between a Performer's creative exploitation of a language's meaning-making resources in a particular context, on the one hand, and a slip of the tongue or a simple mistake on the other. Though Halliday is obviously aware of this problem in his 2004 article on corpus linguistics (cf. Halliday 2004: 21), he never stops to question the status of his 36 tenses in System I as grammatically acceptable or appropriate. Let us look at a couple of concrete examples of unusual verb forms from Collins Wordbanks*Online* corpus (for details of this corpus, see below):

(1)   Mind you you could deduct then all of those that you find that <u>are have got</u> more than one word in them from these totals and then you're okay for that.

(2)   Erm equally as a council <ZF1> you <ZF0> you may feel a respon-sibility <ZF1> to <ZF0> to try to assist er <ZGY> street drinkers <ZGY> in that one instance >ZGY> tangents to that. You <u>are prob-ably be going to be working</u> on half a dozen different <ZGY> at once to try and achieve a safer green area for people to enjoy within the neighbourhood.[5]

Both of these examples are from the subcorpus 'ukspok' [UK spoken], which contains spontaneous, unselfconscious spoken language. The form *are have got* is found not only in (1) but in two other ukspok texts, while the form *are ... be going to be* + present participle in example (2) is a unique occurrence. Neither form is recognised by Halliday as a member of System I. But in each case it is possible to argue that the Performer is drawing on standard re-sources of English and that the particular combination of choices reflects a creative exploitation of the meaning potential of the language. Thus in (1), *are* serves to single out for emphasis both the present temporal meaning of the subsequent perfect ('past in present') form *have got* and the relational nature of the verb group as a whole. In (2), *are ... be going to* reflects a more equally balanced focus on present and future time than either *are going to* or *will be going to*. In other words, both examples could be explained in plau-sible semogenic terms. But are (1) and (2) grammatically acceptable? Should they be included in Halliday's 'System 1'? I think not.[6] It is one thing to be able to offer an ad hoc explanation of why such constructions may occur in performance, quite another to accept them as part of the regular grammati-cal system. But interestingly enough, as we shall see below, both forms are in fact more frequent than some of the forms or constructions accepted as per-fectly normal tenses in Halliday's System I.

The second factor that needs to be addressed when we consider rare constructions in spoken language is their relevance from the point of view of **descriptive adequacy**: to what extent should rare (but obviously potential) occurrences affect the grammatical description of the category under analy-sis? Should infrequent data be as easily and centrally accommodated within the category as highly frequent and perfectly normal data (in which case their exceptional nature may pass unnoticed) or should they be explicitly marked in the description as potential but rare forms which may occur in very special contexts and which may thus serve to supplement the more usual members of the category (in which case their marginal status from the point of view of usage is fully recognised)? In my view, there should be a limit to our efforts to cater for rare and exceptional usage in our general model. Only by having such a limit can we ensure a balanced overall view of usage and meaning potential and at the same time throw appropriate light on rare examples as indeed ... rare examples.

Both the question of the rare occurrence of certain constructions and the question of their descriptive status involve the SFL notion of 'delicacy'. It makes good sense to recognise various degrees of delicacy in a system network (reflecting an increasing specificity and individuality as one moves to the right in the network). But at what point does delicacy turn into idiosyncrasy and simple mistakes? Unfortunately, Halliday has nothing to say about these things in relation to his tense system. While he quite obviously admits to some of his finite tenses being rare, it is not clear exactly what tenses fall into this category and just how rare they are.

In order to get an idea of the relative frequency of the finite active tenses in Halliday's model, I have studied their occurrence in two corpora: the British National Corpus (BNC) of 100,000,000 words and Collins Wordbanks*Online* (CWO) of 57,000,000 words.[7] The BNC includes 10,000,000 words of spoken English, CWO 15,000,000. Of this total of 25,000,000 spoken words in the two corpora, approximately 14,000,000 are spontaneously and unselfconsciously spoken. Just how much speech 25,000,000 words amount to is difficult to imagine because we do not normally think of speech in terms of number of words. But if we assume an average of 120 words per minute in spoken interaction (which is neither very fast nor extremely slow) the spoken part of the two corpora represents almost 3,500 hours of uninterrupted speech.[8] If we 'translate' the number of spoken words into a more easily recognisable measure of written language, we can say that the spoken part of the two corpora corresponds to more than 83,000 standard pages of literary fiction (or about 275 novels). So even though the spoken part of the two corpora is clearly much smaller than the written part, it is still impressively large. In the following investigation I shall initially deal with the BNC and CWO separately because the search facilities are significantly different.

3.6.1   Halliday's System I in the BNC

At the outset it is important to note the following limitation in the search facilities in the BNC when one uses the standard SARA-32 client (SARA = SGML-Aware Retrieval Application): *queries have to be lexically specific.*

SARA cannot handle constructions comprising grammatical variables or combinations of lexical items and grammatical types.[9] Thus there is at present no easy way to determine the exact frequency in the BNC of, say, the 'present in past in present' or the combination of a form of HAVE + *been* + V-*ing*. What one can do instead is test specific constructions like *has been dancing, have been doing, has been working*, etc. By probing a number of frequent verbs as well as some randomly selected ones in such constructions, my empirical investigation does succeed in giving a reasonably clear indication of their status with respect to usage and frequency. In other cases, Halliday's tenses contain enough *invariable material* to allow very precise testing, e.g. the 'present in past in future in past in future' *will have been going to have been taking*, where [will have been going to have been] can be queried and the results skimmed for cases where the string is followed by a present participle of *any verb* (not just *taking*). To identify cases with discontinuous tense constructions, e.g. negated constructions (*will not have been going to have been*), constructions containing other adverbials (*will probably have been going to have been*) or constructions affected by inversion (*will they have been going to have been*), I have used query strings containing the 'anyword' wild card character in post-operator position, which is the most common break-off point in discontinuous constructions (for discussion of adverbial positions, see Bache 2000: 65ff): e.g. [will _ have been going to have been]. I did not test other break-off points or multiple-word constructions in post-operator position. As we shall see below, my procedure ensured default testing of such constructions in connection with low-frequency tenses. Nevertheless, it is important to keep these limitations in mind when we consider the implication of the results of my investigation.

Given the fact that overall precision could not be obtained I decided to settle for a principle of *relative precision* whereby, roughly, precision is *inversely proportional to frequency*. In the kind of study that I wanted to undertake it is not important to establish whether, say, the 'past in present' occurs 139,456 times or 121,989 times in the two corpora, because in either case the 'past in present' is established as a very frequent tense – and that is all we really need to know in the context of this particular study. At the highly frequent end of the scale, a difference of several thousand hits is thus immaterial. By contrast, with extremely rare tenses, the *exact frequency* must be determined. It is obviously important to know whether a form occurs 57 times or just once, or not at all. Here a difference of just a few hits is very significant. With this principle of relative precision in mind, my test was designed in the following way: for each tense, the first query simply involved the verb TAKE, which is Halliday's own example in his list of 36 forms (e.g. the past *took* and the 'present in past in future' *will have been taking*), cf. Halliday (1976c: 153f). For this kind of limited search, I used the abbreviation 'TS' (= Take-Search). If the result of this query was *more than two hundred hits* for a particular tense, no additional queries involving that tense were put to SARA (on the not unreasonable assumption that a comprehensive test of all verbs in English would result in thousands of hits). Morphological variants of the operator with respect to person and number (*am/are/is//were/was// have/has* plus contractions) were recorded separately and the hits were added up in order to provide a total number for the construction as a tense form. The results were double-checked by means of the so-called **query-builder**, which allows complex queries involving several distinct lexical items or several morphological variants of an item at once.

If the result of the first query was *less than two hundred hits* for a particular tense, a new query was put to SARA containing only the unbroken invariable part of the string, e.g. *will have* in the case of *will have taken*, or *had been going to have been* in the case of *had been going to have been taking*. In some cases this resulted in hundreds or thousands of hits, in others very few or none. Many concordances elicited in this way are of course irrelevant because they do not actually contain the missing part of the tense form queried. For example, using [will have] as a query string will elicit not only the 'past in future' *will have taken* but also *will have breakfast*. Using reduced query strings thus requires sifting out the relevant examples. My sifting procedure was the following: when the result was *more than 1,500 hits* I asked for a display of random samples of 100 hits. In these random samples, the *first 12 cases* of the reduced string being followed by a verb form corresponding to the missing verb form in the original query (e.g. infinitive *love*, past participle *brought* or present participle *dancing* depending on the specification of the particular tense) were subsequently tested individually, along with three queries containing verbs not already represented that I predicted would be frequent (such as DO, MAKE, TRY, HAVE, GET). For this kind of search I used the abbreviation SwSS (= Sweet Sixteen Search) because it involved 16 lexical verbs. The hits of these supplementary queries were then added up, and again the results were double-checked by means of the query-builder. In those cases where the reduced string elicited *less than 1,500 hits*, I very carefully went through the material for *relevant* hits (i.e. hits where the query string was followed by the relevant verb form). This part of my investigation shows the exact number of occurrences of the tense in relation to *any verb* in conjunction with the query string. The abbreviation used for this kind of search was ES (= Exhaustive Search). In all cases of a tense not being especially frequent, my search was continued with queries containing the 'anyword' wild card character to identify discontinuous tense constructions, the strategy being to ensure the greatest possible precision for low-frequency tenses.

When the above procedure produced no hits at all, a final query was put to SARA containing only the nonfinite and nonlexical part of the string, e.g. [have been going to have been] representing the 'present in past in future in past in future', as in *will have been going to have been taking*. It is important to note here that in such ES queries the corpus is by default searched also for cases of single- and multiple-word adverbials or subjects in post-operator position as well as cases with prehead (single- and multiple-word) adverbials, as in e.g. the following putative examples of the 'past in future in past in future': *will in any case have been going to have been taking* (with a multiple-word post-operator adverbial), *will your many fine students have been going to have been taking* (with a multiple-word subject in subject-operator inversion) and *will have been going to have been secretly taking* (with a single-word prehead adverbial). The power of this search option is ensured by leaving the potentially isolated parts of discontinuous constructions out of the query string (such as *will* and *taking* in the example just used). Most of these queries in fact produced no hits, but a few did, and the results were here skimmed for examples with relevant operators and heads.

I believe that my test design gives us a fairly reliable impression of the overall relative frequency of the members of Halliday's System I. When considering the implications of the principle of relative precision, it is important to note that there is lack of precision only in connection with highly frequent tenses identified by means of a TS or an SwSS: such tenses are *much more frequent* than I have been able to show (because I only counted hits for a small subset of lexical items). By contrast, my test design ensured a very high degree of precision in the case of infrequent or non-existent tenses identified by means of an ES. In searches involving primary future *will* + infinitive constructions (such as e.g. the 'future', the 'past in future' and 'present in past in future'), the number of hits was not reduced with reference to some of these constructions expressing *modal meaning*. There are two reasons for this, a theoretical one and a practical one. The theoretical reason is that verb forms in English rarely, if ever, profile only one semantic domain (such as temporality *or* modality), for further discussion of this point, see Section 4.4.6 below. The more practical reason is that by not reducing the number of hits for primary future constructions, I am giving Halliday and Matthiessen the benefit of the doubt. Being critical of their tense model, I should be careful not to reduce the number of hits on the basis of what might appear to be subjective interpretation of semantic domains. This means that the test is in this respect designed to give Halliday and Matthiessen the best possible result. A full description of all the queries and the results of my investigation is offered in the appendix. Below I offer a brief summary of the results with a specification for each tense of the number and name assigned to it by Halliday, followed by an example with TAKE in parentheses, the type of search strategy involved and the number of hits elicited by the search(es).

The following members of Halliday's System I are *frequent*:

1.	past (*took*)	TS	37,218
2.	present (*takes*)	TS	11,666
3.	future (*will take*)	TS	3,379
4.	past in past (*had taken*)	TS	3,736
5.	past in present (*has taken*)	TS	1,956
6.	past in future (*will have taken*)	SwSS	945
7.	present in past (*was/were taking*)	TS	1,443
8.	present in present (*am/are/is taking*)	TS	1,559
9.	present in future (*will be taking*)	SwSS	733
10.	future in past (*was/were going to take*)	SwSS	1,972
11.	future in present (*am/are/is going to take*)	SwSS	1,548
16.	present in past in past (*had been taking*)	SwSS	844
17.	present in past in present (*has/have been taking*)	SwSS	779

If these tense forms were tested in relation to *all* lexical verbs, there would of course be many more hits for each tense. We can conclude that they are all perfectly normal, regularly occurring constructions in English and should naturally be recognised as such in our tense description.

The following tenses are *infrequent* or rare (some of them in fact extremely rare) with the upper limit for this category set (somewhat arbitrarily) at 200 hits:

12.	future in future (*will be going to take*)	ES	5
14.	past in future in present (*is going to have taken*)	ES	1
18.	present in past in future (*will have been taking*)	ES	26
19.	present in future in past (*was going to be taking*)	ES	43
20.	present in future in present (*is going to be taking*)	ES	87
22.	future in past in past (*had been going to take*)	ES	41
23.	future in past in present (*has been going to take*)	ES	1

Despite the fact that these results are exhaustive (in the sense that the corpus has been searched for occurrences of the tense forms in relation to any verb, in continuous as well as discontinuous constructions), the number of hits is in each case remarkably low in comparison with the first group of tenses shown above (none of which was tested exhaustively).

Finally, the remaining 16 tenses in Halliday's 'System I' turned out to be *non-existent* in the BNC (each receiving an 'ES 0' in the test):

13. past in future in past (*was going to have taken*)

15. past in future in future (*will be going to have taken*)

21. present in future in future (*will be going to be taking*)

24. future in past in future (*will have been going to take*)

25. past in future in past in past (*had been going to have taken*)

26. past in future in past in present (*has been going to have taken*)

27. past in future in past in future (*will have been going to have taken*)

28. present in past in future in past (*was going to have been taking*)

29. present in past in future in present (*is going to have been taking*)

30. present in past in future in future (*will be going to have been taking*)

31. present in future in past in past (*had been going to be taking*)

32. present in future in past in present (*has been going to be taking*)

33. present in future in past in future (*will have been going to be taking*)

34. present in past in future in past in past (*had been going to have been taking*)

35. present in past in future in past in present (*has been going to have been taking*)

36. present in past in future in past in future (*will have been going to have been taking*)

Before going on to study the frequency of Halliday's System I tenses in CWO, we can conclude that, remarkably, 16 of Halliday's 36 tenses, well over a third, do not occur at all in the BNC, seven are relatively rare, and 13 are frequent, some of them in fact very frequent (especially when we consider the fact that only a limited number of lexical items were tested in this category).

3.6.2   Halliday's System I in CWO

In CWO it is possible to search for constructions containing grammatical variables or combinations of lexical items and grammatical types, such as, say, [*has/have* + *been* + present participle] (which is the formula for the 'present in past in present').[10] This facility of course ensures much greater precision in our attempt to determine the frequencies of tense forms in CWO than in the BNC. In my study of Halliday's System I in CWO, I retained a very similar progression in the queries to the one I used in my study of his tenses in the BNC in that I started out with simple TAKE-searches in connection with the highly frequent simple present tense and simple past tense and ended up with Exhaustive Searches in connection with low-frequency tenses. However, because of the more powerful search options in CWO, the Sweet-Sixteen Search procedure was replaced by what I call a 'General Search' (GS). A General Search queries the corpus for all verbs in a particular tense (such as the 'present in past in present') but does not identify discontinuous data (i.e. examples with post-operator or prehead adverbials or examples with subject-operator inversion). Though it is of course possible in the CWO to operate with single- and multiple-word wild cards, you risk getting too many examples, not of discontinuity, but of the elements of the search-string belonging to two different verbal groups, as in the following examples:

(3)   He has been outstanding in the way he has led Manly this year and <u>will</u> give them what they <u>have been lacking</u>. (oznews/01)

(4)   Hawke told the AIRC it had a legal obligation to protect collective bargaining and reject CRA's approach of offering workers cash in-ducements to leave their union. I believe that if the decision we ask for is not given then commission <u>will have been</u> involved in <u>doing</u> something which will change for the worse the fundamental nature of the Australian society he said. (oznews/01)

Both these examples were elicited by the search string [will+4have+been+2VBG] representing any verb in the 'present in past in future' (such as *will have been taking*) with a post-operator discontinuity option of up to four words and a prehead discontinuity option of up to two words. In the first example *will* belongs to the preceding verbal group and the intervening four words do not constitute a post-operator adverbial or subject. In the second example, it is the prehead discontinuity option that is the problem. Here the VBG form elicits *doing*, which clearly constitutes a separate construction immediately following the relevant verb group. With high-frequency tenses, the more precise queries allowing discontinuity will give you 'too many' hits (and require many hours of tedious work sifting the data), whereas a discontinuity-insensitive GS will give you too few but relevant hits. As a means to identify frequent tenses, a discontinuity-insensitive GS is thus clearly preferable.

The results of my investigation of Halliday's System I tenses in CWO are remarkably similar to the results of my investigation in the BNC: the same 13 tenses are frequent, the same seven tenses are infrequent and the same 16 tenses are non-existent. The following overview shows the frequencies in CWO (again with type of search indicated for each number of hits):

Frequent tenses (inexhaustive searches but thousands of hits)

1.	past (*took*)	TS	20,096
2.	present (*takes*)	TS	7,314
3.	future (*will take*)	GS	69,491
4.	past in past (*had taken*)	GS	60,168
5.	past in present (*has taken*)	GS	137,575
6.	past in future (*will have taken*)	GS	817
7.	present in past (*was taking*)	GS	60,104
8.	present in present (*is taking*)	GS	75,490
9.	present in future (*will be taking*)	GS	3,977
10.	future in past (*was going to take*)	GS	2,780
11.	future in present (*is going to take*)	GS	3,058
16.	present in past in past (*had been taking*)	GS	2,966
17.	present in past in present (*has been taking*)	GS	8,027

Infrequent tenses (exhaustive searches but <200 hits)

12.	future in future (*will be going to take*)	ES	4
14.	past in future in present (*is going to have taken*)	ES	1
18.	present in past in future (*will have been taking*)	ES	20
19.	present in future in past (*was going to be taking*)	ES	42
20.	present in future in present (*is going to be taking*)	ES	161
22.	future in past in past (*had been going to take*)	ES	7
23.	future in past in present (*has been going to take*)	ES	0

Non-existent tenses (exhaustive searches but no hits: 'ES 0')

13. past in future in past (*was going to have taken*)

15. past in future in future (*will be going to have taken*)

21. present in future in future (*will be going to be taking*)

24. future in past in future (*will have been going to take*)

25. past in future in past in past (*had been going to have taken*)

26. past in future in past in present (*has been going to have taken*)

27. past in future in past in future (*will have been going to have taken*)

28. present in past in future in past (*was going to have been taking*)

29. present in past in future in present (*is going to have been taking*)

30. present in past in future in future (*will be going to have been taking*)

31. present in future in past in past (*had been going to be taking*)

32. present in future in past in present (*has been going to be taking*)

33. present in future in past in future (*will have been going to be taking*)

34. present in past in future in past in past (*had been going to have been taking*)

35. present in past in future in past in present (*has been going to have been taking*)

36. present in past in future in past in future (*will have been going to have been taking*)

There was in fact one example in CWO of a 'present in future in past in present' (number 32 in the group of non-existent System I tenses):

(5) You see <ZG0> something like er <u>has been going to be being</u> it doesn't matter what follows it really <M0X> No. <ZGY> <M0X> because <F0X> <ZGY> No. <ZG0> <M0X> er er <ZGY> you've got all the evidence you need in that and all these things are <M0X> Well <ZGY> <M0X> closed sets.

However, a closer look at source and context reveals that this example (which is from the ukspok/04 subcorpus) is part of a linguistic discussion about the English tense system at Birmingham University on 16 September 1991, and that the particular tense construction is a citation of the tense rather than an example of actual usage.[11] For that reason I reject it as a valid concordance line in my examination of tense frequency.

The first and most obvious conclusion of my examination of tense frequencies in the BNC and CWO is that Halliday's recursive tense system is far too powerful: even after the application of stop rules (which seriously constrain the process of recursion), there is an unacceptable overgeneration of tenses. Halliday argues that his inclusion of rare tenses is based on strictly functional criteria, such as an attempt to map the meaning potential of the tense system, but in reality his recursive system generates what looks much more like a *potential inventory of formal combinations irrespective of actual usage* – the kind of thing that formal linguists would be concerned with. Thus, Halliday's tense description may be observationally adequate from a formal linguistic point of view, but hardly from a functional linguistic point of view, where we expect a better balance between considerations of meaning potential and actual usage, i.e. a concern for *genuine choice relations.*

The second conclusion concerns the role of recursion in the generation of tenses. To determine this role more precisely, it is interesting, first of all, to note that there is a striking pattern to the division of tenses into the three main frequency categories (frequent, infrequent, non-existent). The frequent tenses are:

numbers 1–11 plus 16 and 17,

the infrequent ones are:

numbers 18–23 except 21, plus 12 and 14

and the non-existent ones are:

numbers 24–36 plus 13, 15 and 21.

Roughly speaking, the first tenses in System I are frequent, the middle ones infrequent and the last ones non-existent (with some overlap). Moreover, there is a general tendency for the number of hits to decrease as we move down the list of frequent tenses. These tendencies should be considered in relation to the number of recursive cycles involved in the construction of the tenses. System I has the following recursive profile:

1 cycle:	tenses 1–3
2 cycles:	tenses 4–12
3 cycles:	tenses 13–24
4 cycles:	tenses 25–33
5 cycles:	tenses 34–36

At first blush, frequency of occurrence would appear to be inversely proportional to the number of cycles in the recursive process, and this could of course be interpreted as support for the recursive view of the tense category: there is a sense in which it is 'natural' to expect complexity (as a reflection of recursion) to be inversely proportional to frequency. However, the problem with this interpretation is the vast difference between constructions with only one or two cycles (which are generally very frequent) and constructions with three, four or five cycles (which are generally very infrequent or non-existent). To be more precise: the frequent tenses include all three 1-cycle tenses, eight out of the nine 2-cycle tenses (the 'future in future', being rather infrequent), and only two 3-cycle tenses (the 'present in past in present' and the 'present in past in past'). The infrequent tenses include one 2-cycle tense (the 'future in future') and six 3-cycle tenses. And, finally, the non-existent tenses include four 3-cycle tenses, all nine 4-cycle tenses and all three 5-cycle tenses. From the point of view of actual usage, we can conclude that tenses are normally the result of just one or two choices, or cycles. Few tenses are generated by three cycles, and no tenses are generated by four or five cycles. This means that even if we accepted recursion as a plausible mechanism for the generation of complex tenses – which I do not, cf. Sections 3.2–3.5 above – and even if we acknowledged a certain correlation between recursive complexity and frequency of occurrence, it is far from the case that the Performer simply chooses 'again, and again and again' from the basic tripartite system (as indicated by Halliday (1976c: 147f) and Matthiessen (1996: 438f)).

Finally, it is important to note that the secondary future BE *going to* is included in all the non-existent tenses and in all the infrequent ones except one (number 18). At the same time this construction is absent from all the frequent ones, except numbers 10 and 11. This seems to indicate that the more cycles in the recursive process, the more unlikely a choice the secondary future becomes. In fact, it would not be unreasonable to question the status of BE *going to* as a core tense form. At best it is a rather marginal tense, and in my view an observationally more adequate alternative, at least from a functional linguistic point of view, would be to treat it as a special additional means of expressing futurity rather than as an integrated tense form.

3.7   Concluding remarks

I rest my case at this point. I hope to have shown that although the *IFG* tense model has a number of attractive features, there are, regrettably, also quite a few serious problems, especially from a functional linguistic point of view. It was important, I think, to have these problems identified and discussed, not only to be able to arrive eventually at a better description of tense within a systemic functional framework, but also to strengthen the functional aspect of the theory more generally. In the preceding sections, I have tried to identify what I consider to be some of the main problems of Halliday and Matthiessen's approach to tense from the point of view of both descriptive and observational adequacy, thus paving the way, I hope, for a functional tuning of the model.

Notes

1. This is also supported by the fact that they do not provide principles for any variation of values.
2. Strictly speaking, example (1b) is ambiguous: *at noon* may obviously express a relevance time (prior to which Lorna left) but alternatively it may be understood to define the time of her departure (in which case the relevance time is implicit). This ambiguity, however, does not affect my argument, but the distinction between (1a) and (1b) is perhaps more readily perceived if *at noon* in (1b) is interpreted as a relevance time.
3. The source of illustrative examples are given in parentheses and take the form of an abbreviation followed by a page number. A list of all the sources of the examples is offered on p. 207.
4. I use the term 'non-monadic' rather than 'portmanteau' because the latter is normally restricted to morphology and is associated with certain traditional descriptive approaches.
5. The codes <ZF1> and <ZF0> are used to enclose accidental, exact repetitions, and <ZGY> marks 'garbage omitted at this point'.
6. The reason why I do not consider (1) and (2) to be grammatically acceptable is that they violate more general rules for the combination of elements in the verbal group: the 'only one finite' principle in (1) and the 'no bare infinitive after BE' principle in (2) (which also applies to (1) if *have* is interpreted as an infinitive rather than a finite).
7. The 100 million tagged words in the BNC make up six and a quarter million sentences and 4124 texts representing a broad range of genres; for more information, see Aston and Burnard 1998 and www.natcorp.ox.ac.uk. CWO consists of the following 11 subcorpora: oznews (Australian news: 5.3 million words), ukephem (UK ephemera: 3.1 million words), ukmags (UK magazines: 4.9 million words), ukspok (UK spoken: 9.3 million words), usephem (US ephemera: 1.2 million words), bbc (BBC World Service: 2.6 million words), npr (National Public Radio: 3.1 million words), ukbooks (UK books: 5.3 million words), usbooks (US books: 5.6 million words), times (Times newspaper:

5.7 million words), today (Today newspaper: 5.2 million words), for more information see www.cobuild.collins.co.uk.

8. I do not know the actual length of time taken up by the texts of the spoken parts of the two corpora.

9. A new version of the software (called Xaira) is being developed to make such queries possible (Lou Burnard, personal communication). Eckhard Bick, director of the VISL-project at the University of Southern Denmark (VISL = Visual Interactive Syntax Learning; cf. http://www.visl.sdu.dk/), has designed a brilliant local prototype interface allowing licensed users to make advanced, grammatically specified searches in the BNC. This interface enabled me to verify the key results of my queries to SARA.

10. Single-word tenses (i.e. the simple past and the simple present) are important exceptions: you cannot search CWO for all present-tense or past-tense forms.

11. It was Nina Nørgaard who suggested that this example might be a citation, an interpretation which on closer inspection turned out to be correct.

4 Towards an alternative

4.1 Preliminaries

In my critical review of the *IFG* model in Chapter 3, I reached the conclusion
that what we need at this point is a description of tense in English which not
only conforms to the general functionalist axioms of SFL, as formulated by
Halliday and Matthiessen, but which is also more sensitive to function, to
the specific role of context, and to the basic semiotics of the individual tense
markers than Halliday and Matthiessen's particular model of tense. In other
words, we need a more genuinely functionalist account of choice relations as
part of our description of the tense category. The concept of choice should be
understood literally as having to do with the factors affecting the Performer's
selection of a particular tense in a text. A mere description of the inventory of
the tense category (as reflected in system networks) is not enough, nor is a
merely formal specification of how the individual tenses are generated (e.g.
in terms of realization statements and the computer implementation of the
model). Although it is of course important to provide a survey of the various
options available to the Performer, this should not be an aim in itself but a
first step towards a more adequate account of *why* a Performer uses one tense
rather than another in any given case. As I have argued in the preceding
sections, the *IFG* model does not fully meet these requirements.

In this book I shall propose an alternative and more satisfactory approach
to tense and aspect in English. It is one which I believe belongs naturally
within a systemic functional framework, while differing from the *IFG* model
in several important respects. In formulating this alternative, I take my point
of departure in the very different systemic functional description of tense
provided in the Cardiff Grammar (cf. Fawcett, Tucker and Lin 1993; Fawcett
2000a, b, c; Fawcett 2004; Fawcett 2008, Fawcett forthcoming; Fawcett n.d.).
Despite its many virtues, this approach has received less attention than the
IFG model (but see Butler (2003a, b) for a detailed account of the Cardiff
Grammar as a whole). One rather obvious reason for this is that there is no

separate publication available dealing exclusively with the Cardiff approach to modelling 'time' and its realisations in 'tense forms', nor is there a separate chapter in a published grammar. Instead we get glimpses of detailed descriptions of the various 'strands' of meaning in the English clause (where 'time' is treated as experiential rather than logical meaning), their realisations at the level of form and their formalisation in an explicit grammar (which has been computer implemented in the COMMUNAL Project). From these descriptions, however, we can piece together the information we need about primary tense, perfect forms and progressive forms in an integrated 'model of tense'. Significantly, recursion is *not* used as a mechanism for the generation of complex perfect and progressive forms, and far more attention is paid to the different meanings that can be expressed by these forms. The Cardiff Grammar thus provides a giant leap forward in the right direction.

However, in order to reach an even higher level of insight into the functional nature of tense and aspect in English (and thus further enrich the approach adopted in the Cardiff Grammar), I go on to review Harder's work on functional semantics (cf. Harder 1996) and relate it to my own work on grammatical categories, especially tense, aspect and action (cf. Bache 1997, 2002), which is based on extensive empirical work on verbal constructions in English (cf. especially Bache 1985). The model resulting from integrating Harder's approach with my own work has been outlined, but not argued in detail, in Bache and Davidsen-Nielsen (1997) and in Bache (2000), which are general grammars of English. The most important difference between the model I am going to propose in this book and the *IFG* model is that my model does not assume recursion of a simple tripartite tense system for the description of complex verbal constructions while nevertheless retaining seriality as a central principle of tense composition. On the question of recursion as the main organising principle of tense I thus side with the Cardiff approach. But my model, like the *IFG* model and the one proposed by Harder, explicitly recognises the serial nature of tense – an aspect of the model which is far from incompatible with the grammar proposed by Fawcett and his colleagues, but which receives much less emphasis in Cardiff than in Sydney. As I hope to have shown in Chapter 3, the concept of recursion, though not the concept of seriality, is simply at odds with a truly functionalist description of the choice relations involved in the tense category. It should therefore be abandoned, even if it has some descriptive elegance.

Before going into detail on my own theoretical position (in Section 4.4) and my proposals for a new SFL approach to tense in English (in Chapter 5), I shall offer an introduction to the treatment of time and tense in the Cardiff Grammar (Section 4.2). My discussion of this approach will demonstrate that it is perfectly feasible to operate with tense as a nonrecursive category within a genuinely systemic functional framework, and that there is much to be gained from this in a description which aims at a more adequate account of the choice relations involved. There then follows an introduction of Harder's theory of functional semantics and its application to tense in English, in Section 4.3.1 below. Although Harder is very critical of Halliday's version of SFL, his theory is not incompatible with many general aspects of SFL thinking, and a number of his more specific points concerning tense in English will assist me with my proposals for a new SFL model. However, Harder's analysis is not entirely flawless either, and therefore needs to be more carefully examined prior to application. This is done in Section 4.3.2, where I offer a number of critical remarks on Harder's theory and modify his ideas on the basis of my own work on categories.

4.2. The Cardiff approach to time and tense

4.2.1 The Cardiff Grammar

To get a sense of how Fawcett and his colleagues account for time and tense in English, it is necessary first to know the theoretical context in which they make their proposals. The Cardiff Grammar is the result of at least two main ambitions: to develop an alternative to Halliday's version of systemic functional grammar (as presented in *IFG* and elsewhere) which avoids a number of serious problems and inconsistencies in the latter (as identified in Fawcett 2000b,c) but which is no less systemic and functional in orientation; and secondly, to offer a fully explicit grammar that is tested by being implemented in the GENESYS generator of the COMMUNAL project and so offered as an improvement on the Nigel grammar in the Penman Project. The Cardiff Grammar is characterized by a number of interesting and thought-provoking features, the most important of which (for my purposes) are the following:

(A) The emphasis on potential structure

The Cardiff Grammar specifies not only the *meaning potential* of English (in terms of system networks of semantic choices) but also the *form potential*. The latter consists of a complementary set of realisation rules, these being instantiated, for each pass through the system network, as 'one layer of a richly labelled tree structure'. Distinguishing between 'potential' and 'instance', Fawcett offers a model of the main components of the Cardiff Grammar in Figure 4.1 (taken from Fawcett 2000a: 36).

In the Cardiff Grammar there is thus a nice balance between *the level of meaning* and *the level of form*, and there is a specification of the interdependence between the paradigmatic and syntagmatic relations of these levels, respectively.[1] One important aspect of this grammar is that it focuses more precisely on syntax than *IFG* does, but not at the expense of choice relations at the level of meaning. In other words, in addition to a thorough description of system networks and selection expressions, the Cardiff Grammar aims to provide a more consistent theory of both semantics and functional syntax, and in this respect it is very similar to Harder's approach to functional semantics, in which there is an insistence on the relevance of structure as a non-autonomous vehicle for the expression of meaning (see Section 4.3.1 below).

(B) A single two-dimensional structural representation

Second, there is a sense in which *IFG* is in fact more 'structure-oriented' than the Cardiff Grammar in that it provides *several* simultaneous structural representations of a sentence, one for each metafunction. The Sydney grammar thus provides a structure for (a) the interpersonal metafunction in terms of MOOD with Mood (comprising Subject and Finite) and Residue (comprising Predicator, Complement and Adjunct); (b) the experiential metafunction in terms of TRANSITIVITY (e.g. Actor, Process, Goal, Circumstance); and (c) the textual metafunction in terms of both THEME (Theme and Rheme) and INFORMATION (Given and New). In addition, the structure of clause

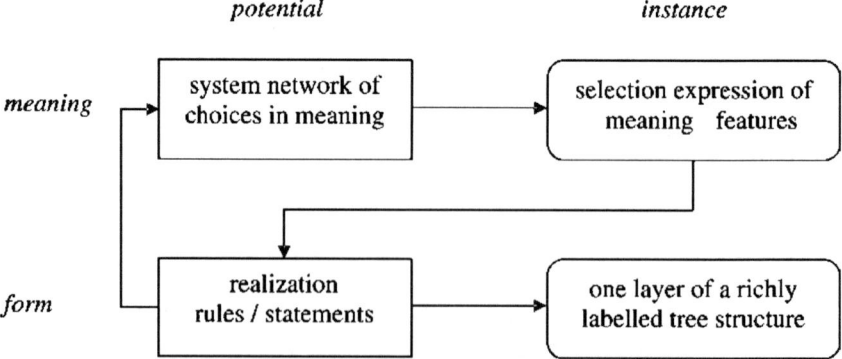

Figure 4.1: Fawcett's main components of a systemic functional grammar

complexes is handled by the logical metafunction. In *IFG* the *multifunctional* approach to the analysis of a sentence is thus matched by a *multistructural* approach. Not so in the Cardiff Grammar. The specification of 'one layer of a richly labelled tree structure' in Figure 4.1 above should be taken seriously. While recognising the central importance of the multifunctional principle in a systemic functional grammar, Fawcett and his colleagues nevertheless argue – in my view very convincingly – that it is both descriptively and explanatorily more adequate to operate with just a single two-dimensional structure at the level of form (for detailed discussion, see Fawcett 2000a). They thus use conventional tree diagrams for the representation of their functional syntax, cf. Fawcett's analysis of a simple clause and its constituents in Figure 4.2 (Fawcett 2000c: 338). In this particular tree diagram the following labels have been used: Cl = clause; O = Operator; RX = retrospective Auxiliary; S = Subject; Ag = Agent; M = Main Verb; C = Complement; Af = Affected; ngp = nominal group; h = head. The slash convention (/) is used to indicate conflation, cf. Subsections C and D.

(C) No verbal group

A potentially even more controversial aspect of the Cardiff Grammar is that it does not recognise the 'verbal group' as a class of unit, and that, more generally, it challenges Halliday's concepts of **rank, rank scale** and **rank shift**. Fawcett (2000b, c) argues – in my view again very convincingly – for treating the elements of Halliday's verbal group as elements directly of the clause. There is no space here to go into the details of all the arguments for

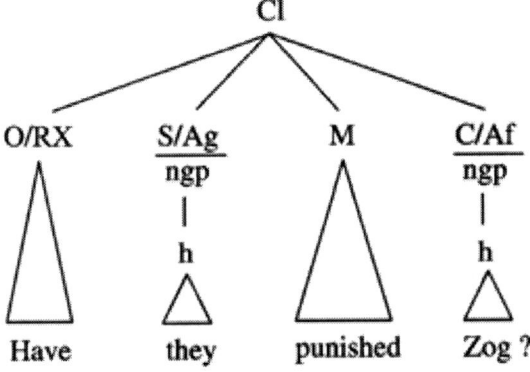

Figure 4.2: Fawcett's tree diagram representation of a simple clause

abandoning the verbal group, but let me give you the main points. Fawcett initially points out that Halliday himself is ambivalent about the status of the Finite as an element of the verbal group or as an element of the clause. In the analysis of MOOD, the Finite co-functions with the Subject, which is clearly an element of the clause, while the 'rest' of the verbal group is part of the Residue. As a result, Halliday promotes the Finite to function as an element of the clause. This has serious implications, not only for the concept of rank (according to which we would expect an element of the clause to have group status) but also for the other verbal group elements with which the Finite is often **conflated**, such as Auxiliaries and the Main Verb. But Halliday never explored these implications. Fawcett is naturally keen to do so. He first of all suggests that we should use 'Operator' rather than 'Finite' as the relevant clausal element (leaving finiteness to be a realisation of primary tense). Strictly speaking, therefore, in the Cardiff Grammar the *conflation argument* extends to auxiliaries only, not to the Main Verb, unless the Main Verb is BE (or more rarely HAVE). But there are many other arguments in favour of abandoning the verbal group, and they apply to all types of Main Verb. These include a number of important syntactic, semantic and computational considerations, such as the unusual amount of discontinuity in the 'verbal group' with intervening clause elements (such as e.g. Adjuncts and Subjects), the ambiguous status in *IFG* of 'particles' (adverbs and prepositions, and combinations) in Main Verb Extensions (as in 'phrasal verbs', 'prepositional verbs' and 'phrasal prepositional verbs'), as well as a number of interdependencies between clause elements and elements of Halliday's verbal group, the most significant of which take the form of **co-realisation** and **portmanteau realisation**.

(D) Co-realisation and portmanteau realisation

As we saw in the preceding paragraph, conflation is an important phenomenon in the Cardiff Grammar (as it is in the Sydney Grammar). In an example like *Jennifer was visiting her friend*, the Operator (O) is said to be conflated with the Auxiliary (X) BE (which together with the suffix *–ing* realises the meaning of 'period-marked' in the Cardiff Grammar terminology, see below), the result being *was* (O/X). If Operator is an element of the clause rather than an element of a verbal group, then surely BE must be, too, unless we were to accept that *was* could be an element of both the clause and a verbal group at the same time – a most peculiar syntactic configuration. Notice next that the finite form of BE co-operates with the present participle form of the Main Verb (*visiting*) to express the meaning of 'period-marked', which is the temporal meaning associated with progressive forms, according to Fawcett. In the Cardiff Grammar terminology, period-marked meaning is **co-realised** by an Auxiliary (a form of BE) and a suffix (*-ing*). Similarly in what is traditionally referred to as the 'perfect' form (e.g. *Jennifer has visited her friend*), 'retrospective meaning' is **co-realised** by an Auxiliary (a form of HAVE) and a suffix (realized as *–en* or *–ed*, or in an irregular form of the Main Verb). Since in both cases the suffix is called upon to co-realise a particular meaning with an element of the clause, it would add considerably to the complexity of the structural analysis (and of the computational implementation) if the suffix was regarded as part of an element of a verbal group, rather than as part of an element of the clause. In examples like *Jennifer was visiting her friend* and *Jennifer has visited her friend*, this supports the status of the Main Verb as an element of the clause too (because the suffix is attached to the Main Verb). In other examples, co-realisation is a further argument for treating Auxiliaries as elements of the clause: e.g. *Jennifer has been visiting her friend* and *Jennifer was being examined by the doctor*.

Another important concept, in addition to conflation and co-realisation, is **portmanteau realisation**, i.e. the blending together of two independent meanings in a single expression without syntagmatic structure, as in e.g. *Jennifer saw everything*, where *saw* realizes both the lexical meaning of 'seeing' and 'past time'. Another example of portmanteau realisation is *Jennifer is brave*, where *is* realises both the minimal process of 'being' and 'present time',[2] and at the same time is a conflation of the Operator with the Main Verb (cf. *Is Jennifer brave?*). As Fawcett (2000c: 339) puts it:

> [I]t is clear that the grammar should treat as elements of the same unit the Operator, the Auxiliaries [...] and the Main Verb (and so too the Main Verb Extension). The descriptive facts of English are that the 'core' elements of the Operator (or Finite), the Auxiliaries and the Main Verb (or Event) are realized by a string of inherently non-adjacent morphemes – or in the case of the Operator and 'irregular' Main Verbs, by portmanteau realizations such as *is* and *ate*. Thus, once the decision has been made to promote the Finite to the clause, that unit has to be the clause.

This very nicely summarises Fawcett's case against the verbal group. As we shall see in Section 4.4 (where I present my own approach to the description of verbal categories, and paradigmatic relations more generally) the notion of a 'portmanteau realisation' is very similar to what I refer to as 'non-monadicness' (see also my earlier comments on this topic in Section 3.5). This phenomenon is not only an argument for abandoning the verbal group:

a full recognition of it is absolutely essential if we want to reach a better understanding of the interplay of various semantic domains underlying choice relations in connection with tense in English.

(E) The multifunctional principle: the many strands of meaning

In the Cardiff Grammar, the fact that there is only one structural representation does not in any way limit the semantic representation of the clause. Quite the contrary. Fawcett and his colleagues in fact elaborate Halliday's multifunctional principle and arrive at a more delicate description in terms of not just four metafunctions but *eight* **strands of meaning** (**experiential, logical, interpersonal, negativity, validity, affective, thematic** and **informational**) of which five are relevant for the description of the Operator:

Interpersonal

Validity

Experiential   a) time reference position, reality and directness
                b) control and disposition

Negativity

Informational   a) contrastive newness in correcting polarity
                b) recoverability of experiential meaning

Some of these five strands of meaning comprise more than one network, so a full description of the possible meanings of the Operator involves a total of 11 networks (for a fuller picture, see Chapter 4 of Fawcett forthcoming). As Fawcett points out, even though not all of these are present at the same time, the Operator is in fact a better example of the multifunctional principle than the Subject, which is often given as the prime example because of its simultaneous function as (a) part of the 'Mood' block (interpersonal meaning), (b) e.g. Agent (experiential meaning), and (c) Theme (textual meaning). He offers the following example of a multifunctional Operator (Fawcett forthcoming: Chapter 4, Section 10.2):

(1)   **A:** We saw an amazing man on TV last night – he can eat virtually anything. He even ate a watch and a razor blade.

       B: Yes, I saw it too. He was amazing. What <u>CAN'T</u> he eat?

Here the Operator *CAN'T* carries the interpersonal meaning of 'information seeker' (in conjunction with the Subject), the experiential meaning of 'ability', a second experiential meaning of 'present time reference position' (cf. Section 4.2.2 below), 'negative' polarity and the informational meaning of 'contrastive newness'.

In the next section, I shall describe the Cardiff Grammar's position on 'time' (including the concepts of 'time reference position', 'reality' and 'directness') and its treatment of the two Auxiliaries that express special aspects of time in the Cardiff Grammar: BE (followed by present participle) for the expression of 'period-marking' and HAVE (followed by past participle) for the expression of 'retrospective' meaning. It is from these sections of Chapter 4 of Fawcett (forthcoming) that we can piece together the Cardiff approach to time and tense.

4.2.2   Time and tense in the Cardiff Grammar

The approach to time and tense in the Cardiff Grammar is refreshingly different from the *IFG* model. As already revealed, recursion is abandoned as a central principle of tense generation, and temporal meaning is regarded as an experiential resource rather than simply as a logical one. One immediate consequence of this is that it becomes possible to fully recognise the contribution of each of the formal markers involved. In the following subsections, I shall introduce the key concepts of the Cardiff approach:[3]

(A) Objective time and performance time

A primary distinction is drawn between the 'objective' model of time and the 'performance' model of time. The former is conceived of as linear (with times such as *in 1998* shown as covering a segment of the time line) and independent of the moment of communication, while the latter is a matter of deictic orientation (centred on the Performer) and thus crucially involves the moment of utterance (more specifically the 'now' of the Performer). The two models are relevant at the levels of both meaning and form: objective time is often expressed by means of 'Time Position Adjuncts' (like *in the nineteenth century* and *on 2 June 2003*), while performance time underlies the tense system. The two models are related through the concept of utterance time, which allows a segmentation of the time line into various 'time spans' with the Performer's 'now' as the anchor. There are three primary time spans: the **past time span**, the **past-present-and-future time span** and the **future time span**, as in the following examples (from Chapter 4 of Fawcett forthcoming):

(2)   Ivy's beloved cat has died.

(3)   Ike likes ice cream.

(4)   Ike will mend the lock by Tuesday.

In (2) the event of 'the cat dying' took place in the past time span; in (3) the 'liking' is true of not just the present but also of the past and future, and thus illustrates the past-present-and-future time span; and in (4) the 'mending' will occur at some unspecified time in the future time span. In addition to these three primary time spans, there is a fourth, very brief present time span in examples like *Rooney shoots*, where the 'shooting' takes place strictly at the same time as the moment of utterance.

(B) Event time and time reference positions

In the setting up of the four time spans, the moment of utterance served as an anchor for the temporal orientation of an event. Thus, as we saw in (2), the moment of utterance defines a point of time from which a time span stretches backwards, and within this time span the event of 'dying' took place. The now of the Performer thus serves as a 'time reference position' (or 'trp' for short). In all three examples above, the present moment serves as a trp; and instead of referring to the 'now' of the Performer as 'the moment of utterance', Fawcett refers to this as 'the present trp' and defines it as the 'pivotal concept in the model of performance time' (Chapter 4 of Fawcett forthcoming). However, in English we often encounter examples with other trps, as in the following:

(5)   Ivy's beloved cat died.

(6)   She'll do well in her exams.

Both of (2) and (5) locate an event in the past time span, but while this event is viewed from a present perspective, i.e. a present trp, in (2), it is viewed from a past perspective, i.e. a past trp such as e.g. *last week*, in (5). This past trp is typically recoverable from the text, either the same clause or a preceding clause. Similarly, in (6), the event of 'doing well' is viewed from a recoverable future trp such as e.g. *next week*.

It is important, Fawcett reminds us, to distinguish between 'event time' and 'time reference position'. Event time is defined as 'the period on the time line that the event occupies' (Chapter 4 of Fawcett forthcoming). Sometimes the event time established in a clause coincides with the trp (as in *Rooney shoots* and *Ivy's beloved cat died*) or includes it (as in *Ike likes ice cream*). In other examples the two are clearly distinct (as in *Ivy's beloved cat has died* and *She'll do well in her exams*). A particularly important type of example in this connection is the use of the past perfect in examples like the following:

(7) (Fi came at ten but) Ivy <u>had arrived</u> at nine.

(8) (Fi came at ten but) Ivy <u>had arrived</u> already.

In these examples, a past event (that of 'arriving') is past relative to an already established past trp. In (8) the Adjunct *already* is used to mark a new dependent past time span: the event of 'arriving' takes place in a past period of time stretching back from the already established past trp.

In order to locate events more precisely in time, the trp can be specified by means of 'Time Position Adjuncts'. Such Adjuncts often evoke the objective model of time (as in *She lived in London in the 1990s*) but may also be deictic (as in *The cat died last week*).

(C) Aspectual types

Another essential difference between the *IFG* model of time and tense and the Cardiff approach is the latter's recognition of the importance of taking certain basic 'aspectual' event types (or 'Aktionsarten', as they are also sometimes called, but see Section 4.2.3 below) into consideration – in addition to the usual experiential process types, etc., cf. Figure 4.3 (from Chapter 4 of Fawcett forthcoming).

Fawcett emphasises the fact that this diagram is not a system network but a classification of conceptual event types that must be taken into consideration in the 'microplanner' that converts the objective time (specified at

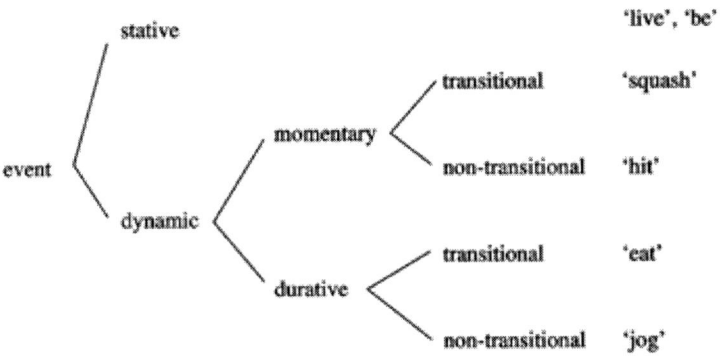

Figure 4.3: Fawcett's 'aspectual types' of event in the belief system

the level of Basic Logical Form) and inherent Aktionsart of the event in the input into performance time (at the level of Enriched Logical Form) for the generation of certain tenses. In addition to the five types in the diagram, Fawcett draws a distinction between 'single event' and 'multiple event'. As an example of the importance of operating with aspectual types, Fawcett offers the following three examples (Chapter 4 of Fawcett forthcoming):

(9)   Ivy <u>lives</u> in Cardiff.

(10)   She <u>jogs</u> to keep fit.

(11)   We <u>squash</u> our plastic bottles (before recycling them).

In these examples, the present tense refers to events in the past-present-and-future time span, but there is an important difference: it can only refer to a single event in this time span if the event is stative, as in (9); if the event is dynamic it refers to multiple events, as in (10) and (11), which are durative nontransitional and momentary transitional, respectively.

Fawcett's inclusion of event types in his description of time and tense is highly commendable, but, as we shall see (especially in Section 4.4), his use of the term 'aspectual' is somewhat misleading and confusing.[4]

(D) Systems for the expression of time

There are three primary systems for the expression of time in the Cardiff model: TIME REFERENCE POSITION, REALITY and DIRECTNESS. Two other important systems (PERIOD-MARKING and RETROSPECTIVITY) will be dealt with shortly. In the first system there are three primary trps: 'past', 'present' and 'future'. Time reference position is expressed by either the Main Verb (if an Operator is not otherwise needed) or the Operator (if it is chosen anyway to express some other meaning). Examples of these would be the past trp in *Joe went along* (trp expressed by the Main Verb) and *Joe did not go along* (trp expressed by the Operator, which is chosen anyway for the expression of negation). It is interesting to note here, incidentally, that time reference position is always included in a portmanteau realization (cf. Section 4.2.1, Subsection D). This fact will be elaborated on in Section 4.4.6 below and elsewhere. Fawcett makes another interesting point in connection with his primary trps: the present trp and the past trp are the two more frequent trps and they are often expressed by the Main Verb, whilst the future trp is typically expressed by *will* (or its first person singular variant *shall*), which always expounds the Operator. Note finally that operating with the 'past', 'present' and 'future' as **primary trps** is in fact the closest the

Cardiff school gets to the *IFG* system of primary tense, especially because Fawcett goes on to say: 'Some of the systems that are dependent on the primary system for TIME REFERENCE POSITION [...] build up secondary – and even tertiary – **dependent time reference positions.**' (Fawcett forthcoming: Chapter 4, Section 3.1, emphasis in original) and exemplifies this with:

(12) She had worked here for five years before she got a permanent post.

(13) He was going to have mended the cupboard door by Tuesday.

In these examples Fawcett identifies, respectively, a 'past from past' trp and a 'past from future from past' trp. The important difference is that in the Cardiff Grammar, such constructions are recognised as the result of combinations of choices in different systems, whereas in the *IFG* model they are generated by re-entering the same system recursively.

The two other major networks for the expression of time are REALITY and DIRECTNESS, both of which interact closely with TIME REFERENCE POSITION and with each other. REALITY offers a choice between 'real' (as in examples (1) to (13) above) and 'hypothetical', as in:

(14) If she had liked her teacher last year, she would have been happier.

(15) If she liked her teacher, she would be happier.

(16) If she likes her teacher next year, she will be happier.

In these examples (cf. Fawcett forthcoming: Chapter 4, Section 3.2), the trp remains the same in the 'conditioning' clause (the subclause) and the 'conditioned' clause (the matrix). Thus in (14) the primary trp in both clauses is past, in (15) it is present, and in (16) it is future.

DIRECTNESS offers a choice between 'direct' and 'reported' speech and thought, which affects the tense of the embedded clause. Examples (1) to (16) all illustrate the choice of 'direct', while the following examples offered by Fawcett illustrate the choice of 'reported':

(17) He said that she had seen Ivy last week.

(18) He thought that she had seen Ivy last week.

(19) He said that if she had liked her teacher she would have been happier.

Again we see an obvious interrelationship between the three primary systems for the expression of time, as well as certain rules at play for the use of tenses within each system. What I find important – and highly commendable – in the Cardiff Grammar is the recognition of the close relationship between TIME REFERENCE POSITION, REALITY and DIRECTNESS. This relationship will also play an important role in the tense model that will be proposed later in this book.

(E) Period-marking and retrospectivity

In addition to the three primary systems discussed above, there are two other very important systems for the expression of certain special aspects of time, PERIOD-MARKING and RETROSPECTIVITY. The first of these systems offers a choice between 'period-marked', realised by a combination of a form of the Auxiliary BE and a present participle (traditionally referred to, of course, as the progressive form), and 'not period-marked', which is realized simply by the absence of this form. Fawcett offers the following examples (Chapter 4, forthcoming):

(20a) They were discussing your case yesterday afternoon.

(20b) They discussed your case yesterday afternoon.

Example (20a) expresses the combination of two different types of time meaning: 'past trp' and 'period-marked'. In examples like (20a) with an inherently durative process (i.e. a dynamic process that lasts for a period of time but typically not as long as in a 'stative' process) the effect of the choice of 'period-marked', according to Fawcett, 'is to draw the period out further, so that the event in [20a] may appear to have lasted longer than that in [20b].' Note here that while the *IFG* model would simply analyse *were discussing* in (20a) as an instance of 'present in past', i.e. as a combination *of two different values of the same type of meaning*, the Cardiff Grammar recognises a combination of *two different types of meaning*. Furthermore, Fawcett very clearly shows that the effect of choosing period-marked differs according to the type of process involved. He offers the following examples:

(21) He lived / was living in Paris at the time.

(22) She hit / was hitting him with a baseball bat.

(23) She squashed / was squashing a plastic bottle.

In (21), Fawcett points out, the effect of period-marking a 'stative' process is in fact to shorten it. In (22) the effect of period-marking a 'momentary nontransitional' process is to express the meaning of *iteration*, i.e a closely repeated series of events. And in (23) the effect of period-marking a 'momentary transitional process' is a focus on *the time leading up to the transition* rather than the transition itself (which is expressed by choosing 'not period-marked').

Finally Fawcett notes that the combination of BE and a present participle can be used to express an entirely different meaning, viz. imminent or arranged future, as in the following example:

(24) I'm seeing him tomorrow.

The system of RETROSPECTIVITY offers a choice between 'retrospective', realised by a combination of a form of the Auxiliary HAVE and a past participle (traditionally referred to, of course, as the perfect form), and 'not retrospective', which is realized simply by the absence of this form. Fawcett offers the following examples (Chapter 4 of Fawcett forthcoming):

(25a) Ike's eaten your chocolate bar.

(25b) He ate some of my fudge last week.

(26a) He has / had lived in Germany.

(26b) He lives / lived in Germany.

As these examples show, the choice of retrospective supplements the choice of trp. Thus in *has eaten* and *has lived* we get a combination of a present trp and retrospection, and in *had lived* we get a combination of a past trp and retrospection. Fawcett points out that there are two different ways of referring to past events: either (a) as located at an unspecified time position within a past time span reaching back from a trp (retrospectivity) or (b) as coinciding with a past trp (the 'nonretrospective' simple past). Here again the Cardiff Grammar – in contrast with the *IFG* model – recognises a combination of different types of meaning. Fawcett also points out that the combination of HAVE and a past participle (like the combination of BE and a present participle) may be used for a different kind of meaning. Somewhat surprisingly, it is also used simply to establish a past trp in cases like the following, where the Performer expresses her evaluation of the validity of the clause by means of a modal verb and a nonfinite perfect form:

(27) Ivy may have eaten some of my fudge last week.

Finally it should be noted that the Cardiff Grammar provides naturally for the combination of positive choices from both the two systems of period-marking and retrospectivity:

(28) Ivy's been eating your chocolate.

In this section I have drawn mainly on Chapter 4 of Fawcett (forthcoming), to illustrate Fawcett's approach to what are traditionally treated as the 'core' options in the English systems for tense. But in the full computer-implemented version of the Cardiff Grammar a central place is given also to the forms and meanings of BE *going to* + infinitive, BE *about to* + infinitive and BE *on the point of* + present participle. There is also provision for a variety of other time meanings and forms.

4.2.3   The Cardiff Grammar as a point of departure

The Cardiff approach to time and tense is obviously a vast improvement over the *IFG* model. Fawcett demonstrates, in my view very convincingly, that it is indeed possible to provide a systemic functional description of English tense without resorting to recursion. At the same time, and perhaps as a natural consequence of not operating with recursion, he offers a more detailed account of both the semantics of tense and the different formal realisations involved. Thus, contrary to Halliday and Matthiessen, he takes event types into consideration, and he draws on five different but related systems: TIME REFERENCE POSITION, REALITY, DIRECTNESS, PERIOD-MARKING and RETROSPECTIVITY. The first system replaces the basic tripartite *IFG* tense system and the last two replace recursion, at least partially. This organisation of the grammar ensures a high degree of adequacy in the description of choice relations. For example, choosing 'period-marked' is not simply a question of choosing 'present' from a basic tripartite system in the second or a later recursive cycle, as the *IFG* model has it. It is clearly different from choosing 'present' as a primary tense (i.e. as a present trp in Fawcett's terms). It is also important to note that the Cardiff description of time and tense is fully integrated in a coherent systemic functional grammar which combines a unitary syntax and a multifunctional semantics in a most elegant way, with realisation rules that provide for conflation, co-realization and portmanteau realisation, among other things.

However, there are a number of reasons why we cannot simply replace the *IFG* model with the Cardiff approach but must attempt to offer an even better model. My first reservation is that with the more individual focus on the various time meanings and their realisations, it is easy to lose sight of tense as *a coherent and integrated model*. The Cardiff approach is admittedly more comprehensive, and so more realistic, than a descriptively decontextualised tense model which ignores interrelated system networks. But what is absent from Fawcett's more comprehensive and realistic grammar, at least in the sources that have been available to me, is a sense that tense is *serial*. Seriality is clearly compatible with the Cardiff approach, it is just not sufficiently emphasised in the descriptive parts of the grammar. In Fawcett

(2008, forthcoming), it is thus not entirely clear what the order of relevant choices is, and what the implications of this order are.[5] It seems to me that if we want to gain a full understanding of tense in English we need to piece together a number of meanings and their realisations in a tight compositional model – even if the achievement of such a model is at the cost of some idealisation and occasionally involves the somewhat artificial extraction of temporal meanings from a number of related factors, such as modality (cf. my discussion of 'monadicness' in Section 4.4.6 and the organisation and inventory of tense proposed in Section 5.1). In other words, I suggest that the best descriptive practice here, at least as a vital first step, is to attempt to bring into close contact just those factors that are relevant to a description of the choice relations involving time and tense.

Another thing which is unclear in the Cardiff approach is the exact status of 'future' in relation to the other time meanings, and how *will*, *would* and BE *going to* fit into the overall scheme of realisations. Like Halliday and Matthiessen, Fawcett seems to treat 'future' as a value on a par with 'past' and 'present'. These three values constitute the set of primary trps and thus correspond to Halliday and Matthiessen's primary tripartite tense system. A three-way time distinction may be attractive from the point of view of our belief system but does not fit very well with either the formal realisations of tense in English or tense usage more generally. One particular problem with such an organisation of the model is that it leaves a number of tense (or tense-like) uses of *would* unaccounted for (cf. Section 5.1). A central aspect of the model to be proposed in Chapter 5 is that it departs from a three-term primary tense system. This has positive repercussions for our account of the seriality of tense and allows us to determine the status of *will*, *would* and BE *going to*.

A third problem in the Cardiff approach is that the description of the semantics of 'period-marking' and 'retrospectivity' (at least as presented in Chapter 4 of Fawcett forthcoming) fails to capture all the relevant meanings and uses precisely enough. For example, saying that period-marking in example (20a) (*They were discussing your case yesterday afternoon*) makes the event appear to have lasted longer than in (20b) (*They discussed your case yesterday afternoon*) is to miss an important aspect (*sic!*) of the progressive form, namely that the distinction in this particular instance is primarily, if not exclusively, a question of the Performer's textual organisation of the proposition. In (20a) the progressive form presents the discussion referred to as unfolding, with a close-up focus on its middle phase, and the statement expressed by the clause may thus well serve as an introduction to more detailed information in relation to the discussion. By contrast, the nonprogressive form in (20b) presents the discussion (potentially the exact same discussion) as a complete whole, as a fact, with no concern for its progression, and the statement expressed by the clause may thus serve as a more self-contained piece of information. That Fawcett's explanation of the difference is insufficient becomes clear when we consider examples like the following, where the presence or absence of period-marking seems to be independent of the use of Adjuncts indicating length of time:

>(20c) They <u>discussed</u> your case <u>briefly</u> yesterday afternoon.

>(20d) They <u>were discussing</u> your case <u>briefly</u> yesterday afternoon.

>(20e) They <u>discussed</u> your case yesterday <u>all afternoon</u>.

>(20f) They <u>were discussing</u> your case yesterday <u>all afternoon</u>.

Here period-marking in (20d) and (20f) does not give an impression of prolongation in comparison with (20c) and (20e). In fact, when we want to indicate that a process went on for a very long time, the nonprogressive is often clearly preferred to the progressive:

>(29a) He <u>walked</u> on <u>for several hours</u>.

>(29b) ??He <u>was walking</u> on <u>for several hours</u>.

As we shall see, it is important to sort out the various semantic domains and the profiling characteristics of the various forms more precisely. In particular it is important to recognise the multifunctional nature of the progressive form, and this requires drawing a quite rigorous distinction between event types (or 'Aktionsart') and aspect (for details, see Section 4.4.7 below). The Cardiff School does not entirely come to grips with the nature of aspectual meaning and the way it interacts with temporal and actional meaning.

So, although the Cardiff approach has taken us a great step closer to our goal, there is still some way to go. Let us now turn to Harder's functional semantics for further inspiration.

4.3   Harder's contribution

4.3.1   Harder's theory of functional semantics

As already indicated, Harder 1996 offers a new, very attractive general theory of functional semantics and applies it to tense in English. Like Halliday, Matthiessen, Fawcett and other functional linguists, Harder focuses on the collaboration of expression and content, and of structure and meaning. He argues convincingly against the common representational, nonfunctional, objectivist view of semantics, and against the formalist assumption that syntax is autonomous. But at the same time he is highly critical of functionalists and cognitivists who deny the existence of structure or shy away from syntax, and who thus leave this essential property of language – the very instrument with which meanings are organised in linguistic expressions – in the hands of linguists who do not accept the functional-interactive view of language, notably generative linguists.

Harder finds much inspiration in the framework of thinking provided by evolutionary biology and is generally much more sympathetically inclined towards functionalism than to formal theories. He views social interaction and cognitive skills as interrelated factors providing the key to our understanding of linguistic meaning. Significantly, interaction is prior to thinking in human evolution and hence both more basic and less sophisticated. To adopt a functional-interactive perspective in one's analysis of language means to take a *top-down* look at structure whereby an item (a linguistic expression) is viewed in terms of its function ('the job done by the item') and its constituent parts in terms of their subfunction, i.e. their contribution to the function of the entity as a whole. Harder (1996: 154–155) provides the illustrative example of a knife which is analysed in terms of a handle and a blade, each contributing in an obvious way to the function of the knife as a whole, viz. the function of cutting or stabbing. The point of this example is that cognition and syntax go hand in hand, and that the intersection and collaboration of the two should be taken seriously in any discussion of linguistic meaning. Harder thus invites hardcore syntacticians to adopt a functional-cognitive orientation without letting go of structure, and invites hardcore functionalists and cognitivists to adopt a structural orientation without letting go of communicative interaction.

Harder's overriding concern is to bridge the unfortunate gap between the traditionally separate fields of function and structure, and of syntax, semantics and pragmatics. At this general level, Harder's mission is very similar to Halliday's: both are concerned with establishing a direct link between grammar and semantics, and both adopt a broad view of semantics which largely includes pragmatics. But on more specific issues there are interesting differences between SFL and Harder's functional semantics. In particular, Harder stresses the importance of operating with both 'expression syntax' and 'content syntax'. Structure, according to Harder, is a two-sided entity: it has an expression side (with expression syntax) and a content side (with content syntax), and expression 'dances to the tune' of content (1996: 498). Rather than operating with complete, unified meanings of complex linguistic structures, like many both formal and functional linguists, Harder advocates a kind of **procedural semantics** that he refers to more specifically as **instructional semantics**. In his view, a complex linguistic expression does not code a denotation or a representation: meaning is not predetermined by the world (and here Halliday and Matthiessen would most certainly agree). Rather, what is coded is *a hierarchically organized set of instructions enabling the Addressee to work out an appropriate interpretation of the utterance.* By operating with a distinction between expression syntax and content syntax and by positing the two as interdependent, Harder in fact offers a functional specification and elaboration of what systemic linguists refer to as their **stratal view of language**; and by viewing the end result of linguistic coding as interpretative instructions, he offers a viable spelling out and refinement of what others refer to as **construal**, a notion which is absolutely fundamental to SFL thinking.

In the course of developing his theory and applying it to tense in English, Harder clarifies a number of important concepts and introduces some new ones. One good example of this is his delimitation of cognitive meaning in language and the consequences of this for his overall theory. Rather than adopting an all-embracing, pan-cognitivist position, Harder argues that cognitive meaning is linked up with conceptualisation but should be kept separate from a number of things often associated with it: (a) external world states (with which concepts are intensionally related); (b) preconceptual skills (which are stimulus-controlled motor routines and perception); and (c) prerepresentational background states of the subject. In practice, cognitive meaning equals the conceptual content of a linguistic expression and is thus an important part of linguistic meaning but does not cover 'everything'. It is distinct from, and in linguistic expressions dependent on, functional-interactive aspects of meaning. As examples of functional meaning Harder includes greetings, terms of address, moods (e.g. declarative), deixis and polarity (assent/negation). Unlike conceptual meanings, these meanings obviously cannot be claimed to exist only inside the head of the Performer, independent of the interactive context of the utterance. Between the two main types of meaning there is a division of labour such that functional meaning **operates** on conceptual meaning. In other words, conceptualization is embedded in interaction (1996: 269): functional meanings knock concepts into communicative shape. This **operator-operand** relationship between function and cognition can be described in terms of two kinds of dependency: **functional dependency** and **conceptual dependency** (1996: 276). For linguistic expressions to work appropriately in communication, concepts are functionally dependent: they require a functional slot to fill.

Conversely, functions are conceptually dependent in the sense that they require conceptual content to operate on.

Harder insists that linguistic meaning is coded function. He compares his theory of content syntax to a recipe. A recipe for grilled salmon contains an ordered set of instructions (coded functions) involving certain ingredients (conceptual meanings) (1996: 214):

> take a salmon, slice it, spice the slices with salt and pepper, put them on the grill and sprinkle them with lemon before serving

In a content-syntactic formula the recipe looks like this (1996: 214):

> serve (sprinkle with lemon (grill (add salt and pepper (slice (salmon)))))

Similarly the meaning of an expression like *Did John go?* can be described informally in this way (1996: 214):

> identify John and construct a mental model of him; make the model instantiate the property 'go'; understand this model as applying to a certain past situation; and consider whether the model is true of that situation.

Or simply:

> interr (past (*go* (*John*)))

These descriptions show the collaboration of meaning and structure, and of functional and conceptual meaning. They also show that we must not confuse linguistic meaning with the Addressee's interpretation of the utterance in terms of extensive, denotational, representational properties: a recipe for grilled salmon is not the same as grilled salmon (1996: 215).

When applied to tense in English, Harder's instructional-semantic approach to meaning leads to important new insights, relating not so much to how tense forms are used in English, but to the linguistic description of tense and its integration with an overall functional theory of language. Like Halliday's recursive tense system, Harder's tense category can be viewed as a **compositional paradigm** (rather than as a traditional **constructional** one), for the members of the category are not immediately and directly organised in a single set but are structured within the paradigm according to certain compositional principles reflecting the fact that some of them are more immediately contrasted than others and that some have scope over others. Unlike SFL's rather densely populated category, Harder's category comprises only eight finite tenses resulting from a structured set of three paradigmatic binary oppositions. The content-syntactic structure of his category looks like this:

past/present (±future (±perfect (state-of-affairs)))

The first subparadigm consists of the choice to instruct the Addressee to apply a **predication** designating some **state-of-affairs**[6] to either the **present** or the **past**, thus turning the predication into a **proposition**. The choice between present and past is a deictic one, being grounded (or 'based') in the time of the utterance. Significantly, the temporal specification is not a property of the state-of-affairs but of the 'point-of-application'. Within the scope of this deictic choice there are two other subparadigmatic choices, one between **future** and **nonfuture** and one between **perfect** and **nonperfect**, the latter embedded within the scope of the former. These two choices are of a relational but strictly nondeictic nature, according to Harder, and involve subjective and objective conceptual meaning, respectively. At the same time they are amenable to an analysis in terms of markedness: the 'look-aheadness' of the future and the 'look-backness' of the perfect are present or absent depending on whether the Performer chooses future and perfect expression syntax or not. By contrast, the choice between present and past is equipollent, each option associated with a definite, positive meaning. Harder is here in deliberate opposition to conventional wisdom, which has the present in English as an unmarked, 'nontemporal' tense. Harder's argument is that deictic tense concerns **application time**, rather than **event time** or **reference time**: a present tense construction instructs the Addressee to apply the state-of-affairs to the 'world as it is now' while a past tense construction instructs the Addressee to apply the state-of-affairs to the 'world as it was then' (for further discussion of this issue, see Subsection C in 4.3.2 below).

Each of the tenses in Harder's system has a **base time** and a **function time**. The base time of both the present and the past is the utterance time, the function time is the application time, i.e. the present or the past, respectively. By having the utterance time as their base time, the present and the past are deictic tenses. Their meaning, Harder argues, is purely functional, subjective and nonconceptual.

The base time of the future is either present or past application time, depending on the first choice in the system. The function time is 'aheadness', or simply future in relation to the chosen base time. The fact that the base time of the future, as in *George will deny it* (1996: 353) is not directly the utterance time but the present application time resulting from the choice of the present form of WILL (*will* as distinct from the past form *would*) means that the future in present future constructions is by itself nondeictic, or only indirectly deictic, despite its deictic associations. In other words, a present future verb form is deictic, but only by way of being applied to the present, not to the future. The anticipation expressed by the future is of a subjective conceptual nature and therefore tied specifically to the Performer and to finite constructions.

The base time of the perfect is a 'time of reckoning' and the function time is 'anteriority' (or 'look-backness'). The perfect provides a cumulative, 'balance sheet' meaning whereby anterior events are summed up with a view to their application to a 'time of reckoning' (1996: 382). The objective, Performer-independent nature of the perfect, which makes it susceptible to truth-conditional analysis (unlike the future), explains the free occurrence of nonfinite perfect forms: in principle, any time may serve as a time of reckoning. According to Harder, this system of interacting base and function times renders the notions of 'event time' and 'reference time' (which play a crucial role in the SFL approach to tense) superfluous or irrelevant (see further Subsection B in 4.3.2 below).

4.3.2   A critical evaluation of Harder's theory of tense

From a purely functional point of view, Harder's approach to tense in English is clearly superior to Halliday and Matthiessen's. Both theories posit a compositional paradigm of tenses, but while the organising principle of the SFL paradigm is automatic recursion constrained by ad-hoc stop rules, Harder's model assumes a hierarchical set of instructions reflecting choice relations and communicative interaction more directly and explicitly in the coding of the individual tenses. It would be tempting, therefore, simply to adopt some of Harder's ideas in our functional tuning of the *IFG* model and the Cardiff approach. However, before giving in to this temptation, we need to examine his theory more critically. In doing so, I shall focus on three important issues: the problem of what may be called 'category architecture' in Harder's compositional paradigm, i.e. its organisation in terms of subsystems and their relations (Subsection A), his rejection of the notions of 'reference time' and 'event time' (Subsection B), and his conception of the primary subparadigm as a binary, equipollent opposition (Subsection C). Although I agree with Harder in most of his views and arguments and certainly recognise that there is a more genuinely functionalist orientation in his work on tense than in Halliday and Matthiessen's, there are also, in my view, a number of possible weaknesses.

(A) The problem of category architecture

One weakness in Harder's approach to tense in English, as I see it, has to do with the actual organisation of his compositional paradigm: it is too diverse in terms of the specific instructions accommodated, yet quantitatively too limited to cover everything we would like to include under the heading of tense. There are only eight members in Harder's tense category (as compared to Halliday and Matthiessen's 36 tenses in 'System I'), and yet the relationship between these eight members, as defined by Harder, is too complex to fit comfortably into just one category. In other words, there is a problem of 'category architecture'.

The members of a category such as tense must normally *share* something (some general meaning or function) to be conceived of as belonging to the same paradigm. At the same time they must *differ* with respect to certain specific characteristics (at a lower level of schematisation) to be conceived of as different members of the same category. In other words, the members of a category must exhibit a certain amount of both sameness and difference (cf. my comments on categories and minimal pairs/sets in Section 3.5 above; for further discussion see Bache 2002). On this, hopefully uncontroversial, view of categories, the individual tenses are expected to share some general category meaning or function (i.e. temporality, defined one way or another) not shared by other constructions but also to differ with respect to specific temporal values (i.e. pastness, futurity, etc.). Interestingly enough, Halliday and Matthiessen's tense category easily meets this requirement despite the large number of tenses accommodated: the common denominator is 'precedence relation', each tense realising a specific precedence relation ('x precedes y', 'x follows y', 'x neither precedes nor follows y'), or a combination of these specific precedence relations. Like traditional constructional paradigms, and like *IFG* recursive tense system, Harder's category is obviously meant to be a *discrete* category in the sense that certain instructions definitely belong to the category while others definitely belong to other categories. It is the quest for discreteness that makes Harder argue at length for 'future' as a temporal rather than modal value (1996: 352ff). Granted that Harder's category of tense is discrete, the question arises: what is the defining characteristic of a tense? What is the general meaning, function or instruction shared by all and only the members of the tense category? What does the common domain that the tenses profile differently look like? At what exclusive level of schematisation, if any, do the individual members merge?

Harder is not very explicit about this. He is understandably reluctant to presuppose the existence of a 'tense system' based on either form alone or on semantic substance prior to the description of structure (1996: 358). But once he has finished his combined expression-syntactic and content-syntactic description of tense, a system (strictly a system of systems) has come into being. This system must be defensible on general criteria (including metalinguistic ones) and should therefore, among other things, provide a common factor shared by all and only the tenses. The notion of deictic time, which characterizes the present and the past, is an attractive candidate: the element shared by the two choices is that of 'directing the addressee towards a point-of-application' relative to the utterance time (1996: 327), the difference between them being the actual point of application (present or past as seen from the perspective of the Performer at the moment of communication). As Harder says, 'the notion of a point-of-application is basic in accounting for tense meaning' (1996: 337). However, although deictic application time constitutes the primary choice in the compositional paradigm, taking the other choices within its scope, thus permeating the whole system, it is not obviously suitable as the common denominator of all tenses because that would *include* finite passive forms and finite progressive forms (which are excluded from Harder's model, if only implicitly so). At the same time deictic time would *exclude* nonfinite perfect forms, which would seem to be included in Harder's model (cf. 1996: 382f) though it is not entirely clear if the perfect form is a tense only when it is inside the scope of the primary choice of deictic time (Is the *nonfinite* perfect a tense? If not, what is it?). If instead of deictic time we adopt a more general common factor, such as having a 'temporal dimension' (cf. Harder's characterization of the perfect on p. 379), we could easily arrive at a more densely populated tense category, including forms associated with the categories of voice and aspect.

While Harder is careful to delimit the tense category from modality (1996: 352ff), he is curiously uninterested in the distinction between tense and aspect, just like Halliday and Matthiessen. In fact, aspect is hardly mentioned at all. There are only two references to it in the index, neither of which throws any light on the categorial issue. This is surprising in view of the fact that many other linguists regard the perfect as a phase or an aspect rather than a tense, or as a combination (cf. Section 2.2 above). The precise categorial status of the perfect is a highly controversial issue in modern linguistics but this is nowhere reflected in Harder's exposition. The same applies to the progressive forms, and if it is strange that Harder *includes* perfect forms in his tense category without arguing explicitly for this inclusion, it is even stranger that he *excludes* progressive forms without discussion. In view of the thoroughness with which Harder introduces his general theory of content syntax within a proper theoretical context, his lack of interest in the precise delimitation of his tense category in the system of verbal categories is rather disappointing. Maybe it is difficult to distinguish precisely between tense and aspect, but then Harder should have dealt explicitly with this interesting and highly relevant problem. I think Halliday and Matthiessen are wrong in not recognising the relevance of aspect for their complex 'tenses', but at least their treatment of the category is deliberate, principled and explicit.

(B) Harder's rejection of the notions of 'reference time' and 'event time'

Another possible problem with Harder's tense category has to do with the notions of 'event time' and 'reference time'. According to Harder, these notions (both of which play a crucial role in the *IFG* approach to tense in English, cf. Section 2.1 above), can be dispensed with if we adopt a procedural account of the tenses whereby each tense has a base time and a function time. Base times and function times are general, functionally defined variables to be further specified for each subparadigmatic choice. Moreover, base times and function times interact in the composition of complex constructions: as we have seen, the function time associated with each choice provides the base time for the next choice. For example, in the case of a past perfect construction (such as *had found*), the base time of the first choice is the time of utterance and the function time is past application time. This past application time, which plugs the expression into the situational context (instructing the Addressee to identify a specific past time in relation to the time of utterance), provides a temporal anchor which may serve as the base time – the time of reckoning – for the perfect form. The function time of the perfect is anteriority (or 'look-backness'): 'it applied then that the state-of affairs expressed by FIND was anterior'. Similarly, in the case of a present future construction (such as *will find*), present application time becomes the base time (the look-ahead time) for the future: 'it applies now that the state-of-affairs expressed by FIND is ahead'. There is thus a sense in which the present future primarily states something about the present, not the future. Harder's system of interacting base and function times is an elegant simplification of Matthiessen's time variable convention in the *IFG* model, it is defined in explicitly functional terms, and, perhaps most important, it directly *reflects the serial character of the tense category without assuming recursion.*

I find that Harder's system works very well indeed without a separate notion of 'event time': by dispensing with this notion he takes the final leap from a representational descriptive mode into genuine functionalism. His system also works very well without the notion of 'reference time' whenever the deictic choice of present or past is combined with only the future *or* the perfect forms, as in *had found* and *will find* (discussed above). However, if all three choices are positive, as in the present future perfect or the past future perfect (such as *will have found* and *would have found*), it is not entirely clear where the anchoring of the perfect form comes from. According to Harder's compositional principle, we would expect the function time 'F' of the future to be the base time (the time of reckoning) of the perfect, on analogy with the interaction of function and base times in other combinations. Certainly, his paraphrase of the present future perfect invites an analysis along these lines:

> All in all, the present future perfect thus tells us that right now there is ahead of us a situation in which a state-of-affairs is anterior. (1996: 397)

The problem here is the typical *specificity* of F (the function time of the future, which becomes the base time of the perfect). Convincing examples of the present future perfect without a specific anchoring of F are few and far between (cf. p. 421), if they exist at all; and Harder openly admits that 'the present future perfect [...] almost always requires some sort of temporal specification of the reckoning time for the perfect'. But if I have understood Harder's definition of 'F' correctly, there is no coding of a *specific* temporal point ('situation') which the perfect may be hooked on to. As Harder states when arguing for the strictly nondeictic nature of the future:

> there is no element of identification: we do not have to pick out the right future point-of-application in order to understand what is meant. The precise time or situation does not matter: the important point is whether there is or is not some situation ahead to which the state-of-affairs applies. (1996: 350)

However, this characterization of the future in terms of 'aheadness' or 'anticipation' rather than in terms of the specific occurrence of the future event (see also p. 387) seems to apply only when the future is the *last* positive tense choice in a construction (as in the present future). When the perfect is added as the third choice (as in the present future perfect) there is typically, in fact almost always, a specific 'F' involved, i.e. a definite point in the future (a reference point?) from which one can look back at some state-of-affairs, as instructed by the perfect form. F appears in such cases to be as much a point of application as S (= present application time) and P (= past application time) in the case of the simple present and past tense, respectively. If this point is not coded by the future, where does it come from? The perfect form *as such* is not an immediately obvious source either, because, as Harder argues, the 'time of reckoning' of the perfect may in principle be unanchored (hence the free occurrence of nonfinite perfect forms (cf. 1996: 383), where he claims that 'No identified base time is necessary to use the perfect'). Can one plausibly argue that the point of time associated with F when followed by the perfect is simply a contextually specified or implicit topic time (i.e. 'the time which is not coded because the interlocutors take for granted that this is the time that the conversation is about' (1996: 405)? Harder's analysis leaves the reader very much in doubt. On the other hand, the possible usefulness and adequacy of a reference point in present future perfects and past future perfects should be weighed against its general redundancy: from the point of view of metalinguistic simplicity, there is no doubt that Harder's solution is preferable even if he does not argue convincingly enough for his position.

One possible solution to the problem is to say that in those cases where a function time is going to be used as the base time for a subsequent choice, in accordance with the serial character of Harder's compositional paradigm, such a shift in status involves the setting up of a *juncture* relative to which the function of the subsequent choice can be realized. In the case of the present future perfect, it means that the function time of the future, the instruction to 'look ahead', remains simply 'look ahead' (not 'identify a *specific* time ahead') but for this function to serve as a base time for a subsequent tense choice, i.e. as the basis for a new temporal orientation, it needs implicit or explicit *grounding* in terms of a juncture along the dimension expressed by the time as a function time. In the case of a perfect chosen after a future, this juncture (whether implicitly or explicitly expressed) becomes the 'time of reckoning', from where the instruction to look back can be carried out. To use Harder's own 'railway ticket' metaphor (1996: 397): on my understanding of his definition, the future is like a ticket that will take you in the right direction (ahead) but to no specific destination. If you want to change direction (i.e. if you add the instruction of the perfect to look back) you normally have to do so at a specific juncture but this juncture is not specified in the original ticket you bought. It is the result of the recategorisation of a function time as a base time, not the application of an independent notion of 'reference time'.

(C) Harder's organisation of the primary subparadigmatic choice

A third problem with Harder's description of tense in English concerns the initial subparadigmatic choice between present and past. As we have seen, these two tenses have the utterance time as base time and application time as function time: choosing either of them turns the predication into a proposition. The difference between them is the actual temporal application of the predication to either 'the world now' or to 'the world then'. The choice is **equipollent** (with two equally balanced, positively defined options), while the other choices in the compositional paradigm (±future and ±perfect) are **privative** (with a marked and an unmarked member of the opposition). There are two issues to be considered in connection with Harder's primary subparadigm: the exclusion of the future (cf. the basic tripartite tense system in the SFL approach) and the equipollent opposition between present and past.

From the point of view of semantic substance alone, it would seem reasonable to operate with a tripartition of the tense system into past, present and future, as suggested by Halliday and Matthiessen, as well as by Fawcett. Such a system would reflect our intuitive division of time into 'now', 'before now' and 'after now' (cf. the discussion of the 'metacategory' of tense in Bache (1997: 244ff); see also Comrie (1985)). But Harder's insistence on a close relationship between expression and content, and more specifically between expression syntax and content syntax, is attractive from a functional linguistic point of view: meaning should be seen not as something separate or in abstraction from expression but as inherent in it, and as its *raison d'être*. Against this background I find Harder's exclusion of the future from the primary subparadigm reasonably justified. The future is expressed periphrastically like the perfect, while the past and the present are expressed morphologically. As noted in my discussion of SFL's recursive system in Section 3.3, the formally very different realisations of the 'same' option in the recursive process are surprising in a grammar which, like SFL, emphasises the naturalness of the relationship between lexicogrammar and semantics. A similar problem applies to the periphrastic future if it is placed in the same subparadigm as the morphologically realised present and past: how does it fit in with these tenses from a formal point of view? Placing it outside the primary subparadigm like other periphrastically realised tenses seems much more *natural*. Moreover, even if Harder's past future (e.g. *would take*) is excluded from Halliday's 'System I' on account of its typical occurrence in projected clauses, the future is clearly *within the scope* of the primary choice between past and present, thus qualifying for a separate subparadigmatic status in the compositional paradigm. Significantly, there is a productive alternation between e.g. *will take* and *would take*, which in some contexts is similar to the alternation between e.g. *has taken* and *had taken* (though, admittedly, the former is more restricted than the latter), for discussion see Section 5.1 below.

As regards the second issue to be considered in connection with Harder's primary subparadigm, the equipollent opposition between present and past, I find the proposed organisation of the subparadigm somewhat problematical. In order to sort out the precise relationship between the past and the present, we must first look more closely at how Harder defines and characterises these two tenses. Harder offers the following formulations as his definitions:

> The meaning of the present tense is to direct the addressee to identify a point-of-application S (a situation as it is at the time S of speech), as that which the state-of-affairs in its scope applies to.
> The meaning of the past tense is to direct the addressee to identify a point-of-application P, (a situation as it is at time P (such that P lies before S), as that which the state-of-affairs in its scope applies to.
> (1996: 327)

He goes on to say:

> There are [...] two aspects of the meaning that need to be kept in mind, and kept separate. One is the element they share: the element of directing the addressee towards a point-of-application, creating a proposition out of a state-of-affairs. The other is the element that keeps them distinct: the temporal specification of the point-of-application. The functions served by the tenses are in the pointing-towards.
> (1996: 327f)

I agree with Harder in most of what he has to say about the present and the past, but I do not fully accept his reason for considering the contrast between them to be an equipollent one. There are three parts to his argumentation (cf. 1996: 441ff). He begins by noting that the traditional argument for treating the present as **unmarked** is its use in so-called 'eternal truths'. This argument, he claims, 'loses its force once it is realised that eternal truths are in the present tense because they are applicable at utterance time', and he continues: 'If the present were really unmarked in Jakobson's sense, it would imply that application time was unspecified' (1996: 341). As we shall see, Harder's view here hinges on what exactly is meant by 'application' and how it fits into the tense category.

The second part of his argument is that the present is 'more semantically cohesive' than the past, the latter having both a temporal and a modal 'distance' interpretation (1996: 441). I find this part of his argumentation rather curious: the way he has defined the two tenses they are equally cohesive from a semantic point of view in that they both direct the Addressee towards a point-of-application. Even if he were right about the present being semantically more cohesive than the past, this would be an argument for treating *the past as the unmarked member* of the opposition and the present as the marked member. It would not be an argument for equipollence. But I do not think that Harder is right: surely there are too many uses of both the present and the past on top of their basic tense function for either of them to be characterised as cohesive, but if one of them were to be picked out as the pragmatically *less* complex, it would be the past, not the present.

Third, Harder notes that the most common reason for treating the present as unmarked is the cross-linguistic tendency to use the present for a variety of different types of what he calls 'imperfective' states-of-affairs (such as, presumably, habituals and mental and physical states), a tendency recognised by typological linguists such as Bybee *et al.* (1994). As Harder (in my view correctly) points out, such considerations have to do with the nature of the states-of-affairs rather than with the tense function of directing the Addressee towards a point-of-application.[7]

The crux of the matter, if we want to determine the nature of the opposition between the past and the present, is the precise relationship between what Harder presents as their *shared* function and their individual *distinct* function (i.e. the actual temporal specification of the 'point-of-application', or the pointing towards it,[8] as past or present). Harder describes this relationship in terms of a single category structure in which the former function – the shared element – is the defining common denominator of the category and the two temporal specifications or points-of-application are immediate members of this category (cf. my discussion of categories earlier in Section 3.5 and Subsection A above). At first blush, this is an attractive account which conforms to the kind of category description argued for in Bache (1997) and (2002). But on closer inspection, the question arises whether 'directing the addressee towards a point-of-application' is a valid schematisation of the two temporal specifications within a single categorial framework. The two temporal specifications clearly presuppose the function of 'directing the addressee towards a point-of-application', but is this function an entry condition for the tense category (and thus strictly speaking outside the tense category as such), is it the superordinate category meaning or function (and thus part of the inherent category architecture of tense), or is it a lower-level concomitant meaning shared with other categories? When considering this question it is important to keep in mind the non-monadic status of the verb forms in English that I argued for in Section 3.5 above: the English verb forms are non-monadic in that they can only be described exhaustively with reference to two or more category domains. Granted that the present and the past in English are non-monadic, the various coded meanings may in principle belong to different (but interrelated) categories rather than to different levels within a single category structure.

Harder sometimes speaks loosely of 'directing the addressee towards a point-of-application' and 'turning a predication into a proposition' as if they were two sides of the same coin or at least causally related phenomena, one following automatically from the other. But, strictly speaking, this is not always the case, as Harder is probably well aware. Consider the following examples:

(1a)   <u>Seeing Janet on May 5</u> will be just great.

(1b)   <u>Seeing Janet on May 5</u> was just great.

In the nonfinite subordinate clause of these examples, the Performer directs the Addressee towards a point-of-application through the use of a circumstantial (5 *May*) without turning the predication of seeing Janet into a proposition. This point-of-application is *absolute* and independent of the moment of communication (hence the difference of temporal orientation between the a-example and the b-example). By contrast, in the finite matrix clause, the point-of-application is *relative* to the deictic zero point, the utterance time: in the a-example we have a present future and in the b-example we have a simple past. So it is important to distinguish between the *general* function of directing the Addressee towards a point-of-application and the *specific* function of directing the Addressee towards a point-of-application *viewed in relation to the utterance time*. Obviously the general function of directing cannot serve as either an entry condition or as the superordinate category function for the present and the past. Harder's definitions of present and past quoted above explicitly presuppose the utterance time S, and this would seem to indicate that it is the specific, deictically based function of directing that Harder envisages as the common category denominator for the two tenses: what the present and the past share is *having the utterance time as the base time*, and it is this deictic grounding of the predication that turns it into a proposition. The two tenses serve this function equally well and are in this respect both positively defined.

However, in my analysis of the two tenses, the deictic grounding of the predication is a question of finiteness, not temporality as such, though temporality is an important, perhaps the most important, aspect of finiteness. What the two tenses share with respect to temporality is having a function time in relation to the deictic base time established (i.e. the time of utterance). This function involves a **temporal orientation**, not of the state-of-affairs but of the point-of-application. The two tenses are not different kinds of finiteness but different kinds of making the Addressee look towards a point-of-application within the framework established by finiteness in the form of a shared base time. The unique status of the present and the past as the primary subparadigm is the result of the categorial interplay between finiteness and temporality. It is in the context of this characterisation of the past and the present that the nature of their opposition should be determined. Since the past establishes a contrast to the base time (the utterance time) it creates a distinct and explicit temporal orientation. By comparison, the present simply confirms the status of the base time as also a point-of-application *without establishing a temporal contrast.* This vague temporal orientation makes it more accommodating of objectively past and future states-of-affairs (such as *In 1952 he <u>leaves</u> New York for good / I <u>hear</u> you are splitting up / On next Tuesday she <u>flies</u> to Toronto*, etc.), as well as eternal truths, generics and laws of nature (such as *The sun <u>rises</u> in the east / Oil <u>floats</u> on water / Two plus two <u>equals</u> four*, etc.). This easy accommodation of certain types of states-of-affairs should not cloud our understanding of the present as a genuine tense in Harder's functional terms, but it is one of the symptoms of it being less strongly marked than the past tense.

A final point: my analysis conforms very well to the assumed close relationship between content and expression in Harder's theory. The present is formally (morphologically) unmarked whereas the past is marked. My analysis thus reflects Harder's general motto: expression dances to the tune of content (1996: 498). Harder is clearly aware of this 'problem' in his analysis of the relationship between the present and the past as an equipollent opposition when he says: 'Regardless of being partially zero on the expression side, on the content side the present tense is a substantially and structurally well-defined paradigmatic alternative to the past tense' (1996: 341). Saying that the present tense is 'partially zero on the expression side' is perhaps slightly misleading: the only morphological variation in the present tense is caused by person and number, not by tense. From the point of view of the tense category, the present is morphologically zero, not partially zero. Despite this morphological quibble, I think Harder is right about the present tense being a 'substantially and structurally well-defined paradigmatic alternative to the past tense', but that does not prevent it from being semantically unmarked, or less marked than the past tense with respect to temporal orientation relative to the moment of communication.

(D) Harder's contribution to a new SFL description of tense in English

In the preceding sections I have offered a number of critical remarks on Harder's work. I have especially objected to the apparently arbitrary delimitation of the tense category, the implicit assumption of monadicness, and the equipollent organisation of the primary opposition in the compositional paradigm. These critical comments should not in any way cloud the general picture of an original and genuinely functional theory of meaning or prevent us from recognising its obvious repercussions for the description of tense in English. In this section I shall briefly recapitulate the points which I think may assist us in our attempt to establish a new SFL description of tense in English.

Harder's insistence on a close relationship between content and expression is a healthy reminder that we should take the functional aspect of expression more seriously, and not just sort out the semantic substance in abstraction from its possible formal realisations. Harder here seems to be very much in line with the Cardiff Grammar. In the case of the tense category, it means that we should pay more attention to the functional contribution of each formal tense marker (e.g. the morphological past tense, the periphrastic perfect form, etc.). But Harder also offers a completely new way of understanding tense meaning in our analysis of the relationship between expression and content: by viewing tense meanings as instructions for interpretation he brings some genuinely functional aspects of the tense system into the centre of our attention, thus providing us with an appropriate procedural framework for sorting out the semiotics and the choice relations involved.

We can also benefit from Harder's view of the tense category as a compositional paradigm – a view which is entirely compatible with a systemic functional way of thinking, as we have seen, but which is unfortunately linked up with recursion in the *IFG* model, and which is underdeveloped in the Cardiff Grammar. By operating with interrelated subparadigms with decreasing scope, Harder manages to preserve the idea of **seriality** rather than just **linearity** in the construction of verbal groups. He does this without assuming recursion and thus avoids all the complications of this process for a functional theory discussed in Chapter 3 above. The seriality of Harder's expression-syntactic description of the verbal group in English is reflected also in the content-syntactic description, where each temporal choice is described in terms of a base time and a function time, and where the function time becomes the base time of the next choice. This dynamic interplay of base and function times makes the notions of event time and relevance/reference time largely if not completely redundant. By getting rid of these concepts, which are inherent in the state-of-affairs rather than in the tense functions as such, Harder performs the final leap from representational semantics into genuinely functional semantics.

Harder does not solve all the problems pointed out in my critical review of the *IFG* model but like the Cardiff Grammarians he makes a substantial contribution to my functional tuning of the SFL description of tense and aspect, as will be evident in the model proposed in Chapter 5 below.

4.4   Principles of category description

Before proposing an alternative description of tense in English, I would like to offer a number of what I consider to be important principles of category description, some of which have already been hinted at in my critical remarks on Halliday's, Matthiessen's, Fawcett's and Harder's work (for a fuller discussion of category description, see e.g. Bache (1997 and 2002)).

4.4.1   Category structure

First of all, **categories** like tense should be recognised as *structured metalinguistic units*. Traditionally, the term 'category' has mainly been used for two different metalinguistic purposes (for discussion, see Bache 2002: 72ff):

1.   to refer to items of a particular 'type' or 'class', such as phonemes, word classes, morphologically marked expressions, syntactic categories, syntactic constructions;

2.   to refer to superordinate units comprising two or more related types or classes of expressions.

Examples of the former are /t/, noun, subject, NP, the genitive, the plural; examples of the latter are tense, aspect, mood, case, number, gender and comparison. When used to refer to superordinate units, categories are *structured* metalinguistic units in that they comprise two levels of description with a specifiable relationship between them: there is a general (or schematized) *superordinate* level representing a common denominator (i.e. the general semantic characteristic of the category as a whole); and there is a subordinate (potentially expression-specific) level representing the **members** of the category (i.e. the different individual types or classes of expression which are associated with the superordinate level). According to this latter metalinguistic practice, rather than being categories by themselves, the singular and the plural are *members of the category of number*, the perfective and the imperfective are *members of the category of aspect*, and e.g.

the present, the past and the future are *members of the category of tense.* Members of a structured category are at once similar and dissimilar: they share the general meaning or function represented by the superordinate level but differ on the specific level with respect to the actual variant of this general meaning or function. Put in slightly different terms, the superordinate level specifies a semantic or functional **domain** and the members share the ability to **profile** this domain, but do it differently. For example, depending of course on how the various terms and labels are defined, one could say that tenses share the domain of temporality but express different specific values of temporality. What exactly 'temporality' is, and what exactly the different specific values are, remain the challenging questions for linguists trying to describe the tense category. But at least the notion of a structured category is an appropriate metalinguistic framework for discussing such questions.

4.4.2   Paradigmatic relations

The kind of structured categories characterised above are **systems** or **paradigms**: the category members are paradigmatically related as **choice options**. The precise nature of the relationship between the members, and between the members and the more general superordinate category level, is determined by means of a substitution test (similar to Hjelmslev's 'commutation test'), carried out within a functional linguistic framework where the alternating forms are viewed as realizations of motivated communicative choices (for discussion, see Bache 1985, 1997, 2002). To determine the range of meanings expressed by certain forms, and indeed their systemic relationship, it is necessary to take a closer look at the substitutional potential of each form. This entails a recognition of the role of forms when establishing systems for choice relations between meanings, despite the fact that forms eventually end up as realisations of choices.[9]

Characteristically, when a large number of examples (say, of progressive and nonprogressive forms) are subjected to such a substitution test (where progressive forms are replaced by nonprogressive forms and vice versa), the result tends to be very different from case to case (cf. Bache 1985: 176–300; 1997: 108ff), and this obviously reflects complex choice relations in operation. Sometimes the resulting example is unacceptable in virtually any context, e.g.:

(1a)   Nefertiti <u>knows</u> him well.

(1b)   *Nefertiti <u>is knowing</u> him well.

(2a) Jack <u>owned</u> a popular pizza place.

(2b) *Jack <u>was owning</u> a popular pizza place.

Sometimes the resulting example is grammatically all right but semantically distinct from the source example. In such cases, it is important to note that the context of the source example may or may not render the resulting example unacceptable, and, second, that the precise nature of the semantic distinction between the source example and the resulting example may vary dramatically from case to case. To get an impression of the semantic diversity often encountered, it is helpful to look again at some of the examples offered in Section 3.5:

(3a) Roger <u>swam</u> across the river.

(3b) Roger <u>was swimming</u> across the river.

(4a) The door <u>slammed</u> behind me.

(4b) The door <u>was slamming</u> behind me.

As noted in our discussion of contrasts and choice relations in Section 3.5, the difference between (3a) and (3b) is one of 'completion' versus 'progression directed towards completion', whereas the difference between (4a) and (4b) is one of 'semelfactive punctuality' versus 'iteration of punctual event'. In both cases, however, the most immediately perceptible difference is of an experiential kind, and it is susceptible to an analysis in terms of truth conditions. In addition to the experiential difference, however, there is a more subtle, truth-conditionally neutral semantic difference: in the a-examples the process[10] is presented with an external focus, as a complete whole, whereas in the b-examples, the process is presented with an internal focus, as something in progress. This distinction is of *a presentational, textual kind* and is in principle independent of experiential meaning. Thus, sometimes it is the only kind of meaning affected by substitution:

(5a) They <u>walked</u> along the beach, arm in arm.

(5b) They <u>were walking</u> along the beach, arm in arm.

(6a) We <u>celebrated</u> Stephanie's birthday at my uncle's the other day.

(6b) We <u>were celebrating</u> Stephanie's birthday at my uncle's the other day.

Here, as argued in connection with (5a) and (5b) in Section 2.5, the nonprogressive form and the progressive form are two different ways of saying exactly the same thing from the point of view of experiential meaning.

The truth of the a-example implies the truth of the b-example, and vice versa ('If it is true that *They walked along the beach, arm in arm,* then it is also true that at some point *They were walking along the beach, arm in arm,* and if it is true that *They were walking along the beach, arm in arm,* then it is also true that *They walked along the beach, arm in arm',* and similarly for (6a) and (6b)). In this respect, examples (5a,b) and (6a,b) differ from examples (3a,b) and (4a,b), which exhibit differences of experiential, propositional meaning *as well as* the textual distinction between an external and an internal focus.[11]

Given the diversity of semantic distinctions identified in the substitution test, the following important question arises: what is the basic (or characteristic, or common) meaning associated with each of the two forms and how can we identify it in a principled manner? How can we explain the many semantic distinctions apparently involved in the formal distinction?

4.4.3 The metalanguage

In Bache (1997, 2002), I have suggested that in trying to tackle such questions we must distinguish very carefully between the language-specific level of usage and the general metalinguistic level of description. To be able to describe language-specific linguistic phenomena, we must have at our disposal a clear and unambiguously defined metalanguage which can serve as an absolute standard. Only with such a metalanguage can we describe language-specific variation and idiosyncratic features with sufficient precision. This means that a metalanguage should be *a useful descriptive tool* rather than *a reflection of linguistic truth* (cf. Bache 1997: 86ff, 324; Bache 2002: 95ff). One important consequence of operating with an abstract, ideal metalanguage is that its categories and the members of these categories are completely regular and characterised by a one-to-one relationship between form (expression) and meaning (content). In language-specific data, of course, we typically see a one-to-many relationship between form and meaning, as in the examples of the progressive and the nonprogressive offered in Section 4.4.2 above.

The kind of metalanguage that I argue for is in fact far from new: my contribution has simply been to make a rather common implicit practice more explicit and to try to present a coherent account of some of the methodological implications. For example, many linguists have asked questions like: Is aspect a category of English? Is the progressive an imperfective form? Is the perfect an aspect or a tense? Not only do such questions, and indeed possible answers to them, presuppose that the metalanguage is reasonably well-defined and serves as an absolute standard, they also show that one-to-one relations are taken as an implicit norm for categories. Not so in a systemic functional approach, where we are always on the lookout for multifunctionality.

4.4.4 Minimal pairs

If we adopt the metalinguistic practice suggested above, we face the problem of how to cope with the semantic diversity of language-specific members of a category. Ideally, we want to be able to identify a basic meaning for each member – a meaning that uniquely defines it as a member of that particular category, and which applies to all and only the realisations of that member. Moreover, we want to be able to account for the semantic variation and complexity characterising each member more generally in addition to its basic meaning. The first step in a comprehensive description of a category and its members is therefore to look for a distinction between the substitutional variants that allows generalisation to the whole set of data. This is most easily and conveniently done in 'minimal pairs', i.e. in pairs of examples which differ with respect to one kind of meaning only. If a fully generalisable distinction exists, it will be present in minimal pairs, and in minimal pairs it will stand out more clearly than in other pairs because it is not part of a semantically complex expression. Predictably, in minimal pairs, choice relations are simple, pure and unambiguously revealed: a substitutional variant is chosen precisely in order to express a basic categorial meaning. In semantically more complex expressions, choice relations are correspondingly more complex.

In the case of the formal distinction between progressive and nonprogressive forms, the various experiential distinctions associated with these forms (cf. my discussion of examples (3a,b) and (4a,b) above) are obviously unsuitable candidates for basic meanings – not because they are of the experiential kind, but because they cannot be generalized across the whole set of data. For example, it is clearly *not* the case that whenever we have a simple, nonprogressive form and a corresponding progressive one, the difference in meaning is one of 'completion' versus 'direction towards completion', or one of 'punctual semelfactiveness' versus 'iteration'. Moreover, in those cases where we find such a particular experiential difference, it is never the *only* difference between the substitutional variants. More generally, if in a substitution test we decided to choose the pairs of examples exhibiting the greatest possible semantic difference as our source of inspiration for defining the basic meaning of each member of the category, our description would not obtain a reasonable degree of observational adequacy and we would have to explain a large number of exceptions.

The opposite approach is much more promising: if we choose examples which exhibit a simple distinction, however small, that can be generalised to the whole set of data, our description will be much more observationally adequate. But it is important to take into account that definitions arrived at in this manner will not necessarily be descriptively adequate if they stand alone. They will go some way towards describing all relevant data, but in many cases not all the way. We want not only breadth but also depth in our description. We must be able to account exhaustively also for semantically more complex or distinct examples. In minimal pairs like *They walked/were walking along the beach, arm in arm* and *We celebrated/were celebrating Stephanie's birthday at my uncle's the other day*, we find – as already mentioned – only one distinction, viz. the presentational, textual distinction between external and internal focus on the process expressed. This distinction applies also to the other, experientially differentiated pairs of examples and may thus serve appropriately as our source of inspiration for the definition of the basic meanings involved in the progressive/nonprogressive distinction. But, obviously, such definitions will not capture all the relevant choice relations in cases like *Roger swam/was swimming across the river* and *The door slammed/was slamming behind me*. In such examples, the choice of expression is motivated by both experiential and textual factors. This means that we need supplementary rules to account for the experiential meanings and for the relationship between the experiential and the textual meanings.

4.4.5   The definition level and the function level of meaning

The advantage of working with minimal formal and semantic pairs, as I suggest, is that the semantic complexity of the formal distinction can be viewed as a *challenge* to find a functional rationale, rather than as an obligation to account for exceptions to the rule. Minimal pairs reveal, or give access to, what I have called **the definition level of meaning**, i.e. the level at which the one-to-one relationship between form and meaning assumed in the metalanguage for category description is revealed most clearly in language-specific data. The meanings found at this level are the meanings that allow pervasive generalization to all the relevant data in the substitution test. If all language-specific forms only expressed one discrete meaning each at the definition level, and displayed no semantic complexity, they would be **monadic**, i.e. they could be described exhaustively in terms of only one category-defining semantic domain. But, of course, language-specific forms are not like that: most, if not all, are far more complex. They are typically multifunctional, or **non-monadic**, i.e. require description in terms of more than one category-defining domain. Such a description involves a specification of **categorial interplay** in terms of (in)compatibility relations and an attempt to identify a rationale for the semantic complexity in terms of rule-governed changes in the substitution test. This level of semantic complexity I call **the function level of meaning**. At this level there is a one-to-many relationship between form and meaning. As argued in Bache (1997) (see especially pp. 196ff), this approach recognises both semantic minimalism or simplicity (at the definition level of meaning) and semantic multiplicity or complexity (at the function level of meaning), and by attempting to sort out the relationship between the two, it amounts to a strong hypothesis concerning the nature of the semantics of grammatical categories.

The examples already discussed in connection with the formal distinction between progressive and nonprogressive may be used to illustrate the difference between the definition level of meaning and the function level of meaning. As we have seen, examples like *They walked along the beach, arm in arm* and *They were walking along the beach, arm in arm* (both spoken with reference to a particular event) constitute a minimal pair, both formally and semantically, and thus reveal a basic distinction at the definition level of meaning. To explain the Performer's motivation for choosing one or the other variant (i.e. to specify the choice relation between them), we can simply refer to the difference of meaning at this level. As noted, the difference between the two examples is one of presentational, textual meaning – it is a question of how the Performer organises her text: the simple, nonprogressive form expresses the process with an external focus, as a complete whole, whereas the progressive form expresses it with an internal focus, as something in progress. The first sums up the 'walking' as a complete unit, while the second dwells on the unfolding of the 'walking'. Exactly the same description applies to *We celebrated Stephanie's birthday at my uncle's the other day* and *We were celebrating Stephanie's birthday at my uncle's the other day*. As the process referred to is construed as homogeneous, with no special importance attached to a single phase (beginning, middle or end), it makes no experiential difference to focus on the middle phase or to focus on the totality of the celebration: the middle phase may adequately represent the totality of the process because the other phases (beginning and end) do not add any significant information. By choosing the simple, nonprogressive form, the Performer gives the celebration a certain factual, straightforward, potentially independent status in the text: she may or may not tell us more about it. But by choosing the progressive form, she invites the Addressee to dwell mentally on the celebration and to expect some relationship between it and some other part of the text: there is something unfinished, incomplete or independent about it as a textual unit. It may serve as a background to some other event, or as a frame, or as an introduction to an account of what happened during the celebration. In a sense the progressive form is thus *textually more cohesive* that the nonprogressive form.

In more traditional terminology, the meanings of external and internal focus expressed by the nonprogressive and progressive forms in minimal pairs belong to the aspect category (as defined by e.g. Comrie (1976), for a critical review of his approach, see Bache (2002)). But while most other scholars, including the Cardiff Grammarians, use the term 'aspect' in a much broader sense (to include many different kinds of meaning), I use it in the narrow sense identified at the definition level of meaning. As we shall see below, one important consequence of this is that we must distinguish precisely between **aspect** and **action** in the metalanguage, the latter being reserved for experiential meanings pertaining to the nature of the process expressed (rather than the textual focus with which it is presented).

Examples like *Roger swam across the river* and *Roger was swimming across the river* constitute a formal pair whose complex semantic distinction involves both the definition level and the function level of meaning. The simple, nonprogressive form does sum up the 'swimming' as a complete unit, and the progressive form does dwell on the unfolding of the 'swimming'. So we clearly have a definition-level difference of aspectual meaning as in the 'walking' and 'celebration' examples discussed above. But that is not the whole story. The process construed by means of the nonprogressive form *swam* contains a natural terminal point (defined by the circumstantial adjunct *across the river*) to which special importance is attached, a point of completion (i.e. the reaching of the other side of the river), beyond which the activity of 'swimming' expressed cannot continue 'as directed', so to speak. This vital end point is outside the scope of the progressive form with its internal focus on the middle phase. The progressive form expresses direction towards this terminal point but does not imply that the actor will reach it. This makes the choice relations more complex than in the case of *They walked/ were walking along the beach, arm in arm*. It is no longer simply a question of whether the Performer wants to express some process with an external or internal focus, but also a question of what exactly the Performer wants to say from the point of view of experiential, actional meaning: if she wants to describe the 'swimming' as an activity which resulted in the actor reaching the other side of the river, she must choose the nonprogressive form. However, if for some reason, she wants to exclude the element of completion, she must choose the progressive form. The Performer's experiential motivation here overrides her textual motivation. Note that although the truth of *Roger swam across the river* implies the truth of *Roger was swimming across the river*, the opposite implication does not hold.

In the case of *The door slammed behind me* and *The door was slamming behind me*, we again see the characteristic definition-level difference of aspectual meaning of the formal progressive/nonprogressive opposition: the nonprogressive form supplies an external focus, summing up a process as a whole, while the progressive form supplies an internal focus, instructing the Addressee to dwell on the unfolding of a process. But as with the 'swimming' example, choice relations are somewhat more complex. The nonprogressive form is semelfactive (construing a single 'slam') unless some (linguistic or extralinguistic) context specifies it as otherwise, whereas the progressive form is iterative (construing several 'slams'). The Performer's choice is here obviously affected by what she wants to say experientially (actionally), and this time it is not a question of choosing between 'completion' or 'direction towards completion', as in the 'swimming' examples. Neither of the two ex-periential distinctions can be generalised to all the relevant data and thus cannot be basic meanings.

What we see in experientially distinct substitutional variants is a subtle interplay between the textual aspectual meanings of external/internal focus on the one hand and various actional, experiential meanings, like 'punctual', 'durative', 'telic', 'directional', 'semelfactive' and 'iterative' on the other. Some actional meanings are compatible with an external focus only ('punctual', 'telic'), others with an internal focus only ('directional'), and yet others are compatible with both ('durative', 'iterative'). Certain lexical and syntactic choices may bring certain actional meanings into play and trigger a dynamic categorial interplay between textual and experiential meaning. For example, if the Performer chooses a nonprogressive form of a verb like SLAM, e.g. *slammed*, which has a clear punctual association, the result is predictably a punctual process because punctuality is compatible with the external focus associated with the nonprogressive form. If, however, the Performer chooses a progressive form of SLAM, *was slamming*, she imposes an internal focus on punctuality, thereby effecting an actional 'change' to 'iteration' because of the incompatibility of punctuality with an internal focus. Thus the actional meaning of 'iteration' can be viewed as a **function** of the definition-level meaning of internal focus in relation to punctuality. The various actional meanings of the progressive/nonprogressive distinction thus belong to the function level of meaning. The descriptive challenge in connection with the progressive/nonprogressive distinction is not just to find the basic semantic distinction involved but also to sort out the categorial interplay, i.e. the relationship between the definition level of meaning (aspect) and the function level of meaning (action).

4.4.6   Monadic versus non-monadic forms

As we have seen, language-specific expressions (forms) are typically non-monadic, i.e. they are most adequately described in terms of *two or more categories in the metalanguage*, i.e. **metacategories**, which by definition are monadic. The concept of non-monadicness is entirely compatible with the Cardiff school use of the term 'portmanteau' and its combination of multifunctionality and a unitary structural representation. One important implication of language-specific category members being non-monadic is that choice relations are always complex: if a particular expression or form requires description with reference to several semantic or functional domains, choosing it is motivated by as many different semantic factors. For example, in the case of *Roger swam across the river*, the choice of the simple past *swam* is not just motivated by an intention to instruct the Addressee to apply the process to a past time relative to the moment of communication but also by the intention to express a telic (or completed) process with an external textual focus (rather than a directional and incomplete process with an internal textual focus).

Two things are important to note in connection with (non-)monadicness. First, this notion should not be confused with the notion of minimal pairs discussed in Section 4.4.4 above. In minimal pairs, the semantic variation resulting from substitution is limited to one kind of meaning, the two variants profiling a single domain differently, cf. our discussion of *They walked/ were walking along the beach, arm in arm* and *We celebrated/were celebrating Stephanie's birthday at my uncle's the other day*. Although in such pairs the semantic variation is minimal, the two variants may well express other meanings – as long as these other meanings are expressed by both examples. In other words, in pairs of examples which differ with respect to one category only, other categories are likely to be present, profiling other semantic domains. But these other categories are kept constant in the substitution. Thus in the two minimal pairs just mentioned, both variants express past temporal meaning as well as a particular aspectual focus.

Second, by definition non-monadic language-specific forms enter multiple systemic relations in that they contrast with two or more other language-specific forms, and for each contrast it is possible to set up minimal pairs as well as more distinct pairs. This makes choice relations very, very complex. For example, as we have seen, there are contexts where *celebrated* contrasts minimally with *were celebrating*. At the same time, there is a more complex, non-minimal relationship between *celebrated* and *celebrate* in examples like *We celebrate Stephanie's birthday at my uncle's* and *We celebrated Stephanie's birthday at my uncle's*. In addition to the temporal difference between present and past application time, there is a potential difference in terms of the kind of process expressed (action). The former example with the present tense form can only be understood as habitual (i.e. 'whenever we celebrate Stephanie's birthday it is at my uncle's'), unless we add a circumstantial adjunct (as in e.g. *We celebrate Stephanie's birthday at my uncle's next Tuesday*) or the context supplies the necessary specification. As it stands, the past-tense example is more immediately ambiguous between a habitual and a nonhabitual reading: the celebration at my uncle's may be a recurring process or a single specific event. An exhaustive analysis of the difference between *celebrate* and *celebrated* would involve not only temporality but also actionality. This is not an accidental feature of the English verb system, but in fact a quite common phenomenon. Thus we find exactly the same complexity in a pair of examples like the following:

(7a) She <u>speaks</u> like a real professional.

(7b) She <u>spoke</u> like a real professional.

As we saw in Section 3.4, the a-example is most readily interpreted in terms of a habit or an ability on the part of the subject, while the b-example is ambiguous between a single specific process (e.g. 'last night at the convention she spoke like a real professional') and a habitual one (e.g. 'As a young woman she spoke (= used to speak) like a real professional').

By contrast, the following examples of the present/past distinction form a truly minimal pair:

(8a) I <u>know</u> Sam well enough to recommend him for the job.

(8b) I <u>knew</u> Sam well enough to recommend him for the job.

Here the *only* difference is one of temporality, the nature of the process expressed being completely identical in the two substitutional variants: the a-example applies 'my knowledge' to the present in relation to the moment of communication while the b-example applies it to the past.

A different way of formulating the choice relations which the simple past in English enters into is to say that it is an aspect (with actional implications) in relation to the past progressive but a tense (with actional implications) in relation to the simple present. In addition, it enters complex relationships with the past perfect and the present perfect.

4.4.7 The metacategories of tense, action and aspect and their categorial interplay

In the preceding sections I have introduced the reader to a number of principles of category description as well as a number of category labels which I find useful in the account of certain choice relations accommodated by the English verb system. Let me briefly summarize my suggestions so far and elaborate a bit.

Verb forms subjected to a comprehensive substitution test usually express meanings which enter complex systemic relationships (cf. Bache 1985). For each contrast we typically find both semantically minimal pairs and more distinct relations between the substitutional variants. Categories in the metalanguage (the so-called 'metacategories' in my proposals) are established on the basis of minimal pairs because they are likely to reveal meanings that can be generalised across whole sets of forms, unlike the meanings in the more distinctly contrasted pairs of examples. While metacategories are monadic (with a one-to-one relationship between member and meaning), language-specific categories are non-monadic (with a one-to-many relationship between member and meaning). It is easy to show that the verb forms traditionally associated with the 'tense system' in English enter complex systemic relationships and thus involve more than just one category. In minimal pairs we find meanings at the definition level of at least three category-defining domains (not counting voice and modality). Tense, action and aspect are appropriate labels for these domains (even if they differ somewhat from their traditional use), but others would of course be possible (e.g. Halliday's 'secondary tense' for 'aspect' and Fawcett's 'event types' for 'action', see Subsection C in 4.2.2 above). Each of these labels designates a metacategorial unit with everything that belongs to it (semantic domain, members, form terms, profiles, etc.), while the derived labels 'temporality', 'actionality', 'aspectuality' are used specifically about the domains as such (i.e. the general category concepts).

On the basis of minimal pairs (which give us access to the definition level of meaning), I can offer the following characterizations of the three metacategories and their members (for a more comprehensive account see Bache 1997: Chapter 7, 199ff):

Aspect is basically a category of textual meaning which provides a choice relation between a **perfective** and an **imperfective** presentation on the process expressed. The general category concept **aspectuality** concerns what may be termed 'situational focus': **perfectivity** offers an external situational focus and **imperfectivity** offers an internal situational focus. In more explicitly functional terms, we can say that with a perfective expression the

Performer instructs the Addressee to look at the process from the outside, as a complete whole, whereas with an imperfective expression, the Performer instructs the Addressee to look at the process from the inside, as something in progression.

Action is an experiential category profiling different kinds of processes, such as **telic** (i.e. 'having duration and reaching a terminal point'), **directional** ('progressing towards, but not necessarily reaching a terminal point'), **punctual** ('having no duration'), **semelfactive** ('happening once'), **iterative** ('happening several times in quick succession'), etc. The general category concept **actionality** thus concerns the classification of processes into types according to the phasal (or procedural) characteristics that we assign to them (cf. Bache 1997: 218). An expression is characterised as actional if, one way or the other, it expresses a process as something **dynamic**, i.e. as something which takes place, or happens, at a particular time and place. Though aspect and action are thus in principle separate categories, and should be kept separate in our metalanguage, they enter a complex relationship in terms of compatibility and incompatibility which serves as a basis for a dynamic categorial interplay.[12]

Tense is a metafunctionally diverse category for the description of the Performer's temporal orientation of processes. This temporal orientation is created by setting up and relating base times (in which the orientation is anchored) and function times (towards which the orientation is directed). The general category concept **temporality** reflects the Performer's temporal projection of processes as preceding, coinciding with or following some designated time (i.e. as **past**, **present** and **future**, relative to some base time such as the moment of communication or some past or future time). In functional terms, tense signals Performer instructions to the Addressee to 'look back' (past), to 'look here' (present) or to 'look ahead' (future) from a base time. The metafunctional diversity of tense becomes clear when we consider the following implications of temporality: (a) the construed temporal location of a process is an important part of what Halliday calls 'representational meaning' and thus clearly involves the experiential metafunction even if it is a function rather than an inherent characteristic of the process expressed; (b) its participation in building up complex expressions (reflecting the serial interplay between base and function times) makes it an important logical resource; (c) its close association with finiteness and deixis, i.e. its regular grounding in the moment of communication, is interpersonally significant; and, finally, (d) its role in organising sequences of processes, e.g. in narration (cf. Bache 1986 and Chapter 6 below), makes it a textual resource like aspect.

On the basis of more distinctly contrasted pairs of constructions (which give us access to the function level of meaning), such as *Roger swam/was swimming across the river* and *She speaks/spoke like a real professional*, we can characterise the categorial interplay between tense, action and aspect in more detail. For example, as we have already noted, if we subject a telic expression like *Roger swam across the river* (which conveys a natural termination point beyond which the process cannot continue) to an internal aspectual focus by using instead the past progressive form *Roger was swimming across the river*, the result is an actional change from something telic to something directional. This is an example of the categorial interplay between aspect and action. Tense is present in those expressions too, but merely as a category which licenses the interplay between aspect and action. However, in other expressions, tense plays a more active part in the categorial interplay. If, for example, in a substitution test we replace the simple past tense form *spoke* with the simple present tense *speaks* in the clausal frame *She __ like a professional*, we not only change the temporal orientation from past to present but we also narrow the actional potential of the expression: the past-tense construction is either dynamic (referring to a particular event) or non-actional (describing a particular characteristic of the subject), whereas the present tense construction is unambiguously non-actional. This example of the categorial interplay between tense and action is the result of the clash between the external aspectual potential of the simple form in connection with dynamic processes and the Performer's mental immersion in the present, which is incompatible with a perfective presentation. A truly dynamic reading is only possible in the past tense variant. The present tense is instead interpreted as a non-actional (and non-aspectual) characterisation of the subject. In the case of nondynamic, stative expressions like *I knew/know him well enough to recommend him for the job*, there is no similar restriction of actionality as we move from the past tense to the present tense because stativity is already specified lexically for the past tense construction. This pair is a minimal pair, the variants differing only with respect to temporal orientation.

To gear the metalanguage to an exhaustive analysis of language-specific expression syntax in relation to both definition-level meanings and function-level meanings, it is important to ensure the accommodation of language-specific markedness relations for each of the metacategories. This is done by marking the category concept as a privative opposition (±TEMPORAL, ±ACTIONAL, ±ASPECTUAL) (for discussion of privative oppositions, see Jakobson 1932, Forsyth 1970: 6ff; Bache 1997: 138, 148f, 310ff). The positive marking of the domain (+TEMPORAL, +ACTIONAL, +ASPECTUAL) indicates that it is open to **specific profiling** by the individual members of the category while the negative marking of the domain (–TEMPORAL, –ACTIONAL, –ASPECTUAL) enables us to handle the possibility that language-specific data with a potentially relevant expression-syntactic realization may not always profile the particular domain positively (for discussion of this descriptive convention, see Bache 1997: 138f). Let us briefly look at an example which involves both non-actionality and non-aspectuality. As already indicated, one of the more radical suggestions in my approach to aspect and action is that expressions of what is traditionally called stativity (including most relational processes) are not imperfective but in fact –ASPECTUAL.[13] Now, stativity is actionally vague and difficult, if not impossible, to visualise mentally. It is not something that *happens* or *takes place*: it simply lacks dynamic manifestation.[14] Stativity is therefore appropriately described as –ACTIONAL, i.e. as unmarked with respect to the action category (lacking positive procedural characteristics). Being non-actional, stativity is also aspectually neutral because one cannot view a process characterised by the absence of dynamic procedural meaning (e.g. action or activity) either perfectively or imperfectively. There is therefore a cross-linguistic tendency for stativity to be expressed by an aspectually unmarked expression, whether this expression is formally perfective (as the English simple present or simple past) or formally imperfective (as the Russian imperfective morphological base form) (cf. Bache 1997: 310ff).

The categorial interplay between metacategories is generated by **incompatibility relations** between domains or between profiles. Such relations should be stated explicitly. For example, the metalinguistic generalization that non-actionality and aspectuality are always incompatible can be formulated by the following incompatibility relation (cf. Bache 1997: 272):

–ACTIONALITY ⇓ +ASPECTUALITY

('–ACTIONALITY is incompatible with +ASPECTUALITY'). Incompatibilities constrain categorial profile selection (e.g. non-actionality cannot be profiled perfectively or imperfectively). Remaining options can be stated in terms of 'co-selection rules', which in effect correspond to incompatibility relations but do not state them explicitly as such. The co-selection rule corresponding to the incompatibility between non-actionality and aspectuality offered above looks like this:

–ACTIONALITY >> –ASPECTUALITY

('if –ACTIONALITY is selected, then –ASPECTUALITY must also be selected'). Note that this rule does not prevent a language-specific form (or construction) traditionally classified as aspectual (such as e.g. the Russian imperfective morphological base form) from expressing non-actionality, but in that case the form is semantically unmarked with respect to aspectuality.

Another example is the incompatibility of punctuality (from the actionality domain) with imperfectivity (from the aspectuality domain):

punctual ⇓ imperfective

('punctuality is incompatible with imperfectivity'). This incompatibility constrains the expression syntax explicitly while the corresponding co-selection rule implies it:

punctuality >> perfectivity, −ASPECTUALITY

('if punctuality is selected, then either perfectivity or non-aspectuality must also be selected'). Note again that this rule does not prevent a particular language from using a form traditionally classified as imperfective for the expression of punctual processes. But the implication is that the form is really aspectually unmarked, i.e. −ASPECTUAL, (at least when used to express punctual processes). Here are some other incompatibilities and derived co-selection rules:

telicness ⇓ imperfectivity

telicness >> perfectivity, −ASPECTUALITY

present ⇓ perfectivity

present >> imperfectivity, −ASPECTUALITY

Telicness (as in *Roger swam across the river*) is incompatible with a positive imperfective reading because such a reading excludes the defining terminal point of a telic process (as in *Roger was swimming across the river*). Language-specific expressions of telicness must therefore be either perfective or non-aspectual (but note that in Russian, for example, telicness may be expressed by the unmarked, formally imperfective form, as in *Ja uže čital ètu knigu*, cf. Forsyth 1970: 13). Similarly, a truly present expression is incompatible with a truly perfective expression because one cannot distance oneself sufficiently from a process taking place at the time of communication to adopt an external situational focus. Thus, in Russian, present processes are expressed by the formally imperfective present tense while the formal perfective present tense is used regularly for the expression of future perfectivity. In English, by comparison, present meaning is expressed either by the present progressive or by the simple present when the process is non-actional (and therefore also non-aspectual) (for more details, see Section 5.5 below).

This concludes my review of some major sources of inspiration and my introduction to a number of important principles of category description and descriptive conventions. I can now move on to suggest a new systemic functional description of English tense and aspect.

Notes

1. The model is in fact rather more complex: there are two further levels of representation (Basic Logical Form and Enriched Logical Form) and a vital component mediating between the two (the 'planner'), and, as we shall see in Section 4.2.2, these are relevant to the generation of tenses.
2. As we shall see shortly, the time span of *is* in *Jennifer is brave* is 'past-present-future' rather than simply 'present' (cf. Fawcett forthcoming: Chapter 4, Section 2.3).
3. This presentation of the Cardiff approach to time and tense, including most of the examples, is primarily based on Chapter 4 of Fawcett (forthcoming).
4. The imprecise terminological practice adopted by Fawcett here is unfortunately very common in current linguistics. It can be traced back to Comrie 1976, among others (cf. Bache 1982, 1985, 1997, 2002).
5. At the time of writing, no published version of the Cardiff Grammar's networks for 'time' is available, so it is hard to judge how far the lack of a sense of seriality is inherent in the model. It may well be clear from the relevant part of the computer implementation of the grammar (in fact it must be for the generator not to mess things up!).
6. Harder uses the term 'state-of-affairs' for what many other linguists call 'situation' and *IFG* calls 'process'. Throughout my discussion of Harder's theory I shall use his term.
7. For exactly the same reason it is in my view misleading to speak of 'imperfective' states-of-affairs. The aspect category and the notions of perfectivity and imperfectivity should be kept distinct from actional meanings such as stativity, habituality, etc. For a critique of Bybee *et al.* (1994) and Comrie (1976), see Bache (2002).
8. There is in fact a slight ambiguity in Harder's way of speaking of the present and the past. Sometimes their meaning seems to hinge on the 'point-of-application', sometimes on the 'pointing towards' the point-of-application. But in either case it is clear that their meaning is functional rather than representational.
9. For a detailed discussion of the problem of 'analytic directionality' ('from form to meaning' versus 'from meaning to form'), see Bache (1997: 26ff).
10. In the rest of this book I shall adopt the SFL practice of using the term 'process' instead of Harder's 'state-of-affairs' or the more common 'situation' (which I

have used in my other writings). It is important to note, however, that the term 'process' is used in a technical sense, i.e. not only for processes in the normal sense of the word, but for all sorts of situations or states-of-affairs, even relational ones and punctual ones (which we do not normally associate with 'processes').

11. The same analysis applies to some of Fawcett's examples: *They discussed / were discussing your case yesterday afternoon,* cf. Section 4.2.3 above.

12. It is this close relationship between the two categories which has induced many linguists to conflate them into a single general category (for discussion, see especially Bache 1982, 1997, 2002). However, such a conflation obscures the nature of the interplay between the meanings involved and is therefore descriptively inadequate.

13. Linguists following Comrie's approach to aspect (cf. Comrie 1976) are likely to be confused by my claim that stative and relational processes are incompatible with a positive aspectual value. Such scholars tend to conflate aspect and action into one general category (without a well-defined coherent semantic or functional domain), and they believe that stative, habitual and relational processes are imperfective (like dynamic processes presented as unfolding), thus failing to draw a distinction between meanings ascribed to the process itself and organizational and presentational meanings of the text describing the process, i.e. between experiential and textual meanings. I have argued (see e.g. Bache 1997 and 2002) that Comrie's definition of imperfectivity captures the essence of imperfectivity but in fact only makes sense in connection with dynamic processes, not states, habits and relations.

14. Significantly, such a process is only called a process in SFL for technical descriptive reasons, not because there is any actual process involved in the ordinary sense of this word.

5 A new SFL description of tense and aspect

Like the *IFG* model of tense in English, my alternative model recognises the serial nature of the category. This seriality, however, is not caused by recursion in relation to a basic tripartite system but results from a limited number of choices ordered by certain dependencies and scope relations. Like Halliday, Matthiessen, Harder and to some extent also Fawcett, I operate with a compositional tense paradigm rather than a traditional constructional one; and in the metafunctional specification of this paradigm, I assume a central logical component (among other things). For presentational reasons I shall remain uncommitted as to whether or not the verbal group should be discarded, as argued by Fawcett, and instead talk of 'verbal expressions'. While I accept Fawcett's arguments (Fawcett 2000b, c) that the elements that Halliday would assign to the verbal group should be regarded as functioning as direct elements of the clause, I am aware that many readers of this book will be unwilling to take that step without reading the arguments for themselves (which I recommend that they should do). For the purposes of the case to be made here, however, it is in fact immaterial whether the elements that I will be discussing are regarded as elements of the clause or as elements of a verbal group filling a Predicator that is an element of the clause. In the rest of this book I shall therefore operate with the *non-theoretical* notion of a '*verbal expression*'. A verbal expression will consist of just those elements that Halliday would assign to the verbal group, but which in Fawcett's model operate directly as elements of the clause. In the structural realisations of tense choices in verbal expressions, I recognise a 'univariate' characteristic, i.e. an element of functional similarity or identity across the serialisation of tense. But that is not the whole story. In addition to the repetition of a single functional principle there are, for each choice, specific functions which imbue the structure with 'multivariate' characteristics, and this has repercussions for the choice relations involved. The individual formal markers of the paradigm are thus not 'just' tense markers but are non-monadic, or multifunctional, as emphasised also by Fawcett, in that they can only be described adequately and exhaustively in terms of more than one functional domain. As we shall see, some of these additional functional domains have other metafunctional characteristics than logical ones.

5.1   Organisation and inventory

From an *expression-syntactic* point of view, the *basic organisation* of a finite verbal expression is determined by five choices of value in relation to the process of the main verb:

	Choice of value	Realisation
(1)	past or nonpast:	± -*ed*
(2)	modal or nonmodal:	± modal verb + infinitive
(3)	perfect or nonperfect:	± HAVE + past participle
(4)	progressive or nonprogressive:	± BE + present participle
(5)	passive or nonpassive:	± BE + past participle
(6)	process	full verb

These choices are interrelated in that the formal realisation of each one of them governs the realisation of the next choice (see also Figure 2.3 in Subsection 2.1.E above): the past/nonpast distinction thus has morphological implications for whatever is chosen next; a modal verb is followed by an infinitive; perfect auxiliary HAVE is followed by a past participle, progressive auxiliary BE is followed by a present participle, and passive auxiliary BE is followed by a past participle, cf. Figure 5.1 (adopted from Bache 2000: 121).[1]

In addition to these choices, the Performer has at her disposal a number of expressions with future temporal (and sometimes also modal) implications:

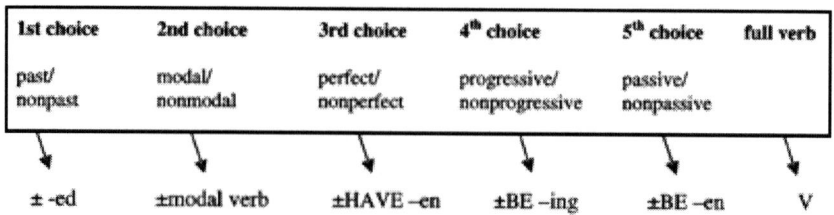

Figure 5.1: The structure of the basic finite verbal expression

BE *going to* + infinitive, BE *about to* + infinitive, BE *on the point of* + present participle, BE *on the brink of* + present participle, BE *to* + *infinitive.*[2] Of these, BE *going to* + infinitive is the most common and also the most neutral alternative to the core future.

All these choices are affected by the tense category and, except for the fifth choice between passive and nonpassive ('active') voice, they are all functionally motivated by considerations of temporality, among other things. The second structural slot, which accommodates the choice between modal and non-modal, is special because it facilitates also future temporal meaning (realised by *will* and *would*; for discussion of the future as a tense, see also Davidsen-Nielsen 1985, 1990). As Harder (1996: 369) puts it: '[...] the English future is therefore a sort of squatter in the modal paradigm, a less than structurally clear-cut entity'. Singling out *will* and *would* as realisations of certain tense choices is thus a central example of the idealisation of tense as a coherent compositional paradigm mentioned in Section 4.2.3. At the same time, however, this descriptive practice is entirely compatible with the non-monadicness of English verb forms more generally (cf. Section 4.4.6), which often renders a rigorous distinction between 'tense forms' and 'modal verbs' irrelevant. The core compositional paradigm which I suggest that we set up thus looks like this in Harder's content-syntactic formalism:

> past/nonpast > future/nonfuture > perfect/nonperfect > progressive/ nonprogressive

The SFL formalism for representing relations between features consists essentially of left- and right-opening brackets. These may be square brackets, representing 'or' or curly brackets, representing 'and'. It is the right-opening square bracket that represents the concept of a **system**, i.e. a choice between two or more features. Because of the strong paradigmatic orientation of SFL, however, systemicists have found little use for the left-opening square bracket, as shown in Figure 5.2, preferring to represent the same possible set of combinations of features (i.e. xa, xb, ya, yb) by two simultaneous systems (i.e. two systems, both entered from a curly, right-opening bracket). Indeed, many systemicists would regard the repeated use of such a bracket in a network as inelegant. In the Cardiff Grammar, however, this relationship is used without any sense of inelegance to represent relations between semantic features that are realised in the elements with which we are concerned here, thus modelling, within the system network itself, the concept of 'seriality' in the meanings as well as in the forms.

Using this formalism, I can offer the system network in Figure 5.3 for my core paradigm.[3]

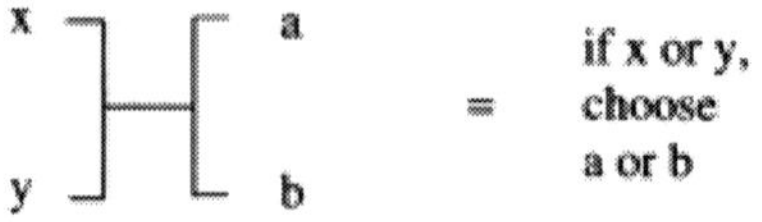

$$
\begin{matrix} x \\[3em] y \end{matrix} \left.\right\}\!\!\left[\begin{matrix} a \\[3em] b \end{matrix}\right. \qquad = \qquad \begin{matrix} \text{if x or y,} \\ \text{choose} \\ \text{a or b} \end{matrix}
$$

Figure 5.2: The SFG convention for showing dependence between systems

Each choice has scope over subsequent choices. All four choices, even the first one, are privative (in that the contrast in each case is between the presence and absence of a particular value). While the first choice is deictic (as well as temporal), the other three are relative (but within the scope of deictic temporality). All positive choices have formal realisations, while all negative choices are formally neutral: content-syntactic markedness is thus reflected by expression-syntactic markedness. Furthermore, as we have seen, the first positive choice is different from the others also in terms of manner of realisation: it is morphologically realised while the other three are periphrastically realised. Again, the special status of the first choice (in terms of finiteness and superordinate scope) is reflected by its special expression-syntactic status. The system thus has a high degree of 'naturalness'. From another point of view it could of course be argued that the system is unnatural, in that it is the result of piecing together only the (sub)systems that are relevant for the tense category. But by ignoring the much more complex relations and groupings of systems in the overall model, we can focus more sharply on the choice relations involved in connection with tense distinctions (cf. Section 4.2.3).

As there are four binary oppositions, the core system comprises a total of 16 active non-monadic 'tenses', i.e. forms which all express complex meanings (including actionality and aspectuality) but which share an element of temporality (cf. Section 4.4.7 above). These tenses are named according to the formal tense selections involved except nonpast, for which I retain the traditional term 'present' despite its unmarked temporal characteristics. The following list shows for each tense its name, the choice of ±past plus addi-

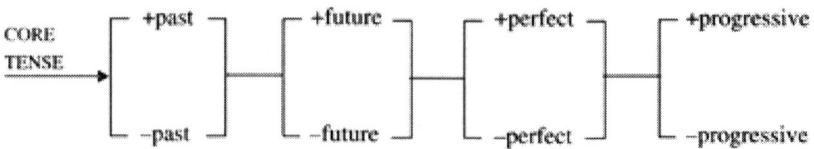

Figure 5.3: Core tense paradigm

tional positive choices,[4] an example with the verb TAKE, and the number in Halliday's 'System I' (cf. Subsection 2.1.H above):

	Tense name / choices	Example	Halliday's model
1.	present −past	*takes*	2
2.	past +past	*took*	1
3.	present future −past (+future)	*will take*	3
4.	past future +past (+future)	*would take*	new
5.	present perfect −past (+perfect)	*has taken*	5
6.	past perfect +past (+perfect)	*had taken*	4
7.	present future perfect −past (+future (+perfect))	*will have taken*	6
8.	past future perfect +past (+future (+perfect))	*would have taken*	new
9.	present progressive −past (+progressive)	*am/are/is taking*	8
10.	past progressive +past (+progressive)	*was/were taking*	7
11.	present future progressive −past (+future (+progressive))	*will be taking*	9
12.	past future progressive +past (+future (+progressive))	*would be taking*	new
13.	present perfect progressive −past (+perfect (+progressive))	*has been taking*	17
14.	past perfect progressive +past (+perfect (+progressive))	*had been taking*	16
15.	present future perfect progressive −past (+future (+perfect (+progressive)))	*will have been taking*	18
16.	past future perfect progressive +past (+future (+perfect (+progressive)))	*would have been taking*	new

This system serves as my **core system** of tenses. Note first of all that it is much more observationally adequate than Halliday and Matthiessen's System I. Tenses 1 to 14 are all frequent in the BNC and CWO, and only tenses 15 and 16 are infrequent (with a total of 46 and 161 hits, respectively). There are no non-existent tenses. My core system thus reflects actual tense usage far more precisely (insofar as the BNC and CWO are reasonably representative of the kind of English we are interested in describing). More specifically it differs from System I in two important respects, both of which concern the secondary future. BE *going to* + infinitive is excluded as a central tense marker (but recognised as an important supplementary form offering the Performer an alternative expression of future meaning). At the same time *would* + infinitive (which is completely absent from System I) is incorporated as a finite past future. Let us consider these two modifications in turn.

In the *IFG* model, BE *going to* + infinitive realises the standard secondary future ('future in') and plays a central role in the recursive tense system, generating a large number of exceedingly rare or non-existent tense forms (such as the 'present in past in future in past in future', e.g. *will have been going to have been taking*) as well as a few very common, regular expressions (the 'future in past', e.g. *was going to take*, and the 'future in present', e.g. *is going to take*). In fact BE *going to* + infinitive helps realise 24 of the 36 tenses in System I, and is thus the second most frequently used building block in the tense system (the secondary past HAVE + past participle tops the list: like BE *going to* + infinitive it is included in 24 tenses, but unlike the secondary future it has two realisations in six of them, thus reaching a total of 30 occurrences). However, as noted in our study of the actual frequency of Halliday's tenses in the BNC and CWO in Section 3.6, BE *going to* is included in all the non-existent tenses and in all the infrequent ones except one (number 18: the 'present in past in future', e.g. *will have been taking*). At the same time it is absent from all the frequent tenses, except numbers 10 and 11 (the 'future in past', e.g. *was going to take*, and the 'future in present', e.g. *is going to take*). This can be taken as evidence that in actual usage, the more cycles there are in the recursive process, the more unlikely the Performer is to choose the secondary future. In fact, it is not unreasonable to conclude that BE *going to* + infinitive is a rather marginal tense, and that it would be observationally more adequate, at least from the point of view of actual usage, to treat it as a special additional means of expressing future meaning than to accept it as a fully integrated tense form. My suggestion, therefore, is that we exclude constructions with BE *going to* + infinitive from the *core inventory* of the category in order *to strike a better balance between trying to capture the meaning potential of tense in English and reflecting actual usage*, both of which are important considerations in a functional grammar. Though this is really a rather modest adjustment of Halliday's System I, the effect is dramatic: the 36 tenses are reduced to 12 (i.e. numbers 1–9 and 16–18). Of the 24 tenses that disappear, 16 are non-existent in the BNC and CWO, six are infrequent, and only two are frequent (the 'future in past' and the 'future in present'). In Section 5.2 below, I shall discuss their status in the description of the tense category as a whole.

The second modification of Halliday's System I that I propose involves the recognition of *would* + infinitive as a member of the core tense system. There are several reasons why I think it makes good sense to include this form as a finite past future tense. First of all, *would* + infinitive may serve as a *neutrally projected form* of another tense, viz. Halliday's primary 'future' *will* + infinitive. As noted in Section 2.1, in this it resembles an uncontroversial tense like the 'past in past' (which is the neutrally projected form of the 'past', the 'past in present' and the 'past in past' itself), and it is thus very strange indeed that *would* + infinitive is absent from Halliday's System II. It will be recalled that System II is a system of finite tenses found in past projected clauses. There are 24 such tenses, according to Halliday, and the system is viewed as a subset of System I. The reduction from 36 tenses in System I to 24 tenses in System II is a result of the neutralisation of 'past', 'past in present' and 'past in past' when projected into the 'past in past'.[5] An example of this neutralisation is *They took / have taken / had taken the key* → *She claimed that they had taken the key.* Similarly, as pointed out in Section 2.1 above, there is neutral projection of the 'present' to the 'past' in examples like *I am very happy for Jim* → *She said she was very happy for Jim* (for critical comments on Halliday's discussion of projection in connection with the tense system, see Subsection 2.1.1). But just like the 'past in past' is a neutrally projected version of the 'past', and the 'past' is a neutrally projected form of 'present', the past future realised by *would* + infinitive may serve as a neutrally projected version of future *will* + infinitive (which Halliday readily accepts as a primary tense marker on a par with the morphological realisations of the past and the present):

There will be another meeting soon
  → The dean said there would be another meeting soon

My commanding officer will regard that as cowardice
  → Peter said that his commanding officer would regard that as cowardice

Just as Halliday's 'past in past' does not in fact express 'past in past' *meaning* in projection, but simply 'reported past', *would be* and *would regard* do not express 'past future' meaning but 'reported future' (for discussion of the last example, see Bache and Davidsen-Nielsen 1997: 311f). There is an obvious parallel between the neutral projection of future *will be* / *will regard* to *would be* / *would regard* and the neutral projections of the 'past' to the 'past in past' and of the 'present' to the 'past'. This clearly indicates that *would* + infinitive serves a function which would be appropriate for a past future form. Furthermore, it clearly qualifies as a natural member of System II, and hence also of System I (since System II is supposed to be a subset of System I). The inclusion of *would* + infinitive as a member of the core tense system allows us to formulate a *tense-internal* generalisation about verbal expressions in projected clauses, which otherwise would not have been possible. As noted by Bache and Davidsen-Nielsen (1997: 312) and others, projection simply affects the first choice between present and past and involves a semantically neutral formal 'backshifting' of this choice. There are only two possible shifts back: from present to past, and from past to past perfect. But these shifts affect a range of more specific tense constructions, simple as well as more complex ones, including some with the choice of +future in them. Thus, if the first tense choice in the original construction is present, the possible backshifts can be summed up as in Figure 5.4.

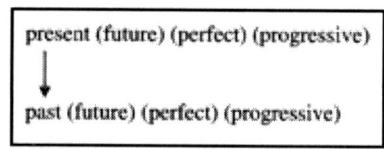

Figure 5.4: Backshifts to the past

The specific shifts accommodated by this generalisation include:

present	→ past
present future	→ past future
present perfect	→ past perfect
present future perfect	→ past future perfect
present progressive	→ past progressive
etc.	

If the first tense choice in the original construction is past, the possible backshifts to the past perfect can be summed as in Figure 5.5.

As indicated, the backshifting from past to past perfect may or may not include the progressive, but past perfect and past future forms remain unchanged when projected:

past	→ past perfect
past progressive	→ past perfect progressive

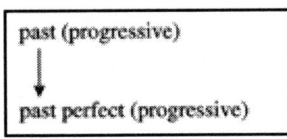

past (progressive)

past perfect (progressive)

Figure 5.5: Backshifts to the past perfect

(for more discussion and examples, see Bache and Davidsen-Nielsen 1997: 312f). We can conclude that by accepting *would* + infinitive as a member of the core system, we have prepared the ground for a more adequate and comprehensive account of projected verb forms in terms of regular backshifting of the primary tense choice, i.e. in terms of a category-internal mechanism. The *IFG* model both fails to include all relevant forms in System II (despite the fact that plenty of low-frequency and non-existent tenses are accepted as members) and misses an obvious generalisation in connection with projection. What I suggest, therefore, is not only that we accept *would* + infinitive as a past future form, but also that we dismantle System II completely and instead account for the projection of verb forms in terms of the two rules of primary tense backshifting. The result of this suggestion is a vast simplification and it has a much higher degree of both observational and descriptive adequacy in our functional grammar.

Another reason for including *would* + infinitive as a past form of *will* + infinitive, and hence as a genuine member of the core system, is that it fits in naturally with (other) tenses in the often tight pattern of forms used for special purposes in connection with *conditional* sentences. The other forms used in this particular sentence type are unproblematically accepted by Halliday as tense forms: e.g. the present, the present future ('future'), the past, the past perfect ('past in past'), etc. As noted by Bache and Davidsen-Nielsen (1997: 269f), in a conditional sentence (which consists of a subordinate clause – the protasis – and a matrix clause – the apodosis) the process described by the apodosis is typically causally dependent on the one described by the protasis and either coincides with it or follows it in time, as in e.g. *If you close the door, I will tell you my innermost secret*, where the telling of innermost secrets is made conditional upon the prior closing of the door.[6] When the finite predicator in the protasis is realised by a present verb form, such as *close*, the finite predicator in the apodosis is realised by a present future ('future') form, such as *will tell*. Both tenses point towards the future. Thus, a present tense form within the scope of a conditional operator, such as *if*, corresponds to a present future ('future') tense form outside this scope. In other words, the two tenses enter what may be termed a 'conditional pair', in that they 'go together' in conditional sentences. When the finite predicator of the protasis is past without past time meaning, the finite predicator of the apodosis is a past future, as in *If she asked him, he would be angry.*[7] The conditional pair of verb forms here regularly consists of the past and the past future, and the effect of using this pair is to indicate that the processes described by the two clauses are unlikely to occur. And finally, when the finite predicator of the protasis is a past perfect ('past in past'), the finite predicator of the apodosis is a past future perfect, as in *If you had told them the truth, they would all have rushed out.* Here the conditional pair expresses counterfactuality: the condition expressed by the protasis instructs the Addressee to imagine an alternative world that negates the real world, and the apodosis offers a scenario in that alternative world. What we see in these three common constellations is a kind of formal 'forwardshifting' (i.e. the opposite of the backshifting of the primary tense choice that we noted in connection with projection):

Protasis		Apodosis	
present	→	present future	(neutral condition)
past	→	past future	(condition + bias towards non-occurrence)
past perfect	→	past future perfect	(counterfactual condition)

The interesting point is that unless we accept *would* + infinitive as a tense form on a par with *will* + infinitive, we cannot capture as a *category-internal* phenomenon the regularity with which finite predicators in conditional sentences are often realised in conditional pairs. As a very general rule of thumb we can say that whichever tense choices are made for the protasis, +future is a regular additional second choice for the apodosis.[8] With Halliday's System I, only the first conditional pair, the one consisting of the 'present' and the 'future' (the present future), belongs unambiguously to the tense category (both forms being proper tenses). Halliday and Matthiessen are forced to consider the other two pairs (consisting of the 'past' and the past future, and the 'past in past' and the past future perfect, respectively) to be combinations of a form from the tense category with a form from another category (only the 'past' and the 'past in past' being proper tenses in their model). Now, since it is in any case relevant to consider the use of tense forms in conditional sentences, adopting *would* + infinitive as a tense allows us to capture a regularity in the formation of conditional pairs in terms of the tense category, something which cannot be done in the *IFG* tense model.

The third, and perhaps most compelling reason for including *would* + infinitive as a past form of *will* + infinitive, and hence as a genuine member of the core system, is that this construction is used with a narrative function which is very similar to narrative functions served by uncontroversial tenses:

(1)   At 16, Eddie O'Hare was suspended somewhere between child-hood and adulthood. In Eddie's opinion, there was no better be-ginning to *any* story that the first sentence of *The Mouse Crawling Between the Walls*: 'Tom woke up, but Tim did not.' In Ruth Cole's life as a writer – and she <u>would be</u> a better writer than her father, in any way – she <u>would</u> always <u>envy</u> that sentence. And she <u>would</u> never <u>forget</u> the first time she heard it, which was long before she knew it was the first sentence of a famous book. (IWOY 13–14).

(2)   The first driver off the ferry was a fool. He was so stunned by the beauty of the woman he saw walking toward him that he turned off the road into the stony sand of the beach; his car <u>would be</u> stuck there for over an hour, but even when he realised his predicament, he couldn't take his eyes off Marion. He couldn't help himself. Marion didn't notice the accident – she just kept walking, slowly.

    For the rest of his life, Eddie O'Hare <u>would believe</u> in fate. After all, the second he set foot on shore, there was Marion. (IWOY 33).

(3)   As for Eddie's favorite book by Ted Cole, he removed it from his duffel bag and read it once more before the ferry landed. The story of *The Door in the Floor* <u>would</u> never <u>be</u> a favourite of Ruth's; her father had not told it to her, and it <u>would be</u> a few years before Ruth was old enough to read it for herself. She <u>would hate</u> it. (IWOY 47).

In these narrative examples the past future is used to point forward to a later process – to 'look ahead' – in the fictional universe created by the author (just as the past perfect *had [...] told* in (3) instructs the Addressee to 'look back' to a previous stage in the development of the narration). Unless we adopt a *genre-biased* approach to our data, giving priority to non-narrative texts, such examples must be taken seriously in our tense description.

The past future is also used in historical accounts where the historian describes past events in the light of later developments (which are future in relation to the past events described but past in relation to the moment of communication). Here is an example from Ronald Wright's *A Short History of Progress*:

(4)   Easter Island's little civilization was one of the last to develop inde-pendently. The earliest of all was Sumer, in what is now southern Iraq. The Sumerians, whose own ethnic and linguistic stock is un-clear, set a pattern that Semitic cultures and others in the Old

World <u>would follow</u>. They came to exemplify both the best and worst of the civilized life [...] (WSHP 65)

In the following example we get two past future forms, the first of which has a clear modal value in contrast to the second one, which is predominantly temporal:

(5)   Gatherers began to notice that seeds accidentally scattered or passed in droppings <u>would spring</u> up the following year. They began to influence the outcome by tending an enlarging wild stands, sowing the most easily reaped and plumpest seeds.

   Such experiments <u>would</u> eventually <u>lead</u> to full agriculture and almost total dependence on a few monotonous staples, but that was several thousand years away [...]. (WSHP 41)

Here *would spring* has an association of 'habitual predictability' in addition to its past future meaning (supported by the adverbial *the following year*), while *would ... lead* simply offers the instruction to look ahead from the past vantage point established by the choice of +past (and the other simple past tense forms in the linguistic context). It is, of course, examples like the latter that provide the best evidence of *would* as a tense form.

It is important to point out that *would* used in narrative and historical contexts entails the actualisation of the process referred to (to use Huddleston and Pullum's terminology, cf. 2002: 198). Thus, in example (2) above, the first driver's car *was* indeed stuck in the stony sand of the beach for over an hour, and Eddie O'Hare *did* believe in fate for the rest of his life, again of course within the framework of the narration offered by John Irving. The two processes come into narrative existence as a result of being referred to by the past future verbal expressions. In this respect, past future *would* + infinitive differs somewhat from expressions with BE *going to* + infinitive. While this expression, unlike *would*, is possible in an ordinary everyday conversation about a process which is future in relation to some deictic past time, it often has a *negative orientation* towards the actualisation of the process referred to:

(6)   They <u>were going to be</u> present at the reception (but didn't make it).

(7)   She <u>was going to kiss</u> him (but then his girlfriend barged in).

In these examples *was/were going to* almost serves as a preamble to a *but ...* and is thus hardly a better candidate for the past future slot in the tense system.

Nevertheless, what I have presented as good reasons to include *would* + infinitive as a member of the core system of tenses in English (its role in conditional pairs and in projection, as well as its use in narration and historical accounts to 'look ahead') could in fact be turned around as an argument for *not* including it: if the construction is never actually used simply to refer to a future time relative to a past time in ordinary, everyday conversation but only seems to have these other, more specialised or genre-dependent uses, why treat it as a central tense form? There is no simple answer to this question. I consider it a matter of choosing the lesser evil. I much prefer coming under pressure from such a challenge than having to defend a system with 16 non-existent forms and seven infrequent ones in the BNC and CWO, i.e. a system with too much of an imbalance between considerations of the meaning potential of language and considerations of actual usage. It is also important, I think, to recognise the particular uses of *would* + infinitive as being relevant to discuss under the heading of tense, for otherwise it would be difficult to explain the widespread occurrence of other, uncontroversial tense forms in such contexts. In dealing with the tense category in English, the task is not simply to sort out in a neat way the semantic substance of tense in isolation but to specify in detail the complex relationship between content and expression in English. An important part of any tense description is to account for all the particular uses of any individual form which serves one or more relevant functions in the system as a whole. A related consideration is how to organise our model in such a way that it reflects both the relative importance of the phenomena to be accounted for and descriptive economy.

Another possible objection to *would* + infinitive as a core tense form is that *would* is primarily a modal verb, not a tense form. There can be no doubt that *would* + infinitive expresses modality in many of its uses (as in the case of the first instance in example (5)), but this is true also of *will* + infinitive (the two items often expressing parallel modal values, such as habitual predictability and 'characteristic behaviour', e.g. *He will/would sit and stare at the mess for hours*). However, this can only be a valid objection if one believes in monadic forms. As I have argued (cf. Section 4.4.6 above), there is plenty of evidence that all the so-called tenses, indeed all verb forms, in English are non-monadic, profiling two or more semantic domains. Both *will* and *would* profile the domains of modality and temporality, and possibly others, but they give different weight or priority to these domains in different contexts. If we restrict our description to monadic forms in English, there would be little or nothing left to describe.

The upshot of all this is that I feel confident in suggesting, as the second modification of Halliday and Matthiessen's System I, that we include *would* + infinitive in our central tense system as a past future parallel to present future *will* + infinitive (which is uncontroversial in an *IFG* context). In addition to the 12 tenses already established after the exclusion of BE *going to* + infinitive, we thus have four new tenses: a past future (e.g. *would take*), a past future perfect (e.g. *would have taken*), a past future progressive (e.g. *would be taking*) and a past future perfect progressive (e.g. *would have been taking*). For a more detailed discussion of *would* as a tense marker, see Bache (2007).

Though my core system looks very different from Halliday's System I in that it comprises only 16 members (as compared to the 36 tenses in System I) and in that four of them are new tense forms (i.e. those with a finite past future expressed by *would* + infinitive), it is really the result of only two modifications of System I: the categorisation of BE *going to* + infinitive as an important supplementary tense form (rather than as a member of the core system) and the inclusion of *would* + infinitive (as a parallel to *will* + infinitive). While the former modification is dictated by considerations of frequency in actual usage – an important indicator of observational adequacy in a functional grammar – the latter is motivated particularly by its function as a neutrally projected tense form, its special role in conditional pairs and, not least, its function to instruct the Addressee to look ahead in narration and historical accounts. All these uses have clear implications for the tense category and thus lend support to the expression-syntactic categorisation of *would* + infinitive as a member of the core tense system.

5.2   The status of BE *going to* + infinitive

In the preceding section I have argued against BE *going to* + infinitive as a member of the core system of tense in English. Instead this construction is to be considered an important supplementary tense marker for the expression of future meaning. In this section I shall comment on its status as a supplementary marker. Furthermore, I shall argue that even if we accept Halliday and Matthiessen's interest in *potential* tense usage rather than *actual* tense usage, there is a descriptively much simpler way of accounting for BE *going to* + infinitive than to consider it a secondary future in a recursive tense system.

As we saw in Section 5.1, there is a certain division of labour between past future *would* + infinitive and *was/were going to* + infinitive in that the latter, but not the former, is used regularly in normal everyday conversation to express future meaning relative to some past time. Here BE *going to* + infinitive has a distinct and extremely important supplementary function, which could have qualified it as a central tense had it not been for the more general distribution of forms viewed in relation to expression syntax. However, with the present variants of the two competing forms (*am/are/is going to*

+ infinitive and *will* + infinitive) the situation is somewhat different. In many cases, Halliday's 'future in present' is more or less interchangeable with his 'future' (my present future):

(1a)   They <u>are going to be</u> present at the reception.

(1b)   They <u>will be</u> present at the reception.

(2a)   He <u>is going to give</u> her a very difficult time.

(2b)   He <u>will give</u> her a very difficult time.

Both tense forms basically instruct the Addressee to look ahead from the present, but there are subtle differences between the variants. In the a-examples, the future process that the Addressee is instructed to look ahead to is presented as part of a present plan or possibly even as being within the subject's present determination or intention, whereas in the b-examples, it is presented more as a Performer assumption. There is in addition a sense in which BE *going to* + infinitive is more closely related to the present than *will* + infinitive is (and this is nicely captured by Halliday's term for it: 'future in present'). Thus, typically, BE *going to* + infinitive, but not *will* + infinitive, is used to instruct the Addressee to look ahead to *the future of a present cause*. As noted by Bache and Davidsen-Nielsen (1997: 291), *It's going to rain* cannot be replaced by *It'll rain* in a situation where black clouds are gathering. Although the basic function of the 'future in present' is the same as that of the present future, namely to instruct the Addressee to look ahead, its special characteristic is to stress the contiguity of present and future meaning. This qualifies it as a variant of the present future but hardly as a separate tense.

Some might argue that the fact that Halliday's 'future in present' is sometimes more or less interchangeable with his 'future' (my present future) is not in itself evidence that it is just a supplementary form without independent status as a tense. Thus, there are with other tenses obvious cases of near-synonymy where we would not consider one of the markers to be merely a supplementary form. Consider the following examples:[9]

(3a)   Mr Forsythe informs me that you <u>retain</u> an attachment to this foreign person. (FFLW 36)

(3b)   Mr Forsythe informs me that you <u>have retained</u> an attachment to this foreign person.

(4a)   Before the war he <u>had admired</u> the British country gentlemen very much, wore English clothes, kept English dogs ... (SMD 29)

(4b)   Before the war he <u>admired</u> the British country gentlemen very much, wore English clothes, kept English dogs ...

In examples (3a) and (3b) there is little difference between the present and the present perfect: in both cases the Performer presents a process as holding in the present, and in both cases there is a time-perspective to the past. In the a-example this time-perspective is signalled exclusively by the lexical verb RETAIN (whose nature is such that it implies a link backwards in time, a past history), whereas in the b-example it is signalled by both lexical choice and grammatical form. The difference, therefore, is one of slight emphasis.[10] The same is true of examples (4a) and (4b), which exemplify the distinction between the past perfect and the simple past. The simple past emphasises pastness in relation to the present moment of communication whereas the past perfect emphasises pastness in relation to some other past point or period of time. But since pastness relative to some other pastness is made explicit in both examples by the adverbial *Before the war*, the difference is again simply one of slight emphasis.

Now, these examples do not induce us to say that the present perfect is merely a supplementary form in relation to the simple present, or that the past perfect is merely a supplementary form in relation to the simple past. The reason for that is that the present perfect and the past perfect are basically distinct from the present and the past, respectively, and have many uses where they are not semantically interchangeable with these two forms:

(5a) A strong pound <u>has made</u> imports cheaper. (NEWS 49)

(5b) A strong pound <u>makes</u> imports cheaper.

(6a) 'You have you. That's more than I have.'
       'No, no, you have me.' He <u>became</u> nervous and active. (UMM 13)

(6b) ... He <u>had become</u> nervous and active.

While the present perfect in (5a) refers to a specific case of cheaper imports resulting from a strong pound, the simple present in (5b) expresses a general rule about the impact of a strong pound on imports. Examples (6a) and (6b) differ with respect to the exact timing of 'his becoming nervous and active'. As noted in Bache (1985: 204), the simple past in (6a) describes a new narrative development whereas the past perfect in (6b) describes the resulting state of 'becoming'. Thus in the a-example 'his becoming nervous and active' follows the reply *No, no, you have me* (or, by way of implication, coincides with it). By contrast, in the b-example this development precedes the reply and may even account for its occurrence, content or formulation. The past perfect in the b-example thus has a kind of textually cohesive, anaphoric function which is absent from the simple past in the a-example.

The fact that the simple present and the present perfect are distinct results more often than not in these forms being unsubstitutable:

(7a)   And you forget that I'm a scientist. I <u>have written</u> a monograph, so I must be. (FFLW 11)

(7b)   *... I <u>write</u> a monograph, so I must be.

The same applies to the simple past and the past perfect:

(8a)   In the first part of this programme, E. G. Cousins, who <u>was</u> then a six years old boy living in China with his family, talks to K. T. Lord about the Boxer Rebellion in 1900. (BBCI)

(8b)   *..., who <u>had</u> then <u>been</u> a six years old boy living in China ...

Basic distinctiveness, distributional patterns and behaviour in substitution thus all indicate that the present, the past, the present perfect and the past perfect are distinct individual tenses – unlike to BE *going to* + infinitive, which is best considered a supplementary form to WILL + infinitive.

However, assigning supplementary status to BE *going to* + infinitive does not mean that it should not be included in a description of tense in English. It simply means that it is not included in the core system of tenses. And though I believe that high priority should be given to actual usage in a functional grammar, it is of course necessary to consider also potential usage: in fact actual usage should be viewed against the background of potential usage. I shall therefore suggest an alternative model for the generation of Halliday's many tenses in which BE *going to* + infinitive is included. This model is based on the fact that there *are two separate grammatical variables* involved in this form: BE and the infinitive. Both of these are realised in a limited number of ways, and the potential tense forms which include BE *going to* + infinitive are restricted to the *possible combinations of the two small sets of realisations*. The rest of the construction, *going to*, remains grammatically invariable.

The realisation of the first variable, BE, is governed by the choices defined by my core tense system except for the choice between progressive and nonprogressive. The reason for this restriction is that BE is already followed by the present participle *going* and thus already forms part of a progressive form. The choice +progressive is inherent in the BE *going to* + infinitive construction. Thus in English we cannot say, for example, *She was being going to make a speech* or *They had been being going to swim across the river*. But potentially we might say *She is/was going to make a speech*, *They will/ would be going to see him* and *They have/had been going to swim across the river*, etc. So the possible realisations of BE can be defined in terms of the three other tense choices of my core system: ±past, ±future and ±perfect.

As for the other variable, the infinitive, there are four different types of infinitive in English:

1.	the simple infinitive:	*(to) laugh*
2.	the perfect infinitive:	*(to) have loved*
3.	the progressive infinitive:	*(to) be running*
4.	the perfect progressive infinitive:	*(to) have been singing*

These infinitives are used for a variety of purposes and are therefore independently motivated, e.g. *She wanted him to laugh*, *Better to have loved and lost, than to have never loved at all*, *It is madness to be running the company like this*, *For her to have been singing for that crowd must have been a gruelling experience*. And, as indicated, in addition to such examples, the four infinitives may complement BE *going to*. The generation of the four different types of infinitive can be described in terms of the following two binary choices in serial relation: ±perfect and ±progressive, i.e. the two choices of my core tense system which are potentially realised by means of a nonfinite form (such as the infinitive): the third and the fourth. The possible specific realisations of the BE *going to* + infinitive construction can thus be described by means of the following formula (with 'inf' standing for 'infinitive'):

$$\pm\text{past} (\pm\text{future} (\pm\text{perfect} (\text{BE}))) + going\ to + \pm\text{perfect} (\pm\text{progressive} (\text{inf}))$$

So the specific realisations of BE *going to* + infinitive are combinations of (i) a core tense form of BE (ii) *going to* and (iii) a nonfinite core tense form of the infinitive. The beauty of this analysis is that BE is realised in terms of those choices of the core system that are relevant for a finite form which is already marked as a progressive construction, and that the infinitive is realised in terms of those choices of the core system that are potentially relevant for a nonfinite form. In other words, we get this description 'for free', as it were, since we do not have to employ rules and systems that are not already needed in the grammar of tense for other purposes. Instead of operating with a recursive mechanism, *the two variable components of the construction select separately for tense in the core system*, the possible choices being restricted by general ('natural') conditions rather than AD HOC stop rules.

The formula that I suggest for BE *going to* + infinitive generates the following 32 potential supplementary tense forms (Halliday's tense numbers are offered in parentheses):

1.	(11)	*is/are/am*	*going to*	*take*	frequent

2.	(10)	*was/were*	*going to*	*take*	frequent
3.	(12)	*will be*	*going to*	*take*	infrequent
4.		*would be*	*going to*	*take*	no hits
5.	(23)	*has/have been*	*going to*	*take*	infrequent
6.	(22)	*had been*	*going to*	*take*	infrequent
7.	(24)	*will have been*	*going to*	*take*	no hits
8.		*would have been*	*going to*	*take*	no hits
9.	(14)	*is/are/am*	*going to*	*have taken*	infrequent
10.	(13)	*was/were*	*going to*	*have taken*	no hits
11.	(15)	*will be*	*going to*	*have taken*	no hits
12.		*would be*	*going to*	*have taken*	no hits
13.	(26)	*has/have been*	*going to*	*have taken*	no hits
14.	(25)	*had been*	*going to*	*have taken*	no hits
15.	(27)	*will have been*	*going to*	*have taken*	no hits
16.		*would have been*	*going to*	*have taken*	no hits
17.	(20)	*is/are/am*	*going to*	*be taking*	infrequent
18.	(19)	*was/were*	*going to*	*be taking*	infrequent
19.	(21)	*will be*	*going to*	*be taking*	no hits
20.		*would be*	*going to*	*be taking*	no hits
21.	(32)	*has/have been*	*going to*	*be taking*	no hits
22.	(31)	*had been*	*going to*	*be taking*	no hits
23.	(33)	*will have been*	*going to*	*be taking*	no hits
24.		*would have been*	*going to*	*be taking*	no hits
25.	(29)	*is/are/am*	*going to*	*have been taking*	no hits
26.	(28)	*was/were*	*going to*	*have been taking*	no hits
27.	(30)	*will be*	*going to*	*have been taking*	no hits
28.		*would be*	*going to*	*have been taking*	no hits
29.	(35)	*has/have been*	*going to*	*have been taking*	no hits
30.	(34)	*had been*	*going to*	*have been taking*	no hits
32.		*would have been*	*going to*	*have been taking*	no hits

Of all these potential forms, only numbers 1 and 2 are frequent. A few others are infrequent (numbers 3, 5, 6, 9, 17 and 18). Number 17 (*am/are/is going to be* + present participle) is the most frequent of the infrequent forms with a total of 161 hits in the BNC and CWO. Generally speaking, the more complex the construction (i.e. the more choices involved in the two variables), the less likely its actual occurrence.

Summing up the discussion of the status of BE *going to* + infinitive, we can say that in its simplest realisations this marker serves important supplementary functions in relation to the core tense system: e.g. *is/was going to take* (i.e. a present or past form of BE plus *going to* followed by a simple infinitive). However, BE *going to* + infinitive is potentially realised in a great number of ways to meet many different context-sensitive expressive needs (not likely to be covered in even an extensive corpus of examples). The potential of this construction is constrained by the variability of BE in relation to the choices of the tense system (except ±progressive, which is already chosen for BE *going*) and of the infinitive in relation to those choices of the system that are relevant to nonfinite forms (±perfect and ±progressive), and which define a set of infinitives with a more general distribution. The proposed description of BE *going to* + infinitive thus meets a high level of both observational and descriptive adequacy.

5.3   Univariate characteristics of verbal expressions: seriality

It is important to stress the fact that my core system is not a pure tense system. Whatever categories are involved in English verbal expressions, their realisation is such that each form/construction is non-monadic (multifunctional), i.e. requires a description in terms of two or more semantic domains. The 16 forms listed in Section 5.1 are thus *not just tenses*, but formal realisations of complex choice relations involving several categories. Nevertheless, I shall continue to refer loosely to my core system as a 'tense system' and to the individual realiations, whether morphological or syntactic, as 'tenses' or 'tense forms'. But it is important to remember that, strictly speaking, tense only accounts for a small part of the semantics of the 16 forms identified in the core system, and that other categories, such as aspect, are also important. Since both tense and aspect meanings involve processes, one way or the other, tense forms profile at least three different semantic domains, traditionally referred to as temporal, aspectual and actional. We should add modality and voice to the list, but I shall have little to say about those two categories. Some markers profile a particular domain more strongly than others but no marker is ever monadic. For example, the simple past in an example like *James owned two small factories* (with reference to some past time) profiles the semantic domain of tense more distinctly than the semantic domain of aspect: the 'owning' is construed as located in the past (at some past time relative to the moment of communication), but the actional nature of the process is such that there are no clear aspectual values associated with it: to own something is a stative relational process and thus does not allow either perfective or imperfective aspect (cf. Section 4.4.7, especially note 13). This is reflected formally by the lack in standard British English of the progressive/nonprogressive contrast in connection with OWN: *James was owning two small factories*. Conversely, with an example like *James talked to Wendy about it*, the process referred to is construable not only as located in the past but also with a definite perfective focus: it is viewed as a complete whole and contrasts with *James was talking to Wendy about it*, which has an imperfective focus conveyed by the progressive form. Though in each case the Performer chooses the simple past (*owned, talked*), the precise choice relations differ somewhat, and this should naturally be explicated in our analysis.

The core system with the four ordered choices represents a continuum of meanings which operate functionally on the lexical verb. The lexical verb is the key element in the expression of processes, but it is not the only element. The other elements assist the lexical verb with the linguistic coding of a number of meanings which are pertinent to our construal of processes, such as their temporal orientation relative to the moment of communication and to other processes (finiteness, tense), their textual presentation (aspect and voice), their procedural characteristics (action), and their relation to reality and interpersonal status (finiteness, mood and modality). Such complexity can easily be accommodated within the SFL framework, which is ideal for handling expression-syntactic phenomena in terms of a diversity of simultaneous meanings. What we see in connection with verbal expressions is not just metafunctional diversity but diversity within each metafunction and a subtle categorial interplay. It is therefore not surprising that we can identify both univariate and multivariate characteristics in the structure of verbal expressions.

Let us first take a closer look at the **univariate** characteristics, i.e. the logical structural principle of the elements making up a verbal expression. If for a moment we disregard the recursive principle of Halliday and Matthiessen's model and focus exclusively on the serial nature of their tenses as such, they have provided an excellent account of the univariate structure of their verbal group. What they say (e.g. Matthiessen 1984: 30ff, Halliday and Matthiessen 2004: 344ff) is that each tense choice in a series of choices creates a point of departure, a temporal setting, for the next choice, so that the temporal value of any choice except the first must be seen in relation to the value of the preceding choice rather than in relation to some common setting for all the choices involved in the construction of the group, such as e.g. the present moment of communication (which is the default setting of the first choice). Thus, if the first tense chosen from their tripartite system is 'future' in relation to the moment of communication, future time becomes the temporal setting for the next choice. If that next choice is, say, 'past', pastness is related to the future time established by the first choice rather than to the present time of the communication. In an example like *She will have finished the report by next Tuesday*, the finishing of the report is construed as past in relation to the future time setting provided by *will* + infinitive (and specified further by the circumstantial adjunct *next Tuesday*), not as past in relation to the 'now' at the time of utterance. The soundness of Halliday and Matthiessen's analysis on this point is not challenged by my alternative approach to tense. Quite on the contrary, it is recognised as a very sensible basic structural principle. What I do challenge is the assumption that seriality can only be a product of recursion, and that an account of the logical, serial structure of tenses has sufficient overall descriptive and explanatory adequacy.

As we have seen, in my core tense system seriality is created by a limited set of four ordered, scope-related choices. In addition there is the possibility of employing supplementary tenses like BE *going to* + infinitive, BE *about to* + infinitive and others. In Harder's instructional-semantic terms, the values that enter the serial relationship can be defined in terms of instructions to the Addressee to assign a temporal orientation to the descriptive content of the verbal expression, i.e. the process. This temporal orientation is the result of an interplay between base and function times chosen by the Performer. The serial nature is realised by turning the function time of a choice into the base time of the next choice, as shown in Figure 5.6.

More specifically, through the deictic component of the first choice between present and past (which has the other choices within its scope), the Performer may instruct the Addressee to turn the process-designating predication into a proposition, i.e. to tag the content of the full verb, i.e. the process, on to the world. The present tense instructs the Addressee to do this *without setting up any temporal contrast* between its base time (the moment of communication) and its function time. This means that the composite instruction of the present tense is in effect to construe the process as applying to the general temporal framework defined by the moment of communication, i.e. a contextually variable 'general present' without any further *specific* temporal orientation. The present is in other words *present by default*, and hence unmarked as a tense form (though it still has the positive deictic effect of instructing the Addressee to tag the process on to the world). Like the present tense, the past tense signals an instruction to tag the process on to the world, but in addition it instructs the Addressee to construe the process as specifically past in relation to the moment of communication. A contrast is thereby created between the function time (pastness) and the base time (the moment of communication), and the past tense becomes a marked tense form. We can sum up the characteristics of the present tense and the past tense by saying that the present tense instructs the Addressee to *tag the process on to the 'world now'* (general present time) while the past tense instructs the Addressee to *tag the process on to the 'world before now'* (specific past time). Instead of tagging the process of the full verb directly on to the world, either choice may set the stage for additional choices, i.e. provides a function time that may serve as a base time for any of the three other choices.

The logical impact of the three other choices is to provide (one or more) directions of 'looking'. Once the process is 'tied to the world' by the present or past tense, further temporal orientation becomes possible. Each additional positively marked choice instructs the Addressee to look towards a time in relation to the base time of that choice, and thus serves to build up the temporal orientation of the expression as a whole:

+future   look ahead (future time, posteriority)

+perfect   look back (anteriority)

+progressive   look here/there (simultaneity)

The univariate characteristics of a verbal expression is a result of the basic serial mechanism whereby the function time of one choice becomes the base time of the next, as well as the bare temporal orientation created by the instructions to look 'ahead', 'back' and/or 'here'/'there'. It is important to note that these instructions are compatible with Matthiessen's definitions of the

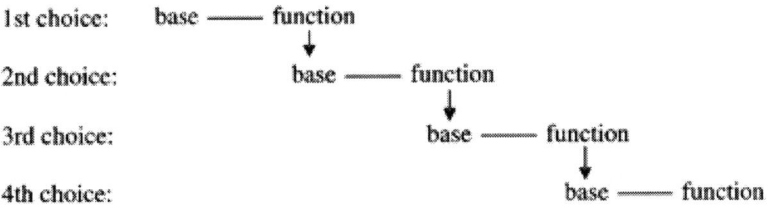

Figure 5.6: The serial nature of tense

tenses of the *IFG* model in terms of precedence relations (cf. Section 2.1 above). The difference is that in my description these relations are given an explicit functional account within Harder's procedural semantics, i.e. they are given a distinct functional tuning. This functional tuning does not change the classification of tense as a (partly) logical resource. The tense category is thus still viewed as being associated with this particular metafunction in the sense that it has obvious logicosemantic characteristics.

The univariate characterisation of the core tense system can be summed up in the following very rudimentary instructional-semantic specifications for each tense (based on Bache and Davidsen-Nielsen 1997: 308f):

1. The present (e.g. *takes*)
   'tag process on to world-now'

2. The past (e.g. *took*)
   'tag process on to world-before-now'

3. The present future (e.g. *will take*)
   'tag on to world-now and then look ahead to process'

4. The past future (e.g. *would take*)
   'tag on to world-before-now and then look ahead to process'

5. The present perfect (e.g. *has taken*)
   'tag on to world-now and then look back at process'

6. The past perfect (e.g. *had taken*)
   'tag on to world-before-now and then look back at process from this vantage point'

7. The present future perfect (e.g. *will have taken*)
   'tag on to world-now, then look ahead to a posterior time and finally look back at process from this vantage point'

8. The past future perfect (e.g. *would have taken*)
   'tag on to world-before-now, then look ahead to a posterior time and finally look back at process from this vantage point'

9. The present progressive (e.g. *is taking*)
   'tag on to world-now and then look here at simultaneous process'

10. The past progressive (e.g. *was taking*)
    'tag on to world-before-now and then look there at simultaneous process'

11. The present future progressive (e.g. *will be taking*)
    'tag on to world-now, then look ahead to a posterior time and finally look there at simultaneous process

12. The past future progressive (e.g. *would be taking*)
    'tag on to world-before-now, then look ahead to a posterior time and finally look there at simultaneous process'

13. The present perfect progressive (e.g. *has been taking*)
    'tag on to world-now, then look back at an anterior time and finally look here at process within that temporal orientation'

14. The past perfect progressive (e.g. *had been taking*)
    'tag on to world-before-now, then look back at anterior time from this vantage point and finally look there at process within that temporal orientation'

15. The present future perfect progressive (e.g. *will have been taking*)
    'tag on to world-now, then look ahead to a posterior time, then look back to an anterior time from this vantage point and finally look there at process within that temporal orientation'

16. The past future perfect progressive (e.g. *would have been taking*)
    'tag on to world-before-now, then look ahead to a posterior time, then look back to an anterior time from this vantage point and finally look there at process within that temporal orientation'

Some of these specifications are very crude. As already indicated, there is much more to the functional description of a verbal expression than the identification of its logical properties, as stated in this list. Choice relations are more complex than indicated by the mere seriality of the tense choices and their basic instructions to look ahead, back or 'here'/'there'. There are several reasons for that. One is that some tenses have developed *special uses*, such as e.g. those containing the combination of +past and +future, i.e. tenses 4, 8, 12 and 16, which, as we saw in Section 5.1, are used primarily in conditional sentences, in projection, in narration and in historical accounts.

Another important reason is that certain combinations of instructions *merge into more complex specific instructions*. This applies to tenses containing the combination of +perfect and +progressive, i.e. tenses 13 to 16. Strictly speaking, in the basic instructional-semantic specifications of these tenses offered above, I should have retained the notion of simultaneity (which was included in the specifications of the progressive in tenses 9 to 12) and left out the formulation 'within that temporal orientation' because that is not part of the instruction originally specified for the progressive marker.

However, without that formulation, the instructions look too inadequate, if not blatantly wrong, when offered as a series of individual instructions for each tense. What happens in perfect progressive tenses is that the progressive marker instructs the Addressee to look more closely at a process, not at the anterior time indicated by the instruction provided by the preceding perfect, but in its progression *from* that anterior time *up to* the primary function time (i.e. the time that the Addressee is instructed to tag the expression on to in the first place, typically either the present or the past). Thus a more precise formulation of the instructions in (13) to (16) above would be:

13a. The present perfect progressive (e.g. *has been taking*)
    'tag on to world-now, then look back at an anterior time and finally look at process progressing from that anterior time towards present time'

14a. The past perfect progressive (e.g. *had been taking*)
    'tag on to world-before-now, then look back at anterior time from this vantage point and finally look at process progressing from the anterior time towards the vantage point

15a. The present future perfect progressive (e.g. *will have been taking*)
    'tag on to world-now, then look ahead to a posterior time, then look back to an anterior time from this vantage point and finally look at process progressing from the anterior time towards the vantage point'

16a. The past future perfect progressive (e.g. *would have been taking*)
    'tag on to world-before-now, then look ahead to a posterior time, then look back to an anterior time from this vantage point and finally look at process progressing from the anterior time towards the vantage point'

The third, and perhaps most important reason why the description of the core tense system in terms of seriality is inadequate by itself, is that each of the formal markers making up the system has additional meanings and functions which imbue the structure of verbal expressions with multivariate characteristics. We have already discussed the finite deictic nature of −past and +past, which make up the first complex choice relation, and briefly commented on the modal meanings often associated with the distinction between +future and −future (such as the subject's determination or intention to carry out a future process or the Performer's assumption of the future occurrence of a process). It is important to note that some of these concomitant meanings potentially apply to all the tenses (finiteness, active voice) whereas others serve as discriminating features, characterising a subset of tenses (such as modal meanings in connection with +future). The latter, but not the former, are thus relevant from the point of view of choice relations. For example, finiteness or voice are not likely to motivate, or even partly motivate, a choice *between* the present and the present perfect, or between the past and the past progressive, because all these forms share, or potentially share, values from these categories.

In the following, I shall look into some of the discriminating features that affect the choice relations between perfect and nonperfect forms and between progressive and nonprogressive forms, apart from the instructions to decode the bare temporal orientation of an expression already identified in our discussion of the univariate characteristics of verbal expressions. But before doing so it is perhaps necessary to settle an important question once and for all: can a particular structure have both univariate and multivariate characteristics? In *IFG* there seems to be an assumption that a structure is *either* univariate (e.g. verbal groups) *or* multivariate (e.g. nominal groups). At the same time, however, Halliday's multifunctional analysis at clause level is matched by a multistructural analysis (not simply by a single structure, as in the Cardiff grammar, cf. Section 4.2.1 above). This would seem to indicate that it is perfectly all right within a systemic functional framework to view a particular wording from different perspectives, and that is in fact what I am proposing for verbal expressions: there is in the relationship between the individual elements a combination of univariate and multivariate characteristics, and that combination is a result of multifunctionality.

5.4   Multivariate characteristics of verbal expressions: perfect forms

I have defined the basic function of the perfect as an instruction to the Addressee to 'look back' in time from the base time provided by previous choices in the core system. For simplicity's sake, let us focus on the choice relations in −future and −progressive constructions, i.e. the present (nonfuture) perfect (nonprogressive) and the past (nonfuture) perfect (nonprogressive) in relation to the simple present and the simple past. In the following I shall thus discuss the contribution of these forms to the multivariate semantics of verbal expressions (above and beyond their logical, univariate characteristics).

We have established that the basic instructional-semantic function of the *present perfect* is to make the Addressee 'tag on to world-now and then look back at process'. Put more informally, we can say that the present perfect is used to indicate that 'it applies now that something is anterior in time'. The basic instructional-semantic function of the *past perfect* is to make the Addressee 'tag on to world-before-now and then look back at process'. Hence the basic temporal orientation provided by the past perfect can be paraphrased as 'it applied at a past time that something was anterior in time'. However, the semantics of the perfect forms is somewhat more complex. There are two reasons for this complexity: one is the *dual nature* of perfect forms, a feature which affects their choice relations; the other is the non-monadic combination of meanings characterising perfect forms. Let us first take a closer look at the complex choice relations. Normally, the present perfect is choice-related to the simple present, and the past perfect is choice-related to the simple past, as in the following pairs of examples:

(1a) I always <u>visit</u> her on Sundays.

(1b) I <u>have</u> always <u>visited</u> her on Sundays.

(2a) They <u>arrived</u> in London early next morning.

(2b) They <u>had arrived</u> in London early next morning.

These choice relations are a natural consequence of the serial nature of my core system: in setting up the relevant complex temporal orientation you first choose between present or past, then you go on to choose perfect or nonperfect (skipping the choice between future or nonfuture for convenience). Having chosen, say, present, the next choice is either to leave it at that (in which case you choose nonperfect) or to choose perfect.[11] The immediate choice relation is thus between present (nonperfect) and present perfect. Similarly, the immediate choice relation is between past (nonperfect) and past perfect. But from a functional semantic point of view, the situation is more complex, especially in the case of the present perfect. Since the present perfect instructs the Addressee to look back at a past process, it often overlaps more directly with the simple past (which instructs the Addressee to tag a process on to the world before now) than with the simple present (which instructs the Addressee to tag the process on to the world now). Thus in the following two examples the present perfect and the simple past may refer to exactly the same real-world process of 'becoming' but impose a different temporal orientation on it (among other things):

(3a) Her achievement <u>has become</u> part of the folklore.

(3b) Her achievement <u>became</u> part of the folklore.

This means that when we look for definition- and function-level meanings in connection with the present perfect (cf. Sections 4.4.4 and 4.4.5 above), we should do so by considering its choice relation not only to the simple present but also to the simple past (for a more thorough discussion of 'valid pairs' of perfect and nonperfect forms, see Bache 1985: 184ff). Interestingly enough, we find the full range of possible substitutional relations in both pairs.

Present perfect vs. simple present

(4a) Mr Forsythe informs me that you <u>retain</u> an attachment to this foreign person. (FFLW 36)

(4b) Mr Forsythe informs me that you <u>have retained</u> an attachment to this foreign person.

(5a) A strong pound <u>has made</u> imports cheaper. (NEWS 49)

(5b) A strong pound <u>makes</u> imports cheaper.

(6a) And you forget that I'm a scientist. I <u>have written</u> a monograph, so I must be. (FFLW 11)

(6b) *... I <u>write</u> a monograph, so I must be.

(7a) Almost everyone is a regular everyday drug taker, and before you <u>say</u> 'not me!' let me ask you a question: did you have a cup of tea today? (BBCY)

(7b) *[...] before you <u>have said</u> 'not me!' [...]

As noted in our discussion of these examples in Section 5.2 above, examples (4a) and (4b) form a **minimal pair**, examples (5a) and (5b) a somewhat more **distinctive pair**, and examples (6a) and (6b) an **unsubstitutable pair** (with the present perfect as the unsubstitutable form); examples (7a) and (7b) also form an unsubstitutable pair, but this time with the simple present as the unsubstitutable form (for comments on the semantics of the first two pairs, see Section 5.2). The very same distributional categories are relevant in the case of present perfects contrasted with simple past forms.

Present perfect vs. simple past

(8a) I <u>brought</u> some paper cups because I knew you wouldn't think of it. (UMM 13)

(8b)   I <u>have brought</u> some paper cups because I knew you wouldn't think of it.

(9a)   For weeks, the signs <u>were</u> visible, though scarcely credible. (NEWS 20)

(9b)   For weeks, the signs <u>have been</u> visible, though scarcely credible.

(10a) In April nineteen twelve the passenger liner Titanic *sailed* from England on her maiden voyage to America. (BBCI).

(10b) *In April nineteen twelve the passenger liner Titanic <u>has sailed</u> from England on her maiden voyage to America.

(11a) I am suddenly aware that he <u>has opened</u> his eyes and is looking at me.

(11b) *I am suddenly aware that he <u>opened</u> his eyes and is looking at me.

Examples (8a) and (8b) form a minimal pair. The two variants express the same or almost the same experiential meaning: the simple past in the a-example construes the 'bringing' process as occurring in the past without an explicit link to the present moment and thus leaves its present relevance as a contextual implication whereas the present perfect in the b-example construes the occurrence of the past process of 'bringing' as a present fact or condition.

Examples (9a) and (9b) are more clearly distinct than (8a) and (8b) because they differ with respect to propositional meaning: the exact temporal location of the period expressed by the circumstantial adjunct *For weeks* depends on the choice of tense form: in the a-example with the simple past the period is located (and has ended) in the past, whereas in the b-example with the present perfect the period starts in the past and extends up to (and possibly continues beyond) the present moment of communication.

Finally, in examples (10a) and (10b) the simple past cannot be replaced by the present perfect in standard British English. The present perfect is generally incompatible with circumstantial adjuncts identifying a precise location in the past of the process expressed by the verbal expression (for a brief discussion of restrictions on the use of adverbials in connection with the present perfect and the simple past, see Bache and Davidsen-Nielsen 1997: 293ff). This indicates that though both the simple past and the present perfect may construe a process as past relative to the moment of communication, only the simple past can be used when the Performer's attention is focused on this past time. Conversely in examples (11a) and (11b): here the

Performer's attention is focused on the nonpast, and therefore the present perfect *has opened*, but not the simple past *opened*, is possible.

Now, the important conclusion to draw on the basis of examples (4a–b) to (11a–b) is that the present perfect is choice-related to both the simple present and the simple past. Though this is of course a complication for our description of this form, it may actually help delimit its precise nature. A more comprehensive analysis of the substitutability of the present perfect with the simple present and the simple past (cf. Bache 1985: 160ff, 176ff, 193ff, 223ff; Bache 1994) shows that the choice relations involved are very much context-dependent. In other words, the present perfect is not usually choice-related to the simple present and the simple past *at the same time*, i.e. in the same contexts: it is choice-related to the simple present whenever it is the Performer's communicative intention to express a present fact or condition (as in examples (4a–b) and (5a–b)). However, when the Performer's communicative intention is to express a relevant past process, the present perfect is more naturally choice-related to the simple past, as we see in examples (3a–b), (8a–b) and (9a–b). What this substitutional behaviour shows is that the present perfect contains two semantic components (which we can loosely refer to as 'present condition' and 'past process'), and that these components potentially overlap with meanings that are characteristic of the simple present and the simple past, respectively. Choice relations are affected by these potential overlaps, and whether one affiliation or the other is relevant in a particular case very much depends on the Performer's communicative intention in the context. Thus, the complex instruction to tag on to the world now and then look back on a past process (the present perfect) will sometimes overlap with the instruction simply to tag on to the world before now directly (the simple past), sometimes with the instruction simply to tag on to the world now (the simple present).

Though the present perfect is clearly to be considered a coherent unitary expression (i.e. 'a tense form'), the two semantic components can in fact be associated fairly closely with the two formal components making up the present perfect: the present form of HAVE (*has* or *have*, depending on the number of the subject) and the past participle. The present form of HAVE signals 'present condition' and the past participle signals 'past process'. In an atomistic approach to the present perfect within an SFL framework, the present form of HAVE could be said to express not just a temporal meaning but a kind of process by itself. Despite its status as an auxiliary serving as finite, HAVE can be attributed process-like qualities. Thus the typical experiential function of the full verb HAVE as a 'relational Process' (usually 'Possessive') is perceptible also in the auxiliary HAVE employed in the present perfect. The reason why we hesitate to grant present perfect auxiliary HAVE full status as a Process is that it is actionally and aspectually vague. In fact, the relational meaning in a present perfect is not only strictly −past (rather than present as such, cf. Section 5.1 above), it is also −ACTIONAL and −ASPECTUAL (like relational meaning more generally). In contrast, the experiential meaning of the past participle is unrestricted. It may be material (e.g. *He has broken the window*), mental (e.g. *I have always believed him*), relational (e.g. *He has been a sailor for more than five years*), etc. And these process types may be further specified for actional values, such as punctual, directed, iterative, etc. In an example like *Alex has turned off the telly*, there is thus an obvious contrast between the stative non-actional present state of 'the telly having been turned off' and the punctual material process of 'turning it off'. Sometimes the process expressed by the past participle may be represented with a definite aspectual value (as in present perfect progressive constructions like *She has been dancing* and *It has been raining*, where the processes of dancing and raining are represented with an imperfective focus), sometimes it is aspectually more neutral (as in *I have always thought that she would succeed*). Potentially, therefore, the two semantic components of the present perfect ('present condition' and 'past process') are not just temporally distinct but often also actionally and aspectually distinct. It is the precise specification of this dual nature of the present perfect that has led linguists and grammarians to establish different types of perfect. Thus we typically get a 'resultative perfect' when the actionality of the past participle is dynamic and presented with a perfective aspect, as in *He has broken the window* and *Alex has turned off the telly*, but a 'continuative perfect' when the actionality is stative (i.e. unmarked for actionality), as in *I've lived in Copenhagen since 1958* and *For weeks, the signs have been visible*, or when dynamic actionality is presented with an imperfective focus, as *She's been talking to her boyfriend for over an hour* and *It's been raining since last night*.

A final point about the present perfect as a form for the expression of past processes is that though it is regularly used in competition with the simple past, unlike this tense it does not require temporal anchoring in the past. In the case of the simple past, the function time of logging on to some past time provides such an anchor, whether explicit or implicit. Thus an expression like *I was in Paris*, is well-formed only if the context is such that there is already a past temporal framework for the Performer's utterance, i.e. there must be a definite past time to log on to and which could be made explicit by means of a circumstantial adjunct, as in *I was in Paris last August*. Without such a circumstantial adjunct or a contextually clear framework for the temporal location of the process, the expression *I was in Paris* is incomplete. But the present perfect does not need such a temporal anchor. It does not in-struct the Addressee to log on to a past time, but to the general present, and then to look back. This looking back does not require an awareness of the particular past context of the process. In fact, in standard British English the present perfect is incompatible with a circumstantial adjunct explicitly lo-cating the process temporally in the past. Thus we may say *I've been in Paris* as a complete statement but not **I've been in Paris last August*. The clause *I was in Paris (last August)* is thus a statement about some past time, whereas the clause *I've been in Paris* is a statement about some present condition deriving from some past process (i.e. the construction serves to update the Addressee on my past experiences).

If we relate the componential analysis of the present perfect proposed above to the scope relations defined for my core system of tenses, we can characterise the present perfect as a form which expresses one process as embedded within another: a +past process of any type within a –past rela-tional process. Put differently, it expresses a present (strictly speaking nonpast) fact or condition deriving from a past process. In Harder's terms, the present in a present perfect is 'a time of reckoning' (Harder 1996: 382). An exhaustive analysis of the present perfect thus requires a non-monadic specification of both components in terms of temporality, actionality and aspectuality. There is always a contrast within the temporal domain (–past versus +past) and typically one within the actional and aspectual domains as well (e.g. –ASPECTUAL versus perfective and –ACTIONAL versus punctual). It is this semantic complexity that makes the present perfect so flexible in con-text – and so difficult to describe in terms of choice relations.

Moving on to the past perfect, we first of all notice that its substitutional relationships are simpler than those of the present perfect. The past perfect is directly choice-related only to one other form, the simple past (as dictated by the seriality of the core system). English does not have a 'remote past' with which the past perfect could enter a second choice-relation. The choice rela-tion between the past perfect and the simple past parallels the choice rela-tion between the present perfect and the simple present, not the choice relation between the present perfect and the simple past. As with the pairs of forms discussed in connection with the present perfect above, substitutions of the past perfect with the simple past, and vice versa, result in the full range of construction types showing different kinds of substitutional behaviour, i.e. minimal pairs, more distinctive pairs, and unsubstitutable forms:

> (12a) After we <u>parked</u> the car, I peeped through a flap in the tent and saw it all. (cf. Bache and Davidsen-Nielsen 1997: 296)

(12b) After we <u>had parked</u> the car, I peeped through a flap in the tent and saw it all.

(13a) When the second half began, Rush <u>had scored</u> two goals. (cf. Bache and Davidsen-Nielsen 1997: 195, 313)

(13b) When the second half began, Rush <u>scored</u> two goals.

(14a) In the first part of the programme, E. G. Cousins, who <u>was</u> then a six years old boy living in China with his family, talks to K. T. Lord about the Boxer rebellion in 1900. (BBCI)

(14b) *[...] E. G. Cousins, who <u>had</u> then <u>been</u> a six years old boy [...]

(15a) By then, Alex and Sally <u>had been</u> lovers for ages.

(15b) *By then, Alex and Sally <u>were</u> lovers for ages.

Examples (12a) and (12b) are a minimal pair, the only difference being a slightly greater emphasis on the derived condition of 'having parked' than just the actual parking itself prior to the process of peeping. At the level of the clause complex, the basic temporal layout seems identical in the two examples. Though the simple past in the a-example merely instructs the Addressee to log the process of parking on to some past time, and the past perfect in the b-example instructs the Addressee not just to log on to a past time but also to look back at the process of parking, the overall timing of the parking relative to the peeping is the same. The reason for this is that the sequence of the two processes is made explicit by the subordinate *after*-clause. Hence there is little difference between the two variants (apart from the association of derived non-actional condition of the past perfect in example (12b)). Since the difference in terms of basic temporal orientation is thus neutralised or suppressed, we are in a better position to evaluate any other difference between the two forms, however slight it may be. Interestingly enough, the one difference that emerges in this neutralising framework has to do with the duality of the past perfect: this form expresses not only the actual parking of the car but also the derived state or condition of having parked the car: the peeping takes place after having reached the state or condition of having parked the car. In contrast, the simple past merely mentions the actual parking of the car as prior to the peeping.

In examples (13a) and (13b), the basic temporal meaning of the two tenses are very similar to those identified in examples (12a) and (12b): the simple past instructs the Addressee to log the process of scoring on to some past time whereas the past perfect offers the additional instruction to look back from the past time logged on to, but here the effect of this distinction between the variants is much more perceptible and clearly involves an accentuation of logical meaning with propositional repercussions: the actual sequence of processes in the a-example differs from that in the b-example. In the a-example with the past perfect, the scoring of goals took place before the second half began whereas in the b-example with the simple past it takes place just after the second half began. The difference thus involves the relative timing of processes (cf. also my comments on examples (6a) and (6b) in Section 5.2 above).

Finally, in the two pairs (14a–b) and (15a–b) we see cases of the simple past and the past perfect being unsubstitutable with each other. In the first pair, the Performer's attention is simply on a specific past time with no further temporal orientation, and therefore only the simple past is possible. In the second pair, further temporal orientation is specified by the combination of two circumstantial adjuncts, *By then* and *for ages*, the first of which helps log the expression on to a specific past time while the second specifies a period leading up to that past time, thus requiring a further look back.

As noted in Section 5.2, the basic temporal meaning of the past perfect is a combination of an instruction to log on to the world before now and an instruction to look further back from that past time. In other words, its meaning is 'it applied at a past time that something was anterior in time.' But like the present perfect, the past perfect may be subjected to an analysis in terms of actionality and aspectuality in addition to the bare temporal orientation in terms of the two instructions to log on to some past time and to look back from there. The past perfect thus adds to the multivariate characteristics of verbal expressions by stating a past fact or condition deriving from an anterior process. More technically, it expresses one process as embedded within another: a +past aspectually specifiable process of any type within another +past process which is –ACTIONAL (more specifically, relational) and –ASPECTUAL. That the past perfect is parallel to the present perfect (just one step further back in time) becomes obvious if we 'transpose' the present perfect examples discussed above into the past perfect: *Her achievement had become part of the folklore / A strong pound had made imports cheaper / I had brought some paper cups because I knew you wouldn't think of it / For weeks the signs had been visible / He had broken the window / I had always believed him / He had been a sailor for more than five years / She had been talking to her boyfriend for over an hour*, etc.

However, there is an important difference: while the base time of the present perfect is *unmarked* general present time, the base time of the past perfect is *marked* past time, i.e. it expresses a specific time of reckoning. The effect of this is that the past perfect is felt to be more clearly a marker of temporal orientation (a past in the past), than the present perfect, which in context is often felt to be as much an actional and aspectual marker than simply a temporal marker (a past in the present). The past perfect is therefore less dependent on the supplementary non-monadic description than the present perfect. A possible reason for this difference between the two forms is that with the past perfect, the Performer instructs the Addressee to relate a base time and a function time which are both distant from the moment of communication, whereas with the present perfect only the function time is distant. The Performer and the Addressee are themselves very much part of, or immersed in, the temporal setting, the base time, of the present perfect, and this both reduces the force of the basic temporal orientation of this form and enhances the element of non-aspectually presented derived fact or condition.

5.5   Multivariate characteristics of verbal expressions: progressive forms

As we have seen, the basic function of the progressive marker BE V-*ing* is to give the Addressee an instruction to look at a process happening or taking place at its own base time. This base time is provided as a function time (i.e. application time) by previous choices in the core system, but it is turned into a base time – as well as a new function time – by the progressive. The effect is to make the Addressee 'look here/there' rather than 'look back' or 'look ahead'. As with the perfect/nonperfect distinction, it is practical to try to determine the choice relations involved in the progressive/nonprogressive distinction by examining constructions with the fewest possible other interfering factors, i.e. nonfuture and nonperfect constructions. In the following discussion of the contribution of progressive forms to the multivariate semantics of verbal expressions (above and beyond their logical, serial characteristics), I shall therefore deal mainly with the present (nonfuture nonperfect) progressive and the past (nonfuture nonperfect) progressive and their choice relation(s) to the simple present and the simple past, respectively, as in e.g. *Civilisation has a habit of walking into what Ronald Wright calls / is calling progress traps* and *Amazingly, the jungle reclaimed / was reclaiming the old Maya fields.*

It has further been established that the basic instructional-semantic function of the *present progressive* is to make the Addressee 'tag on to world-now and then look here at simultaneous process'. The temporal orientation provided by the present progressive can thus be paraphrased in this way: 'it applies now that a process is simultaneous', i.e. there is some overlap between its present base time and its function time (as argued convincingly by Matthiessen (1984: 30), see also Section 3.4 above). The basic instructional-semantic function of the *past progressive* is to make the Addressee 'tag on to world-before-now and then look there at simultaneous process', the temporal implication thus being 'it applied then that a process was simultaneous'. Again there is some overlap between base time and function time (but this time the overlap is in the past relative to the moment of communication).[12] The basic temporal orientation provided by present progressive and past progressive forms (as well as other progressive forms) is part of the serial nature of the tense category and is clearly associated with the logical metafunction. However, as in the case of perfect forms, progressive forms can only be described adequately and exhaustively if we take other factors into account as well, such as especially aspect and action. In other words, we have to consider not only logical, serial meanings but also both textual and experiential meanings (for the association of aspect with textual meaning and of action with experiential meaning, see Section 4.4.7 above).

As pointed out in Section 3.4 above, Matthiessen (1984: 30) argues that the *IFG* 'secondary present' (i.e. the progressive) does not simply express simultaneity but a more specific kind of simultaneity, viz. **inclusion**. I believe Matthiessen is right here, but I also believe that it is important to look at the metafunctional implications of this particular kind of simultaneity in order to determine more precisely the choice relations that progressive forms enter with nonprogressive forms. Unlike 'mere' simultaneity (or, to put it in my terminology, the bare instruction to 'look here/there' from some base time), the kind of inclusion provided by progressive forms imposes certain conditions on the process presented as including the base time. For example, even if we interpreted the base time of a −past or +past tense as strictly punctual, for a process to *include*, this base time *in the intended sense*, it must itself be durative: a punctual process cannot include another punctual process. I do not think this interpretation of the concept of inclusion in any way challenges Matthiessen's: he is quite explicit about distinguishing between the special meaning of inclusion provided by his secondary present (i.e. the progressive) and **co-extension**. This means that the inclusion of, say, y in x should be considered in its everyday 'container' sense (where 'y is less/smaller than x'), rather than in the sense: 'y is less/smaller than, *or equal to*, x'. In other words, the intended sense of inclusion is what may be termed **proper inclusion**.

Another implication of proper temporal inclusion is that the including *process* is sufficiently delimited and substantial (i.e. sufficiently 'situation-like') to serve a container function in a nontrivial sense, and that what is included is privileged by the inclusion. This condition excludes non-actional processes such as relations and states. Thus, in an example like *Miranda is my best friend*, even though the relational process of 'being' overlaps with the base time of the present (i.e. the moment of communication), and can be said to be 'true of the present', there is no sense of proper inclusion: the process may extend indefinitely into both the past and the future, and the present base time is not in any way thought of as being in a privileged relation to it, one way or the other. The process of *being* is only related to the present base time in a very general, loose sense.[13] By contrast, in an example like *I was doing the dishes*, we get a clear sense of nontrivial proper inclusion: the choice of +progressive instructs the Addressee to transform the past function time of the choice +past to a base time and to view it as being in the middle of the process of *doing*. As a result, this process is related specifically to the past base time, in contrast to other times, present or past. This relationship becomes especially clear when another situation is applied to the base time of *doing*, as in *I was doing the dishes when suddenly the telephone rang*. The association of interruption here hinges on the base time being properly included in the process of *doing*. The obvious paraphrase of the relation 'y is properly included in x' is that 'y is in the middle of x'.

The relevant notion of inclusion associated with progressive forms in English thus has definite experiential, actional repercussions: no punctual situations and no relations or states qualify as the including process.[14] This means that we are left with delimited but durative processes. Unlike punctual, relational and stative processes, such processes share the property of **representational variability**. They can either be expressed with an instruction to the Addressee to dwell mentally on the progression of the process, i.e. to focus on it from the inside, or, alternatively, with an instruction to mentally sum up the process as a whole, i.e. to look at it at a distance, from the outside. Thus, the notion of proper inclusion that we operate with in connection with progressive forms has not only actional repercussions but also aspectual ones. The choice between progressive or nonprogressive forms is extremely complex, being often determined by a mixture of logical, experiential and textual considerations, and therefore resulting in structural relationships imbued with both univariate and multivariate characteristics.

These observations seem to be supported empirically when we submit progressive and nonprogressive forms to a substitution test (we have already seen examples behaving in a predictable way in Section 3.5 and especially Section 4.4.2 above). The following account is based on the results of a large number of substitutions where progressive forms are replaced by nonprogressive ones, and vice versa; for a more thorough empirical examination, see Bache (1985) (and for further discussion of the results, see Bache 1997). In substitution tests with the nonprogressive, the progressive clearly turns out to behave like a marked imperfective form, instructing the Addressee not only to look at a process which is simultaneous with the present or past base time selected but also, given its additional inclusive meaning, to focus situation-internally on its **progression**. In an example like *It was raining in Dublin*, the Performer hence instructs the Addressee to form a mental image of the unfolding process of raining, i.e. to focus on the middle phase of this process. Similarly, in an example like *Walter was moving to the door*, the Addressee is invited to dwell on the unfolding process of *moving*. The nonprogressive counterpart is aspectually the unmarked member of the opposition, expressing sometimes perfective meanings, sometimes non-aspectual meanings. In *It rained in Dublin* and *Walter moved to the door*, the simple past forms present the two processes perfectively as complete units, i.e. with an external focus, provided that the expressions refer to single-occasion processes. But there is a difference between the two pairs of examples with respect to their procedural characteristics: the process of 'raining' is phasally more homogeneous, self-contained and, alas, indeterminably extensive than the process of 'moving to the door.' In the latter, but not in the former, there is an explicit terminal point beyond which the process cannot continue as before. This terminal point is expressed by means of the circumstantial *to the door*. The choice of perfective rather than imperfective focus thus involves a distinct 'change' of experiential meaning in the substitution test. While the choice between *It rained in Dublin* and *It was raining in Dublin* is primarily, if not exclusively, a question of textual meaning (depending on the context), the choice between *Walter moved to the door* and *Walter was moving to the door* is motivated by both textual and experiential meaning. If the perfective form is chosen, Walter is presented as reaching the door, i.e. the terminal point beyond which the process cannot continue as before is within the referential scope of the expression. If, on the other hand, the imperfective form is chosen, Walter is presented as being on his way towards the door, but not necessarily as reaching it, i.e. the terminal point is outside the referential scope of the expression. In other words, the two substitutional variants differ with respect to both aspect and action: the progressive is imperfective and directional while the nonprogressive is perfective and telic. The actional variation is a result of the interplay between action and aspect on the functional level of meaning (cf. Section 4.4.5). By contrast, the two alternative ways of expressing the process of raining in Dublin on a particular occasion differ only with respect to the aspectual focus which the Addressee is instructed to adopt: both the perfective and the imperfective variant express a homogeneous self-contained durative process, i.e. a process where each phase is potentially representative of the process as a whole. On this evidence we can conclude that the choice relations between the progressive and the nonprogressive are subtly different in the two pairs of examples, and this should of course be explicated in our description.

The fact that the choice relations of the progressive/nonprogressive opposition are complex and variable is even more obvious in cases where the perfective nonprogressive form is used in an aspectually unmarked, neutral manner to express non-actional processes (relations or states), e.g. *Lawrence possessed a certain wildness* and *In those days I knew him well, of course*. In these examples, the imperfective progressive form is not possible: **Lawrence was possessing a certain wildness* and **In those days I was knowing him well, of course*. The experientially stative character of these examples makes them aspectually invariable: they are not compatible with either a perfective or an imperfective focus. The fact that we can use the nonprogressive form for the expression of such processes is related to the status of this form as the aspectually unmarked member of the opposition. The choice of the simple past nonprogressive in such cases is very differently motivated from the choice of the same form in the pairs discussed in the previous paragraph.

Since neither non-actional processes (relations, states) nor punctual processes can be said to progress in any meaningful way, or to allow an imperfective focus, the progressive form is incompatible with these actional meanings in the final analysis. This incompatibility, however, often prompts a dynamic interplay between temporal, aspectual and actional values at the function level of meaning, cf. Section 4.4.5 above, and in the initial stages of this interplay the progressive may well be brought into contact with verbs with a clear potential for expressing non-actionality and non-aspectuality (as in e.g. *I don't know what was possessing him*). Below I shall examine in more detail the extent to which aspect and action imbue verbal expressions with multivariate characteristics in addition to their univariate characteristics.

If we assume that the progressive is an aspectually marked imperfective tense form (expressing imperfectivity in addition to the temporal orientation of 'looking here/there' in relation to some base time established as a function time by previous tense choices) and that the similarly non-monadic nonprogressive form is an aspectually unmarked perfective tense form (expressing sometimes perfectivity sometimes aspectually neutral meaning, i.e. −ASPECTUALITY, in addition to the temporal orientation it provides), we should expect the two choice options to conform to the metalinguistic specifications of the interplay between tense, action and aspect outlined in

Section 4.4.7 above and presented in much more detail in Bache (1997).[15] First of all, the incompatibility relation:

–ACTIONALITY ⇓ +ASPECTUALITY

and the corresponding co-selection rule:

–ACTIONALITY >> –ASPECTUALITY

can be translated into the following language-specific specification:

–ACTIONALITY is expressed by nonprogressive forms.

This means that in a corpus of examples we should expect to find no progressive constructions expressing –ACTIONALITY. Furthermore, if in a substitution test a –ACTIONAL nonprogressive form is replaced by a progressive form (or vice versa), we should expect the result to be either unacceptability or a change of meaning from –ACTIONAL and –ASPECTUAL to +ACTIONAL and imperfective (or vice versa). This is indeed what we see in a more extensive substitution test.

Unacceptability

(1a) Nobody <u>knows</u> how many stars there <u>are</u> in the Milky Way. (BSHE 48)

(1b) *Nobody <u>is knowing</u> how many stars there are in the Milky Way.

(1c) *Nobody knows how many stars there <u>are being</u> in the Milky Way.

(2a) Until the time of Julius Caesar, Rome's conquests <u>were</u> essentially private enterprises. (WSHP 89)

(2b) *Until the time of Julius Caesar, Rome's conquests <u>were being</u> essentially private enterprises.

(3a) The box <u>contained</u> little else than handwritten notes.

(3b) *The box <u>was containing</u> little else than handwritten notes.

As we see in these present and past tense examples, only nonprogressive forms may express –ACTIONAL processes: the result of replacing them with the corresponding progressive forms clearly lead to unacceptability. By themselves, constructions like *is knowing, are being, were being* and *was containing* are not ungrammatical. Thus we might find examples like *The big jar <u>was containing</u> more and more water* and *They <u>are being</u> really silly* but such cases illustrate precisely the change of meaning we would expect to arise in the functional categorial interplay involved (see below). Having said that, it is important to add that we are unlikely to find any contexts in which the full sentences in (1b), (1c), (2b) and (3b) would be acceptable.

Change of meaning

{–ACTIONAL, –ASPECTUAL} ⇔ {+ACTIONAL, imperfective}[16]

(4a)   Mrs Wentworth speaks Greek to her mother.

(4b)   Mrs Wentworth is speaking Greek to her mother.

(5a)   He's being a soldier the way a lot of men would be politicians. (SMD 40)

(5b)   He is a soldier the way a lot of men would be politicians.

(6a)   She was being invincibly polite, trying to conceal her patience with his stupidity. (LMTW 19)

(6b)   She was invincibly polite, trying to conceal her patience with his stupidity.

(7a)   Molly laughed in a very contagious manner.

(7b)   Molly was laughing in a very contagious manner.

In these examples, the present or past nonprogressive forms express the subject's ability (*speaks*) or a characteristic description of the subject (*is, was*). Example (7a) with *laughed* is ambiguous between a habitual reading (where this particular kind of laugh characterises Molly more generally) and an occasion-specific reading (where the construction refers to just one instance of laughing). Only the former reading is relevant at this stage. The corresponding progressive forms express occasion-specific 'processes in progress' (*is speaking* and *was laughing*) and 'enactment of behaviour' (*'s being a soldier* and *was being invincibly polite*), both of which are of course {+ACTIONAL, imperfective}.[17]

Note that when the verb *as a lexical item* is inherently actional (e.g. SPEAK, LAUGH, RUN, WRITE, PLAY, etc.), the nonprogressive present tense form cannot refer to a process going on at the moment of communication:

(4c)   *Mrs Wentworth speaks modern Greek to his parents right at this very moment.

(8a)   *(I'm afraid Mr Wilson is unable to see you this morning.) He writes up the GOP report and must finish before noon.

The nonprogressive present tense form of an inherently actional verb thus typically expresses not a present instance of the process but a more general habit or characteristic of the subject (as in (4a)), or is used in e.g. the historical present mode or some similarly well-defined specialised mode, such as e.g. sports commentaries and demonstrations (cf. Section 3.4 above):

> (9)   Now that Maya inscriptions can be read, they have dispelled old notions of Classic Period life as lofty and serene. For all the grand explorations of cosmic time, public texts are also royal propaganda, proclaiming births, accessions, deaths, victories and *coups d'état*. During the eighth century, as trouble <u>begins</u> to brew, these statements <u>become</u> more strident, betraying a scramble for power and resources in a shrinking world. Militarism <u>takes</u> hold, old alliances <u>break</u> down, dynasties <u>become</u> unstable, the ruling class <u>exalts</u> itself with extravagant building projects. (WSHP 98)

(for this particular use of the nonprogressive present in narration, see Bache (1986) and Chapter 6 below, where example (9) is discussed in more detail). In everyday communicative contexts that require reference to a strictly present instance of the dynamic process, only the progressive present form is possible, as in (4b) above and (8b):

> (8b) (I'm afraid Mr Wilson is unable to see you this morning.) He <u>is writing</u> up the GOP report and must finish before noon.

The inability of nonprogressive present tense forms to refer to a dynamic instance of a process going on at the moment of communication is related to another metalinguistic incompatibility relation:

present ⇓ perfectivity

This relation, which is a generalisation over our cognitive inability to adopt an external holistic focus on a process taking place at the moment of communication (i.e. at a time in which we as Performers and Addressees are completely immersed), leads to the following co-selection rule:

present >> imperfective / −ASPECTUALITY

In other words, reference to a strictly present process requires either an imperfective form or an aspectually unmarked form. The former is only possible when the process is +ACTIONAL, whereas the latter is in principle independent of actional value. In English, however, although the nonprogressive present tense is sufficiently unmarked to be used to refer to −ACTIONAL processes (states and relations) in the present, it cannot be used to refer to strictly present +ACTIONAL processes in everyday deictic communicative interaction. In English we thus get either progressive present tense forms with imperfective meaning, as in (4b) and (8b), or nonprogressive present tense forms with both −ASPECTUAL and −ACTIONAL meaning, as in (4a) and (8c): [18]

(8c) Mr Wilson <u>writes</u> GOP reports for his company.

The fact that nonprogressive present tense forms typically express states, relations, habits and characteristics of the subject (i.e. −ACTIONAL processes that tend to apply more generally than just to the moment of communication) is part of the reason why the primary tense distinction in English is a privative one between +past and −past (rather than an equipollent one between past and present, as argued by Harder, cf. Section 4.3.2 above). In metalinguistic terms, the change of meaning from {−ACTIONAL, −ASPECTUAL} to {+ACTIONAL, imperfective}, and vice versa, which we see in examples like *Mrs Wentworth <u>speaks / is speaking</u> modern Greek* and *He <u>is / is being</u> a soldier the way a lot of men would be politicians*, is often associated also with a change of meaning from −TEMPORAL to present or −past, and vice versa.

The next metalinguistic specification which is relevant to our discussion of the progressive/nonprogressive distinction is the following incompatibility relation:

punctuality ⇓ imperfectivity

with its corresponding co-selection rule:

punctuality >> perfective / −ASPECTUALITY

This metalinguistic specification can be translated into the following language-specific specification for English:

punctuality is expressed by nonprogressive forms

The prediction here is that in a corpus of examples we find no progressive forms expressing punctuality and further that if in a substitution test a punctual nonprogressive form is replaced by a progressive form (or vice versa), the result is either unacceptability or a change of meaning from (semelfactive) punctuality to an actional value compatible with imperfectivity (iteration, direction, homogeneous self-containment) (or vice versa). This is indeed what we see in a more extensive substitution test:

Unacceptability

(10a) He <u>slaps</u> Joe's face once only, then drags him over to the kitchen table.

(10b) *He <u>is slapping</u> Joe's face once only, then drags him over to the kitchen table.

(11a) Granny <u>dropped</u> the glass on the floor and started to cry.

(11b) *Granny <u>was dropping</u> the glass on the floor and started to cry.

(12a) Jenny <u>reached</u> the second mark in less that 10 seconds.

(12b) *Jenny <u>was reaching</u> the second mark in less than 10 seconds.

(13a) As soon as he <u>switched</u> the light off, the sound disappeared.

(13b) *As soon as he <u>was switching</u> the light off, the sound disappeared.

(14a) The rumours of the illness, came a chanting Etonian voice, were very much exaggerated. It was utter nonsense to suggest that he <u>was dying</u>. All that had happened was a 'minor cardiac incident.' (SCP 65)

(14b) *... It was utter nonsense to suggest that he <u>died</u>. ...

(15a) He found the gate padlocked on the inner side. It must have been forgotten that he <u>was arriving</u> that afternoon. (FET 4)

(15b) * ... It must have been forgotten that he <u>arrived</u> that afternoon.

As already mentioned, the use of the nonprogressive simple present tense is found only in special modes, such as the historical or narrative present in (10a). Even though the present progressive is called for to refer to present dynamic processes, example (10b) is blocked because of the cotextually required punctual interpretation of the process of 'slapping.' The same constraint applies to the past tense examples in (11a,b) to (13a,b). Conversely, in examples (14a,b) and (15a,b) only the progressive form is possible in the particular contexts in which the examples occur. The nonprogressive form is blocked precisely because of its perfective punctual meaning. The only exception to the incompatibility relation between punctuality and the imperfectivity of the progressive that I have come across (cf. Bache 1985: 290f) is in examples like:

(16a) The clock <u>was striking</u> the half-hour as she entered the room.

(16b) She entered the room just as the clock <u>was striking</u> the half-hour.

In these examples, the progressive form is perfectly acceptable even if the process of striking the half-hour is strictly punctual, i.e. consisting of just a single non-extended sound signal.[19] The reason for this is that the process referred to is presented as co-occurring with another situation (someone entering the room). This relationship is made explicit by means of the conjunction *as* (in 16a) and *just as* (in 16b). In the first example the progressive construction is in the matrix clause, in the second it is in the subordinate clause, but in both cases the progressive form has the effect of providing a narrative context for the expression of the process referred to by the nonprogressive form.

Although there are many cases of unsubstitutable perfective expressions of punctuality, we also encounter examples where substitution leads to a change of meaning.

Change of meaning

{punctual, perfective} ⇔ {iterative, imperfective}

(17a) Sally <u>hits</u> Alex hard on the chest.

(17b) Sally <u>is hitting</u> Alex hard on the chest.

(18a) Somebody in the next room <u>coughs</u> and Harriet becomes distracted.

(18b) Somebody in the next room <u>is coughing</u> and Harriet becomes distracted.

(19a) A door <u>slammed</u> behind him, a loud door.

(19b) A door <u>was slamming</u> behind him, a loud door.

(20a) She <u>tapped</u> him lightly on the shoulder.

(20b) She <u>was tapping</u> him lightly on the shoulder.

Other frequent verbs in this category are BANG, BEAT, CLICK, DRIP, KNOCK, NOD, POP, RING, SHOOT, STRIKE, SHAKE, TICK, TWITCH and WINK. As with the other examples looked at so far, the present nonprogressive tense forms are restricted to special modes of communication (such as narration and dramatic historical present accounts). What the present and past nonprogressive forms in (17a) through (20a) (and similar constructions with other verbs) have in common is that they have a clear punctual potential in addition to their holistic perfective meaning, although in some cases we cannot rule out an interpretation of the process in terms of limited number of repetitions. Thus, although *He knocked on her door* (versus *He was knocking on her door*) could simply be taken to mean 'knocked once', it could also mean 'one quick succession of knocks, e.g. two or three knocks'. The same vagueness applies to *coughs* in (18a) and *tapped* in (20a), but probably not to *hits* in (17a) and *slammed* in (19a) unless some circumstantial adjunct or context actively supports a multiple-instance reading (e.g. *Sally hits Alex hard on the chest until finally he stops laughing at her* and *A door slammed behind him again and again, a loud door*). In some cases, the nonprogressive form is associated with inchoative punctuality, e.g. *Suddenly a telephone rang* (versus *A telephone next door was ringing*). Here *rang* implies 'gave a first ring' or 'began to ring', and is clearly punctual (again unless a different interpretation is explicitly prompted, as in *The telephone rang three or four times before he picked it up*). By contrast, the present and past progressive forms in (17b) through (20b) (as well as the progressive examples mentioned with 'knocking' and 'ringing') are unambiguously iterative and imperfective. We can conclude that with verbs with a strong punctual potential, the progressive/nonprogressive distinction involves a regular actional difference between imperfective representation of iteration and perfective representation of punctuality, though the less strongly marked nonprogressive form often does not exclude an interpretation in terms of limited iteration and indeed is open to adverbial or contextual quantification more generally. Needless to say, this regularity significantly affects the choice relations between the two forms.

The same is true of the next change of meaning detected in the substitution procedure.

Change of meaning

{punctual, perfective} ⇔ {directional, imperfective}

(21a) He paused, she <u>began</u> to cry.

(21b) He paused, she <u>was beginning</u> to cry.

(22a) She <u>slipped</u> into a dark fructifying dream.

(22b) She <u>was slipping</u> into a dark fructifying dream (cf. LMTW 287).

(23a) The truck <u>stopped</u> for a red light.

(23b) The truck <u>was stopping</u> for a red light.

(24a) Norah <u>died</u> of cancer.

(24b) Norah <u>was dying</u> of cancer.

With the possible exception of (21a,b) these examples may well be unsubstitutable in a larger context precisely because of the clear semantic distinction involved. The nonprogressive forms have perfective punctual meaning while the progressive forms have imperfective directional meaning. In pair (21a,b) this difference affects the exact relation between the processes expressed by the two clauses: in the a-example 'her beginning to cry' follows 'his pausing' (in fact a possible implication being that 'her beginning to cry' is prompted by the pause), while in the b-example the crying begins before the pause sets in, and the pause could well be caused by her emotional behaviour. In the other pairs of examples, the process referred to by the progressive or nonprogressive form is not explicitly related to another process (but could of course well be so in the broader linguistic or extralinguistic context). As they stand, the substitution of forms simply triggers a change of meaning from perfective punctuality (nonprogressive forms) to imperfective direction (progressive form). In all three pairs there is an implication in connection with the directional meaning of the progressive form that unless something interferes, the terminal point (as expressed by the nonprogressive form) is imminent, but strictly speaking, this point is outside the scope of the progressive. In other words, the directional movement could potentially be stopped or diverted before reaching its conclusion (e.g. *She was slipping into a dark fructifying dream when suddenly the telephone rang / The truck was stopping for a red light when unexpectedly it picked up speed again / She was dying of cancer but was miraculously saved by a new much improved kind of radiation treatment*).

I turn now to yet another metalinguistic specification which is relevant to the choice relations involved in the progressive/nonprogressive distinction, viz. the incompatibility relation between actional telicness and aspectual imperfectivity:

telicness $\Downarrow$ imperfectivity

Telicness is here defined as a durative process which involves movement towards, *and including*, a terminal point beyond which the process cannot continue as before. The incompatibility of this actional value with imperfectivity leads to the following co-selection rule in our metalanguage:

telicness >> perfective / −ASPECTUALITY

This co-selection rule can be translated into the following language-specific rule for English:

telicness is expressed by nonprogressive forms

The prediction here is that in a corpus of examples we find no progressive forms expressing (semelfactive) telicness as defined, and further that if in a substitution test a telic nonprogressive form is replaced by a progressive form (or vice versa), the result is either unacceptability or a change of meaning from telicness to an actional value compatible with imperfectivity (or vice versa). As with the other predictions that we have examined so far, this is indeed what we see in a more extensive substitution test:

Unacceptability

(25a) In her room that afternoon she <u>unbuttoned</u> her dress and stood before her mirror in her chemise and petticoats (FFLW 29).

(25b) *... she <u>was unbuttoning</u> her dress and stood before her mirror ...

(26a) Gerald <u>assembled</u> all the pieces in less than five minutes.

(26b) (*)Gerald <u>was assembling</u> all the pieces in less than five minutes.

(27a) Over the next month world grain reserves <u>fell</u> to only 22.4% of consumption.

(27b) (*)Over the next month world grain reserves <u>were falling</u> to only 22.4% of consumption.

(28a) Lisa <u>translated</u> the summary of his thesis into Spanish and returned it to the editor.

(28b) *Lisa <u>was translating</u> the summary of his thesis into Spanish and returned it to the editor.

(29a) At the time he <u>was building</u> a small garden shed, but he never quite managed to finish it.

(29b) *At the time he <u>built</u> a small garden shed, but he never quite managed to finish it.

In these examples, the nonprogressive past tense form expresses perfective telic meaning, and in each case the corresponding progressive form is blocked because of the cotextually required reading of the process referred to as having reached its crucial terminal point. Thus in (25b) and (28b), the process in question is followed by another process (*stood* and *returned*, respectively) which presupposes the completion of the first process. In other words, the realisation of the second process is dependent on the telicness of the first process. In (26b) the telic nature of the process referred to is supported by the specification of a time limit for its completion (by the circumstantial *in less than five minutes*). The only marginally possible interpretation of (27b) is that Gerald got involved in assembling all the pieces in less than five minutes (so that the circumstantial *in less than five minutes* specifies the time within which the process was initiated rather than the time within which it was completed).[20] In (27b) the imperfective focus on the 'falling', i.e. the gradual downwards movement, is incompatible with the precise specification of the end result of the decline (*to only 22.4%*) in the period specified (*Over the next month*). But as with (26b), special interpretations are possible in special contexts. Thus, for example, if the process is interpreted as applying **distributionally** to different 'grain reserves' (such as wheat, barley, rye, etc., or different reserves in different countries), and if some of these reserves had reached (or were sure to reach) the 22.4% mark and others were on their way down towards this mark, then (27b) would be a possible construction. In the last pair of examples in (29), unlike the other pairs, only the progressive form is possible: here the cotext makes it clear that the terminal point of the telic process of 'building a small garden shed' was never reached, thus inviting an imperfective focus on the building process.

As the examples reviewed above indicate, the progressive/nonprogressive distinction often involves the following change of meaning in a substitution test:

Change of meaning

{telic, perfective} ⇔ {directional, imperfective}

(30a) He <u>wrote</u> another letter.

(30b) He <u>was writing</u> another letter.

(31a) They <u>climbed</u> the steep dune with difficulty.

(31b) They <u>were climbing</u> the steep dune with difficulty.

(32a) Nolan <u>walked</u> to the university.

(32b) Nolan <u>was walking</u> to the university.

(33a) She <u>drove</u> through Randwick.

(33b) She <u>was driving</u> through Randwick.

In these pairs, the nonprogressive a-variants express perfective telic meaning and the progressive b-variants express imperfective directional meaning. These meanings are created in conjunction with the following complement (*another letter, the steep dune*) or circumstantial (*through*

Randwick, to the university), which in each case defines a limit to the process, i.e. the crucial terminal point of a telic process beyond which the process cannot continue as before. Whether this point is actually reached (i.e. whether it is inside or outside the scope of the tense form) is here not determined by the cotext. The main difference between these examples and examples (25a,b) to (29a,b) is that they do not contain an explicit restriction of the telic or directional meaning potential (either through circumstantials or an imposed sequence of processes), but leaves it to the tense form to freely instruct the Addressee to construe the exact value. There is thus room for variation between, on the one hand, the perfective telic meaning of the nonprogressive form (which includes the terminal point in its scope) and, on the other hand, the imperfective directional meaning of the progressive form (which excludes the terminal point from its scope). In a larger context, one of the constructions would most likely be blocked precisely because of the meanings associated with each form.

In the paragraphs above I have examined a number of meaning changes in the substitution test which derive from what is basically a metalinguistic incompatibility of imperfectivity with expressions referring to a decisive point, whether this point is all there is (punctual processes) or an inherent or natural terminal point (telic processes). In either case, imperfectivity imposes on the situational referent an element of duration leading up to the point, or turns the process into an iterative or otherwise multiple-instance process which allows a close-up focus on progression. My account of this behaviour so far is admittedly somewhat simplified and sketchy. Thus, in addition to the major types of actional relations involved in the formal distinction, we find a number of other factors affecting the Performer's choice of form in relation to this particular incompatibility. Consider the following examples:

(34a) Mrs Parkes, wearing a discarded floral overall of Susan's, <u>was stooping</u> to slide something into the oven. (LMTW 282)

(34b) Mrs Parkes, wearing a discarded floral overall of Susan's, <u>stooped</u> to slide something into the oven.

(35a) I <u>looked</u> up at the dark clouds that were gathering.

(35b) I <u>was looking</u> up at the dark clouds that were gathering.

(36a) We had sat down in the armchairs. He <u>pointed</u> to a cigarette box on the desk. (SSR 199)

(36b) We had sat down in the armchairs. He <u>was pointing</u> to a cigarette box on the desk.

In these pairs of examples, the nonprogressive form is {perfective, punctual} and the progressive form is {imperfective, self-contained} (i.e. durative but nondirectional). The special relationship between the substitutional variants here is that the nonprogressive form, instead of referring to the final point of a process, or its completion, refers to the ingression or initial point of a self-contained process while the progressive form refers to the progression of this self-contained process. For example, *looked* in (34a) marks the transition from not looking to looking, and *pointed* in (36a) similarly marks the occurrence of a new process, that of pointing, while the corresponding progressive forms dwell on the subsequent middle phases of looking and pointing, respectively.

Another interesting change of meaning encountered in the substitution test as a result of the incompatibility of imperfectivity with expressions referring to a decisive point is of a more temporal nature:

(37a) I couldn't imagine why Louise <u>was marrying</u> him. (DSB 9)

(37b) I couldn't imagine why Louise <u>married</u> him.

(38a) Roger told me he <u>was spending</u> the week-end at Basset, Dianna Skidmore's house in Hampstead. (SCP 48–49)

(38b) Roger told me he <u>spent</u> the week-end at Basset, Dianna Skidmore's house in Hampstead.

(39a) Osbaldiston told me that Roger <u>was taking</u> over the final draft of Gilbey's speech. (SCP 31)

(39b) Osbaldiston told me that Roger <u>took</u> over the final draft of Gilbey's speech.

These examples are all in the narrative mode and they all involve projection. In each of the b-examples, the nonprogressive past refers to a punctual or telic process occurring at an earlier stage than the past-tense process of projection and is thus close or identical in meaning to a past perfect (in accordance with the rules of projection, cf. Section 5.1 above):

(37c) I couldn't imagine why Louise <u>had married</u> him.

(38c) Roger told me he <u>had spent</u> the week-end at Basset, Dianna Skidmore's house in Hampstead.

(39c) Osbaldiston told me that Roger <u>had taken</u> over the final draft of Gilbey's speech.

By contrast, in the a-examples, the progressive form dwells on the simultaneous progression towards a point of completion *ahead* of the time of projection. This construction is thus close in meaning to a 'past future' (cf. *In two weeks Louise would marry him* and *Louise was going to marry him in two weeks*). The contrast in nonprojected constructions would thus be between a past nonprogressive and a present progressive, e.g. *'Why did Louise marry him?'* versus *'Why is Louise marrying him?'*. In Chapter 6, I shall go into further detail with the use of tenses in the narrative mode of communication.

Outside the narrative mode, the temporal implication of actional direction is evident in pairs of present tense examples like the following:

(40a) Louise <u>marries</u> him on Saturday.

(40b) Louise <u>is marrying</u> him on Saturday.

(41a) We <u>leave</u> Sydney on 2 April.

(41b) We <u>are leaving</u> Sydney on 2 April.

These substitutions are only possible in examples specifying a future time (cf. the circumstantials *on Saturday* and *on 2 April*). The difference between the two variants is quite subtle: the simple present is used in factual statements about a process scheduled for some future time whereas the present progressive is used to indicate present intention, preparation or activity leading to the future process scheduled. In corresponding examples in the past tense, nonprogressive forms report the definite occurrence of the full process including the final point, while the progressive forms report intention or preparation towards this final point:

(40c) Louise <u>married</u> him on Saturday.

(40d) Louise <u>was marrying</u> him on Saturday.

(41c) We <u>left</u> Sydney on 2 April.

(41d) We <u>were leaving</u> Sydney on 2 April.

Here things are in fact slightly more complicated than in the present tense. While the simple past tense offers factual information about a wedding and a departure at a definite past time specified by a circumstantial adjunct, the past progressive construction could be used to refer to past intention, preparation or activity directed towards a past future marriage or departure even in contexts where these events get cancelled. Thus we could say:

(41e) We <u>were leaving</u> Sydney on 2 April but when we got to the airport our flight had been rescheduled.

(41f) We <u>were leaving</u> Sydney on 2 April but on 1 April QANTAS cancelled our flight.

But there is also the possibility of changing the time perspective expressed by the circumstantial adjunct. Thus in example (40d), as a substitution variant of example (40c), the most immediate interpretation of *on Saturday* is 'last Saturday' (relative to the moment of communication) or another contextually specified past Saturday, i.e. with the same time value as *on Saturday* in example (40c) with the simple past tense. For example, we could say:

(40e) Louise <u>was marrying</u> him on Saturday but she changed her mind late Friday evening.

However, it is also possible to interpret *on Saturday* as referring to 'next Saturday' relative to the moment of communication:

(40f) Louise <u>was marrying</u> him on Saturday but now she *isn't*.

If the context is sufficiently specific, or if we change the word order, the circumstantial adjunct may even be interpreted as expressing the temporal location not of the wedding but of the intention:

(40g) On Saturday Louise <u>was marrying</u> him but on Sunday she changed her mind.

Finally, in an example like the following, the progressive seems at first capable of referring to the actual marriage as having taken place:

(40h) Louise <u>was seducing</u> Steven on Friday, <u>marrying</u> him on Saturday, <u>deceiving</u> him on Sunday, and <u>going</u> back to her folks on Monday. She's really something!

Contrary to our expectations the progressive form is here used to refer to the processes of 'seducing', 'marrying', 'deceiving' and 'going' as complete processes. But when we look at this example more closely, we find a textual explanation for the use of the progressive form. Compared to the factual account in (40i):

(40i) Louise <u>seduced</u> Steven on Friday, <u>married</u> him on Saturday, <u>deceived</u> him on Sunday, and <u>went</u> back to her folks on Monday.

Example (40h) offers a much more vivid and intense description of Louise's rash behaviour and her keen, unstoppable involvement in each process. Each of the progressive forms refers to a process as a part (or phase) of an amazing (and hardly credible) series of processes. In other words, together they express the progression of a complex macro-process and the choice of the progressive is likely to be the result of the Performer's wish to represent the totality of Louise's adventures with this particular situational focus. The imperfectivity imposed by the use of progressive forms is therefore not on the individual process but on a higher textual level.

Most of the examples discussed so far in this section have shown actional and/or temporal variation in conjunction with aspectual variation. However, as indicated in my comments on *It rained/was raining in Dublin*, and the examples dealt with in previous sections, we sometimes encounter constructions which, when subjected to the substitution test, display variation only on the definition level of aspectual meaning:

Change of meaning

perfective / −ASPECTUAL ⇔ imperfective

> (42a) I <u>had</u> a chat the other day with an old friend of mine from South Wales.

> (42b) I <u>was having</u> a chat the other cay with an old friend of mine from South Wales. (ALJ 81)

> (43a) We <u>celebrated</u> Stephanie's birthday at my uncle's.

> (43b) We <u>were celebrating</u> Stephanie's birthday at my uncle's.

> (44a) They <u>walked</u> along the beach, arm in arm.

> (44b) They <u>were walking</u> along the beach, arm in arm.

> (45a) I spotted Marion in the corner, and as promised she <u>wore</u> her famous see-through blouse.

> (45b) I spotted Marion in the corner, and as promised she <u>was wearing</u> her famous see-through blouse.

> (46a) It was a tricky process, and perhaps because she <u>tried</u> too hard she became flustered.

> (46b) It was a tricky process, and perhaps because she <u>was trying</u> too hard she became flustered.

In these examples, the simple past is perfective (representing the process as complete) or −ASPECTUAL (merely stating a fact, with no particular focus on the process), while the past progressive is positively imperfective (focusing on the internal constituency of the process, i.e. its development or progression). We get a sense of the meaning potential of the unmarked nonprogressive form, which ranges from the aspectually neutral to the positively perfective, when we compare examples in the everyday mode of communication with examples in the narrative mode. Thus in a narrative example like the following:

(47a) Their bodies <u>sought</u> with the gradualness of actual growth to enlarge and refine their fit. (UMM 12)

(47b) Their bodies <u>were seeking</u> with the gradualness of actual growth to enlarge and refine their fit.

In its narrative context, there is no sense of completion about *sought* in example (47a). In fact, the circumstantial adjuncts *with the gradualness of actual growth* and *to enlarge and refine their fit* invite a close-up internal focus on what is going on. The function of the nonprogressive is simply to introduce a new process at the stage reached in the narration in a factual, detached manner and leave the elaboration of how the process develops to the circumstantial adjuncts. By comparison, insofar as examples (42a) to (46a) are envisaged in a non-narrative context, i.e. as reports of past processes relative to the moment of communication, the nonprogressive offers a past holistic representation in contrast to the imperfective counterpart. In Chapter 6, I shall go into more detail about the use of tense forms in narration.

Since the variation in aspectual meaning in examples (42a,b) to (47a,b) are on the definition level, no intercategorial incompatibilities or co-selection rules are involved. Nevertheless the substitution of forms sometimes results in a clash between the aspectual meaning conveyed by the replacement form and the context or cotext. Thus in isolation both the following sentences are all right:

(48a) He <u>worked</u> very efficiently on the proposal all through the night.

(48b) He <u>was working</u> very efficiently on the proposal all through the night.

But if the intention is to express the process of 'working' as a complete process, or if a holistic representation is otherwise textually required, only the perfective nonprogressive variant is entirely felicitous:

(48c) He came into the office early in the evening. He <u>worked</u> very efficiently on the proposal all through the night, only interrupted by one or two phone calls, and managed to submit it before the deadline at 8am.

(48d) ??He came into the office early in the evening. He <u>was working</u> very efficiently on the proposal all through the night, only interrupted by one or two phone calls, and managed to submit it before the deadline at 8am.

The variants in (42a,b) to (48a,b) form minimal pairs and as such provide evidence of the basically aspectual, textual nature of the progressive/ nonprogressive distinction (cf. my discussion in Section 4.4.4 of the importance of minimal pairs in determining the defining properties of categories). But, as is clear from all the previous examples discussed in this section, these aspectual meanings often interact with actional and temporal meanings on what I have called the function level of meaning, i.e. the level on which variants differ in terms of more than one category and hence reveal their non-monadic character. In Figure 5.7 I have summed up the main changes of meaning identified when we subject the progressive and nonprogressive to a substitution test.

Even though I have not attempted an exhaustive analysis of the distinction between progressive and nonprogressive forms, I believe that I have provided plenty of evidence for my claim that the choice relations involved are extremely complex and not just a question of serial temporal orientation. When the Performer has to make a choice between the two forms, this choice is affected not only by lexical availability and the univariate, serial nature of verbal expressions, but also by aspectual, actional and more specific temporal considerations. Thus, although the tense system is basically assumed to consist of a set of instructions to 'log on to the world' and 'look back', 'look here/ there' and 'look ahead', arranged serially in terms of interacting base and function times, the Performer's choice of form is much more complex. On each occasion he or she is faced with experiential and textual considerations that may prove decisive, and the exact nature of these factors is likely to change from one occasion to the other. If we aim at descriptive and explanatory adequacy, this complexity should be recognised in our functional description. In Halliday's systemic functional terms, the most obvious way of doing this is to accept multivariate characteristics in the structuring of elements in verbal expressions in addition to univariate seriality. This is hardly at odds with general SFL assumptions and premises. Quite the contrary, SFL is ideally suited to a description of the relationship between expression and content in terms of multiple functional characteristics.

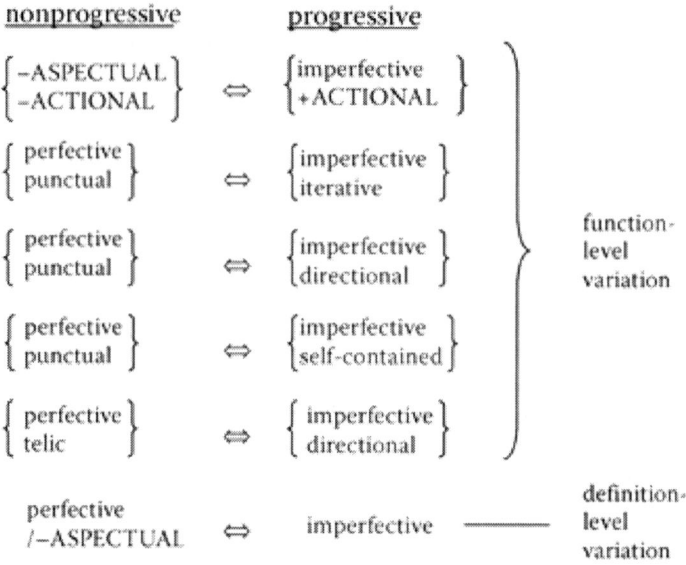

Figure 5.7: Multivariate characteristics of the progressive/nonprogressive distinction

Notes

1. In principle the choices indicated are choices between meanings and the forms pointed to by the arrows are formal realisations. However, as we shall see, the choices are often very complex because of the categorial interplay between tense, aspect and action, cf. Sections 4.4.7, 5.4 and 5.5.
2. The term 'present participle' is here used in its broad sense, including what was often referred to as the 'gerund' in traditional grammar.
3. I am grateful to Robin Fawcett for pointing out possible formalisations of my tense model and for taking the time to discuss a number of complex issues in connection with its potential computer implementation. In the network offered here, possible extensions and all the realisations rules have been left out. In this book, I have given priority to a discussion of the nature of relevant choice relations rather than the technicalities involved in the generation of tense forms within a particular formalisation.
4. I have simplified the specification of choices by leaving out the the three negative values which do not affect the name of the tense: –future, –perfect and –progressive.
5. Since this neutralisation takes place in six 'triads' of System I tense forms, there are six times two tenses fewer in System II (cf. Halliday 1994a: 201).
6. I am here disregarding conditional sentences like the following, in which the dependence of the conditional subclause on the main clause is reduced to a

much looser sense of relevance or inference: *If you are hungry there's some left-overs in the fridge* and *If today is Friday, he is here already.*

7. A past form in a protasis may also express genuine past meaning, as in *If you really saved her from her violent husband, you are a hero!* In such cases the condition hinges on the actual past occurrence or truth of the past process, and there are fewer restrictions on the tense of the apodosis.

8. An alternative is of course to modalise the apodosis, as in *If you forget your passport, you may well get into trouble, If you closed the door, they might get very upset* and *If you had brought your wife, we could have settled the matter once and for all.*

9. The discussion of these examples is based on Bache 1985: 193ff and 223ff.

10. Interestingly enough, the simple present *informs* in the matrix clause is also near-synonymous with the present perfect *has informed.* As noted by Bache (1985: 197), there is just a slight difference between the two forms in terms of how much emphasis the Performer puts on the fact that his or her present knowledge depends on the past process of receiving information (which is greater in the case of the present perfect than in the case of the simple present).

11. This is of course a schematic representation of the systemic order of choices, not necessarily identical to the order of choices in the Performer's mental processing of the expression.

12. The description of the temporal orientations of the present and the past pro-gressive offered here differs somewhat from the account provided in Bache and Davidsen-Nielsen (1997: 302f), where the two forms are defined right away in terms of both 'simultaneity' and 'progression'. The reason for this is that the present description distinguishes much more rigorously between 'univariate' and 'multivariate' characteristics.

13. The reason why I have chosen a *simple present* example *Miranda is my best friend* to illustrate the difference between general simultaneity and inclusion is that in nonprogressive examples there is only a potential overlap between base time and function time in present constructions. In the corresponding *simple past* example *Miranda was my best friend*, the base time and the function time are completely separate (present and past, respectively) and thus not relevant for the argument presented here for recognising the notion of inclusion as a specialisation of the notion of simultaneity.

14. Apparent counter examples like *I am understanding/liking him more and more as time goes by* should be interpreted rather as involving a change, i.e. as dynamic or developmental in nature.

15. This claim of conformity is not as circular as it may seem at first. Although I have presented this kind of metalinguistic analyses of English tense forms be-fore, and hence more or less know in advance what to expect, the metalanguage with all its (in)compatibility relations and co-selection rules is established on the basis of definitions arrived at in a principled manner and a much broader range of linguistic data (including Russian examples), cf. Bache (1997). For example, the fact that imperfectivity is incompatible with punctuality is not just

a useful metalinguistic specification derived from and subsequently applied to English with guaranteed success, but a simple conceptual consequence of the definitions of imperfectivity and punctuality more generally.

16. I use curly brackets to indicate feature bundles.

17. Depending on the context, these progressive examples could also be interpreted as expressing recurring activity within a limited period of time, e.g. *This week Mrs Wentworth is speaking Greek to her mother* and *During her stay with his parents she was being invincibly polite*.

18. In Russian the co-selection rule arising as a result of the incompatibility of present temporality with perfectivity is borne out by a different distribution of forms: only the unmarked imperfective present tense is used to refer to present processes (including both actional and non-actional processes). The marked perfective present tense refers to the future and forms an aspectual pair with the periphrastic imperfective future consisting of BYT' + an imperfective infinitive, cf. imperfective future *On budet pisat'* versus perfective present *On napiset* (both meaning 'He is going to write' or 'He will write'). The difference between English and Russian is thus simply one of markedness relations. While in Russian it is the imperfective that is the unmarked aspect, in English it is the perfective (for discussion, see Bache 1997: 198ff, 322ff).

19. An alternative is of course to interpret the process of 'striking the half-hour' as a durative process involving more than just a single ding, in which case the progressive form may receive its normal inclusive interpretation.

20. This interpretation is more plausible if the circumstantial is moved to the front of the sentence: *In less than five minutes Gerald was assembling all the pieces*.

6 The narrative mode

In Section 5.1, I argued that the inclusion of *would* as a past future tense marker in the core system made it possible to account for tense usage in projected clauses and in conditional sentences as *category-internal mechanisms*, the former in terms of 'backshifting' and the latter in terms of a kind of 'forward-shifting'. With the core system I have proposed as a revised SFL-model of tense in English we can offer a comprehensive, yet very simple, account of both phenomena. However, it is important to notice that the use of tense forms in both projected clauses and conditional sentences is significantly different from the use of tense forms we should expect on the basis of the definitions offered for the members of the core system. In examples like:

(1)   She <u>claimed</u> that they <u>had taken</u> the key.

(2)   I <u>really</u> thought she <u>was</u> happy.

(3)   The dean <u>said</u> that there <u>would be</u> another meeting soon.

the process in the projected clause is governed temporally by the process in the projecting clause in that it adopts the function time of the process in the projecting time (which is +past in all three examples) as its base time: *had taken, was* and *would be* relate to the past time of 'claiming', 'thinking' and 'saying' respectively and are only indirectly related to the moment of communication. At the same time, there is a neutralisation of the temporality of the original proposition ('They took/have taken/had taken the key', 'She is/was happy' and 'There will/would be another meeting soon'). This means that an isolated description of *had taken, was* and *would be* in terms of the instructions specified for the past perfect, the simple past and the past future does not capture their special use:

> The past perfect: 'tag on to world-before-now and then look back at process'
>
> The past: 'tag process on to world-before-now'
>
> The past future: 'tag on to world-before now and then look ahead to process'

(for the full list of instructions, see Section 5.3). In all three examples, the 'tagging on to world-before-now' has been taken care of by the past tense form of the projecting process and in all three cases the full instruction misses possible interpretations as well as the relationship between the projected and the projecting process.

Similarly, in examples like:

(4)   If you <u>close</u> the door, I <u>will tell</u> you my innermost secret.

(5)   If she <u>asked</u> him, he <u>would be</u> angry.

(6)   If you <u>had told</u> them the truth, they <u>would</u> all <u>have rushed</u> out.

the tense forms clearly do not signal the instructions we should expect, with the exception of *will tell* in (4), which does in fact instruct the Addressee to 'tag on to world-now and then look ahead to process'. Contrary to the specifications of the members of the core system, the simple present in (4) has an element of aheadness (triggered by the combination of the conditional marker *If* and the present tense). The same is true of the simple past *asked* and the past future *would be* in (5), which in addition to aheadness expresses a bias towards non-occurrence. In example (6) the past perfect *had told* and the past future perfect *would have rushed* do instruct the Addressee to 'tag on to world-before-now' but instead of the usual further orientation of these tense forms they express counterfactuality. As argued in Section 5.1, the distribution of tense forms in this particular kind of conditional sentences can be described in terms of 'conditional pairs' which are formed by 'forward-shifting':

conditional marker + present $\Rightarrow$ present future

conditional marker + past $\Rightarrow$ past future

conditional marker + past perfect $\Rightarrow$ past future perfect

What the use of tense forms in projection and conditional sentences shows is that in certain well-defined contexts, the instructional characteristics of the core system realisations are overruled, or assimilated, by higher-priority considerations. These higher-priority considerations can be described as special communicative, or textual, functions. When the Performer projects utterances or thoughts or stipulates conditions, these special functions enlist tense forms for their own special purposes, thereby often overruling or assimilating the usual functions of the tense forms in a broader communicative frame.[1] As I have argued (cf. Section 5.1), it is not enough in a description of tense in English to sort out the basic structuring of temporal meaning in isolation; rather we need to account for the particular uses of any individual form which realises one or more basic functions in the system. Tense usage in projection and in conditional sentences is a clear case in point.

Another very important special communicative function is narration, or as I have called it elsewhere, the narrative mode of communication (cf. Bache 1986). Like the projection of speech/thought and the stipulation of conditions, narration introduces a particular communicative framework, a kind of stage or mental space, which overrules or assimilates the 'normal' function of tense forms to suit narrative purposes. Within this framework, each verbal expression expresses a process or development in the narration, and in each case the Performer instructs the Addressee to locate this process or development, not in real time relative to the moment of communication, but in the story which the Addressee is prompted to 're-create'. This re-creation involves *mental presence* at the 'occurrence' of the processes expressed. Each process 'takes place' in 'story time' and both the Performer and the Addressee are 'present there', as it were, the Performer as the 'creator' and the Addressee as the 're-creator'. By comparing the examples in (7a) (which is a real-time account) and (8a) (which is a story-time account), one can get a sense of this mental presence in the latter:

(7a) 'I am not sure he <u>knew</u> what he <u>was doing</u>. It <u>looked</u> to me as if he <u>was trying</u> to get out of the building before suffocating. He <u>was</u> probably desperate and <u>thought</u> the only option <u>was</u> to break the glass wall by toppling over all the book shelves.' (e.g. a statement in a court case by a Vatican library security guard)

(8a) Finding the glass wall again, he <u>placed</u> one hand on it to guide him as he <u>raced</u> in the dark toward the far end of the vault. The back wall <u>loomed</u> suddenly, and he <u>collided</u> with it, crushing his shoulder. Cursing, Langdon <u>circled</u> the shelf and <u>grabbed</u> the stack at about eye level. Then, propping one leg on the glass behind him and another on the lower shelves, he <u>started</u> to climb. Books <u>fell</u> around him, fluttering into the darkness. [...] He <u>scrambled</u> toward the upper shelves, stepping on books, trying to gain purchase, heaving himself upward. Then, like a rock climber conquering a rock face, Langdon <u>grasped</u> the top shelf. Stretching his legs out behind him, he <u>walked</u> his feet up the glass wall until he <u>was</u> almost horizontal.

Now or never, Robert, a voice <u>urged</u>. *Just like the leg press in the Harvard Gym.*

With dizzying exertion, he <u>planted</u> his feet against the wall behind him, <u>braced</u> his arms and chest against the stack, and <u>pushed</u>. Nothing happened.

Fighting for air, he <u>repositioned</u> and tried again, extending his legs. Ever so slightly, the stack <u>moved</u>. He <u>pushed</u> again, and the stack <u>rocked</u> forward an inch or so and then back. Langdon <u>took</u> advantage of the motion, inhaling what felt like an oxygenless breath and heaving again. The shelf <u>rocked</u> farther.

Like a swing set, he <u>told</u> himself. *Keep the rhythm. A little more.*

Langdon <u>rocked</u> the shelf, extending his legs farther with each push. His quadriceps <u>burned</u> now, and he blocked the pain. The pendulum <u>was</u> in motion. *Three more pushes*, he <u>urged</u> himself.

It only <u>took</u> two.

There <u>was</u> an instant of weightless uncertainty. Then with a thundering of books sliding off the shelves, Langdon and the shelf <u>were falling</u> forward.

Halfway to the ground, the shelf <u>hit</u> the stack next to it. Langdon <u>hung</u> on, throwing his weight forward, urging the second shelf to topple. There was a moment of motionless panic, and then creaking under the weight, the second stack <u>began</u> to tip. Langdon <u>was falling</u> again.

Like enormous dominoes, the stacks <u>began</u> to topple, one after another. Metal on metal, books tumbling everywhere. [...] (BAD 384–6)

As a first approximation we can say that while the past tense forms in (7a) instruct the Addressee to 'tag on to the world-before-now', i.e. to look back at earlier events relative to the moment of communication, in (8a) they build up the narrative universe with a complex sequence of events. There is no sense of a moment of communication, the Performer (author) and the Addressee (reader) being not necessarily either temporally or spatially close or at all related, and therefore there is no base time relative to which the events can be specifically located. In other words, deixis is suspended (or perhaps rather, transformed). As the Addressee reads on, each event adds to the storyline. The feeling of curiosity or suspense is, at least partly, a result of the Addressee being mentally present at the 'occurrence' of each process. The Addressee is simply keen to see what *happens next*. In such texts, the past tense accordingly signals a somewhat different instruction, namely the instruction to 'tag on to story line and look at process'. This instruction is a neutral instruction to switch mentally out of sync, so to speak, and into the narrative mode. In a sense, temporal distance is replaced by narrative distance from the actual temporal and spatial context of the production and the reception of the text.

The narrative mode is not restricted to written texts. In fact it probably originated in orally transmitted accounts of real events in the past, i.e. in contexts with an intense moment of communication, with an explicit temporal orientation and with real past situational referents. However, even in such contexts, once the events form a complex pattern of relationships and structural coherence in an extended text, the force of narration exerts itself and invites the listener to adopt a mentally closer stance to the development of the storyline, thus increasingly neutralising the deictic nature of the past tense. The thin line between the narrative mode of communication and what for want of a better term I call the ordinary everyday deictic mode of communicative interaction is still present: when does a deictic account of past events turn into a narrative? It is hard to give any definite criteria but it is certainly not a question of whether the events are real or fictional, as some may believe. As we shall see, real events can be presented in narrative form and fiction can be presented as real past events. But when the accumulation of processes expressed reaches a certain point of complexity the balance tips in favour of the narrative mode. To see this, we need to have a closer look at the two examples provided in (7a) and (8a).

Given the assumed deictic nature of example (7a), we expect as a matter of course that a different choice of the first value in our core system (±past), i.e. a choice of −past instead of +past, *will affect the deixis of the construction dramatically*. Indeed this is what happens:

(7b) 'I am not sure he <u>knows</u> what he <u>is doing</u>. It <u>looks</u> to me as if he <u>is trying</u> to get out of the building before suffocating. He <u>is</u> probably desperate and <u>thinks</u> the only option <u>is</u> to break the glass wall by toppling over all the book shelves.'

By changing the past tense forms in (7a) into present tense forms in (7b) we turn the account of past processes into an account of present processes relative to the moment of communication. The Performer has been asked to watch someone trying to get out of a building and to comment on what she sees. The reason that (7b) survives this transposition of tense and in fact may serve perfectly well as a deictic, real-time account of present processes is that all the nonprogressive tense forms (*knows, looks, is, thinks, is*) express −ACTIONAL processes (relations and mental states) and are thus comfortable with the simple present tense, while the +ACTIONAL processes (*is doing, is trying*) are already in the progressive form. Another good reason is that there are no circumstantial adjuncts specifying the past application time in (7a).

By contrast, given the nondeictic nature of the narrative mode of communication we should expect a similar change of tense forms from past to present in example (8) to be *neutral with respect to temporal orientation*. Indeed this is the case:

(8b)   Finding the glass wall again, he <u>places</u> one hand on it to guide him as he <u>races</u> in the dark toward the far end of the vault. The back wall <u>looms</u> suddenly, and he <u>collides</u> with it, crushing his shoulder. Cursing, Langdon <u>circles</u> the shelf and <u>grabs</u> the stack at about eye level. Then, propping one leg on the glass behind him and another on the lower shelves, he <u>starts</u> to climb. Books <u>fall</u> around him, fluttering into the darkness. [...] He <u>scrambles</u> toward the upper shelves, stepping on books, trying to gain purchase, heaving himself upward. Then, like a rock climber conquering a rock face, Langdon <u>grasps</u> the top shelf. Stretching his legs out behind him, he <u>walks</u> his feet up the glass wall until he <u>is</u> almost horizontal.

Now or never, Robert, a voice <u>urges</u>. *Just like the leg press in the Harvard Gym.*

With dizzying exertion, he <u>plants</u> his feet against the wall behind him, <u>braces</u> his arms and chest against the stack, and <u>pushes</u>. Nothing <u>happens</u>.

Fighting for air, he <u>repositions</u> and <u>tries</u> again, extending his legs. Ever so slightly, the stack <u>moves</u>. He <u>pushes</u> again, and the stack <u>rocks</u> forward an inch or so and then back. Langdon <u>takes</u> advantage of the motion, inhaling what <u>feels</u> like an oxygenless breath and heaving again. The shelf <u>rocks</u> farther.

Like a swing set, he <u>tells</u> himself. *Keep the rhythm. A little more.*

Langdon <u>rocks</u> the shelf, extending his legs farther with each push. His quadriceps <u>burns</u> now, and he <u>blocks</u> the pain. The pendulum <u>is</u> in motion. *Three more pushes*, he <u>urges</u> himself.

It only <u>takes</u> two.

There <u>is</u> an instant of weightless uncertainty. Then with a thundering of books sliding off the shelves, Langdon and the shelf <u>are falling</u> forward.

Halfway to the ground, the shelf <u>hits</u> the stack next to it. Langdon <u>hangs</u> on, throwing his weight forward, urging the second shelf to topple. There <u>is</u> a moment of motionless panic, and then creaking under the weight, the second stack <u>begins</u> to tip. Langdon <u>is falling</u> again.

Like enormous dominoes, the stacks <u>begin</u> to topple, one after another. Metal on metal, books tumbling everywhere. [...] (cf. BAD 384–6)

This text is still very much in the narrative mode of communication. Like the past tense forms in (8a), the present tense forms in (8b) contribute to the formation of the storyline and the Addressee is still mentally present, in fact perhaps even more so than in (8a). The difference between the two variants of the texts is a stylistic one, not one of temporal orientation: the present tense forms convey a higher degree of immediacy and make the narration slightly more dramatic. However, as the text unfolds, this stylistic effect weakens and the use of the present tense becomes less marked. The difference between the two tenses is more perceptible when a largely past-tense narration suddenly employs the present tense, which is not an uncommon stylistic phenomenon. For example, as the tension increases towards the end of the passage in example (8a), Dan Brown could at any time have decided to suddenly switch into the present tense (e.g. in the last few paragraphs) and then back into the past tense after Langdon's escape from the suffocating enclosure of the Vatican library.

My own favourite example of such narrative tense switching is the ending of John Fowles's small novel *The Ebony Tower*, where the main character, artist and art critic David, is meeting up with his wife Beth after having visited the painter Henry Breasley and his two muses, Anne and Diana, at Coët:

(9)   He got to Orly to find that the flight was delayed for half an hour. There was fog at Heathrow. David hated airports at the best of times, the impersonality, herding, sense of anonymous passage; the insecurity. He stood by the window at the visitors' lounge, staring out into the flat distances. Dusk. Coët was in another universe; one and an eternal day's drive away. He tried to imagine what they were doing. Diana laying the table, Anne having her French lesson. The silence, the forest, the old man's voice. Macmillan barking. He suffered the most intense pang of the most terrible of all human deprivations; which is not of possession, but of knowledge. What she said, what she felt, what she thought. It pierced deeper than all questionings about art, or his art, his personal destiny. For a few terrible moments he saw himself, and all mankind, quite clear. [...]

The flight arrival was announced and he went down to where he could watch for Beth. He had brought her holiday luggage in the car, and she came out with the first passengers. A wave. He raised his hand: a new coat, surprise for him, a little flounce and jiggle to show it off. Gay Paree. Free woman. Look, no children.

She <u>comes</u> with the relentless face of the present tense; with a dry delight, small miracle that he <u>is</u> actually here. He <u>composes</u> his face into an equal certainty.

She <u>stops</u> a few feet short of him.

'Hi'

She <u>bites</u> her lips.

'I thought for one ghastly moment.'

She <u>pauses</u>.

'You were my husband.'

Rehearsed. He <u>smiles</u>.

He <u>kisses</u> her mouth.

They <u>walk</u> away together, talking about their children.

He <u>has</u> a sense of retarded walking, as in a post-operational state of consciousness some hours returned but not till now fully credited; a numbed sense of something beginning to slip inexorably away. A shadow of a face, hair streaked with gold, a closing door. *I wanted you to.* One <u>knows</u> one dreamed, yet cannot remember, the drowning cry, jackbooted day.

She <u>says</u>, 'And you, darling?'

He <u>surrenders</u> to what is left: abstraction.

'I survived.' (FET 105–6)

Up until the moment Beth arrives, the novel is in the past-tense narrative mode, describing David's visit to Coët and how he has been hurled into dreamlike confusion, soul-searching, passion, love, self-realisation, and new knowledge. Then, when he finally returns from Coët to resume his relationship with Beth, with whom he has planned to go on a holiday after the visit to Coët, the narration switches to the present tense. Fowles knows exactly what he is doing here: *She comes with the relentless face of the present tense.* A powerful stylistic device to mark the contrast between Coët and the reality David returns to: the past tense marks a narrative distance even if the Addressee is mentally present at the unfolding of the storyline while the present tense is immediate, close-up and dramatic, having 'a relentless face'. It is significant, I think, that while this kind of switch from past tense narration to present tense narration is not an uncommon device for creating vividness and contrast, I have actually never encountered the opposite: a present tense narration that suddenly switches into past-tense narration in order to create a less vivid impression of what is going on. In the narrative mode, the past tense is the unmarked member of the opposition.[2]

The following text, which is a historical account of the collapse of the Mayan civilisation, and thus basically an account of real events, also switches from real-time past tense reference to present-time narrative mode and back again. The first switch is possibly triggered by the use of real-time present tense forms to describe Maya inscriptions that are available today and important to our understanding of Mayan culture (for easy reference each finite verbal expression is numbered):

> (10) Each city [1]had its distinctive style. Copan [2]produced intricate sculpture, the statues of its kings [...] radiating order and refinement. Palenque's palaces [3]were light and imaginative [...] Tikal [4]became a massive, vertical place [...] – a Manhattan of art deco towers. (The resemblance [5]isn't fanciful: Maya architecture [6]influenced modern styles [...])
>
> Now that Maya inscriptions [7]can be read, they [8]have dispelled old notions of Classic Period life as lofty and serene. For all the grand explorations of cosmic time, public texts [9]are also royal propaganda, proclaiming births, accessions, deaths, victories, and coups d'etat. During the eighth century, as trouble [10]begins to brew, these statements [11]become more strident, betraying a scramble for power and resources in a shrinking world. Militarism [12]takes hold, old alliances [13]break down, dynasties [14]become unstable, the ruling class [15]exalts itself with extravagant building projects. Tikal [16]was built up over 1,500 years, but all the high towers that still [17]watch over the forest [18]went up in the city's final century, costly [19]blooms on the eve of collapse.
>
> When the great cities [20]wobbled, upstarts [21]began to assert themselves, as [22]happened in Greece during the Peloponnesian Wars. (WSHP 98–99).

The first part of this text is in the ordinary real-time, deictic mode of communication: verb forms 1 to 4 plus 6 are in the past tense, referring to past processes (*had, produced, were, became, influenced*), while verb forms 5 and 7 to 9 are in the present tense (including present modal and present perfect: *isn't, can be read, have dispelled, are*). Then the narrative mode sets in with nondeictic present tense forms: verb forms 10 to 15 (*begins, become, takes, break, become, exalts*). My interpretation of this part of the passage is that the narrative present is triggered by the real-time present evidence that we have (the inscriptions with the statements that became more strident, cf. verb form 11). In the last part of the text, the author switches back to his real-time historical account with deictic past tense forms 16, 18 and 20–22 (*was built, went, wobbled, began, happened*) and deictic present tense forms 17 and 19 (*watch, blooms*). When the present tense is used as with verb forms 10–15 in the narrative mode of communication, it is often called 'the historical present' precisely because it refers to real past (and often historical) events. This use of the narrative mode to refer to real past events is not restricted to the written language:

> (11) 'We took a bus from Castlereagh Street and got off the usual place on Clovelly just after Frenchman's Road. As we were walking down Glebe Street, this tall dark bloke suddenly <u>comes</u> up to me and <u>says</u>: 'Do I know you?' It was really spooky.'

Again we see a switch from the deictic past tense to the narrative present tense and back. Jespersen's comment on this vivid use of the present is very apt. He says that the Performer 'steps outside the frame of history, visualising and representing what happened in the past as if it were present before his eyes' (Jespersen 1929: 258). The effect is the more dramatic because the contrast is between real past time and 'mentally present time', but in fact Jespersen's description applies to the narrative mode more generally. Mental presence at the occurrence of the process is a central characteristic of the narrative mode, whether the present or the past tense is selected, and whether the contrast is to real-time past events or a stylistic one in the narrator's building up of a storyline.

As we have seen, the narrative mode may be employed both when the reference is to real past events and when it is to fictional ones. Interestingly, the deictic, real-time mode is similarly unrestricted: as we expect, it may of course be used for expressions of real events with one of the usual temporal orientations relative to the moment of communication, but significantly it may also be used in fiction, especially, but not only, in representations of dialogues, as in the following example:

> (12) 'Mister Law,' she says, at ease with practice, 'I <u>need</u> you to be as transparent as possible in your dealings with me.'
>
> He cracks the last of the pill between his teeth. 'Then I<u>'ll try</u> not to disappoint you. [...] When I <u>created</u> Soft Gold, the code <u>required</u> a place it could be housed. It <u>needed</u> dedicated power, and a financial institution behind it that people <u>could trust</u>. [...] Three years after the new money <u>was set</u> up, I <u>was paid</u> a previously agreed quantity of SoftMark shares. [...] The new money <u>was</u> somewhat more successful than SoftMark <u>had anticipated</u>. Eventually I <u>came</u> to hold a controlling stake in the corporation. But I <u>did</u> so because Soft Gold <u>is</u> here. My code <u>is</u> here. My fortune <u>is</u> largely theoretical. [...].'

She types, *Nature of Business: Money*. The words look ludicrous even as she completes them, and she is angry again. 'Thank you.'

'You<u>'re</u> welcome,' he says, and without looking she knows he is smiling.

'And what <u>did</u> they <u>get</u>?'

'<u>I'm</u> sorry?'

'I <u>can see</u> what you <u>got</u> from this. I <u>can't see</u> what they <u>gained</u> from you.'

'I <u>see</u>, yes. Alright.' For the first time since they have sat down he looks away from her. [...] 'When I <u>came</u> to them, SoftMark <u>was</u> already one of the most successful companies in the world. Now there <u>is</u> no need to qualify the term. I <u>take</u> full responsibility for that. I <u>offered</u> the corporation the most forceful advertising tool money <u>could buy</u> – their own money.' (HC 40–41)

In this passage, the storyline is developed in two different ways: by means of present tense narration (i.e. the narrative mode of communication) and by means of a dialogue between two characters. Examples of the former are: *He cracks the last of the pill between his teeth* and *She types* Nature of Business: Money. *The words look ludicrous even as she completes them, and she is angry again.* In addition there are explicit present-tense narrative markers of the dialogue: *she says, he says.* This dialogue itself contains more of a variety of tense forms. To the characters there is a continuing 'present' moment of communication, as in real life, with a deictic present and a deictic past which may form the basis of all the usual orientations specified in the core tense system. Hence we get examples of the simple past (e.g. *created, needed, required*, etc.), the simple present (e.g. *need, is, think*, etc.), the present future (*'ll try*), the past perfect (*had anticipated*), all used with the normal functional content. In addition we find projection (*would take*) and a number of modalised verbal expressions (*could trust, can't see, could buy*). In imitating the everyday mode of communicative interaction, the text establishes a kind of fictional deixis with the narrative stage reached as the deictic zero point, i.e. 'present' moment of communication, and each turn-taking marks a progression in the storyline, continually updating this 'present' moment.

So far we have established the following characteristics of the narrative mode of communication:

(a)   The focus is basically on the development of a coherent complex of processes – a narrative universe – with each verbal expression adding to the storyline, rather than on providing the temporal orientation of each process in relation to the moment of communication.

(b)   The Addressee 'mentally witnesses' each process as they are expressed, i.e. he is 'mentally present' at the 'occurrence' of each process.

(c)   The basic concern in the narrative mode is thus the sequential relationship between the processes whereas the basic concern in the everyday mode of communicative interaction is the temporal orientation of the process relative to the moment of communication.

(d)   There is sometimes an indeterminate transition from the everyday mode of communicative interaction to the narrative mode: what starts out as reference to past processes related to the present moment of communication may slip into the narrative mode as a collection of processes begins to form a storyline with its focus on the sequential relationship between processes.

(e)   The neutral tense form in the narrative mode is past but without its usual deictic function of instructing the Addressee to tag on to the world-before-now.

(f)   In the narrative mode present tense forms may be employed instead of past tense forms without creating a temporal contrast.

(g)   The difference between present-tense narration and past-tense narration is of a stylistic nature: both tenses help develop the storyline and invite the Addressee to witness the processes expressed, but while the past tense is neutral, with an association of narrative distance, the present tense offers a close-up, vivid, dramatic account, especially when the narration switches from the past to the present, thus creating a contrast.

(h)   In the narrative mode it is hence the present tense that is the marked member of the opposition, not the past tense as in the everyday mode of communicative interaction.

(i)   The transition between modes mentioned in (d) above is sometimes made explicit by means of the marked narrative present-tense form in the context of deictic past-tense forms (this is often referred to as 'the historical present').

(j)   There is no one-to-one relationship between mode of communication and the reality of the processes expressed: in both the narrative mode and the everyday mode of communicative interaction we encounter fictional processes as well as real (historically more or less accurate) processes.

There is an important qualification to be made in connection with these characteristics of the narrative mode. They apply first and foremost to those processes which carry the storyline forward. But of course, there are other kinds of process: narration is typically not just the listing of processes in a simple sequence, one after the other, but a combination of such processes and processes which partially or fully overlap with them, or precede or follow them. In this respect narration seeks to reflect 'real life' complexity. In other words, there is in this mode an orientation of processes which is very similar to the temporal orientation of processes in the everyday deictic mode of communication but which is related to the point or stage reached in the storyline rather than the present moment of communication. Like the deictic zero-point, this point or stage is in constant movement as the plot develops and it serves as the basis for the orientation of processes in the narration. I shall therefore call it **the narrative zero-point**.

This is not the place to provide a full-scale description of tense usage in either the everyday deictic mode or the narrative mode. But let me just offer a few characteristics of the orientation of processes relative to the narrative zero-point. Basically, except for the neutralisation of deixis in connection with the ±past distinction, the tense system remains intact. However, as we shall see, there are some notable special applications of the other core distinctions, especially ±perfect and ±progressive, which derive from the temporal neutralisation of ±past.

In present-tense narration, the perfect with its instruction to 'look back' provides a means of referring to processes at an earlier stage than the narrative zero-point, and this is very appropriate because earlier processes typically only get mentioned for their particular contribution to our understanding of the storyline at the narrative zero-point:

(13)   The local train is late in, and she misses her connection. At Central Station she looks for the linctus-scented guard, but the shifts <u>have</u> inevitably <u>changed</u> and he <u>has gone</u>, leaving behind two younger men who have little time for her. (HC 261)

Sometimes the earlier process is very close to the narrative zero-point, in fact so close that it helps move the story-line forward, as in the following examples:

(14)   She is leaving on lights, dimming them, when her mobile rings. It is downstairs, she is upstairs, and by the time she reaches it, it

has vibrated its way across the kitchen table, sideways, like an escaping crab. She catches it as it falls.

A message has been left. (HC 217)

Sometimes the earlier process is in fact quite distant from the narrative zero-point:

(15) For these things she has the Internal Revenue Service to thank, and Lawrence to thank for the IRS. It is an organisation she has dealt with several times in her years at the Revenue, but she knows no one there well enough to call them herself. (HC 221)

However, the past tense is also available in present-tense narration and is used for events located at specific past points or in contrast to the narrative zero-point:

(16) She sits and reads her unread books, unpacking boxes of those texts that never interested her before, the ones she can sell, if it comes to that. Engels and Marx, the histories of Israel and gunpowder. The several lives of Albert Einstein. The secret codes of Sparta, the city that turned its back on money. (HC 239)

(17) It is several years since she has even seen the sea. As a child she did so all the time, though she has never travelled much. Summer and winter there were holidays in Holland, where her grandparents lived, her father's father and mother at first, then only his mother. (HC 222)

The past tense is particularly frequent in projection or implicit projection of thoughts and recollections of the past:

(18) His movements are economical with experience. It is how she remembers him. Not here but at the Revenue. Not doing these small things, but what he cared for most. Keeping watch. Setting the record straight.

She remembers the way he worked. A kind, instinctual, and relentless man. When he was like, lost in the investigation, he was the perfect inspector. People said so, and Anna still believes it. [...]

Later he became other things. When his drinking became more extreme Lawrence could be cruel. His exactitude became unforgiving [...] (HC 24)

(19) She narrows her eyes, remembering. One year there was a fair and a raffle for some local cause. She and Martha bought two tickets and won a kilo bag of tiger prawns. There is a photograph of them

somewhere: two children with the sack held between them, proud as anglers. They <u>ate</u> nothing else for days, sucking the prawns still frozen, like ice cubes. (HC 222)

We rarely encounter the past perfect in present-tense narration but it is not ruled out. Immediately before the following passage, Anna has been reading a letter which indicates where she can find John, viz. with his mother on the Scottish Isle of Coll, and suddenly remembers an old article about John's mother living there:

(20) Coll. She <u>had</u> almost <u>forgotten</u> the article, years old and only half believed. She wonders if Carl remembers it too, and if so, how far ahead of her he is already. (HC 242)

The past perfect is used to 'look back', not directly from the narrative zero-point but via the slightly earlier point where Anna reads the particular passage in the letter mentioning John's mother. In other words, it is a narrative 'past in the past'.

While present-tense narration quite regularly looks back from the narrative zero-point, using especially present perfect forms, it may also look ahead, although this is much rarer:

(21) What is happening upstairs is something Howard <u>will hear</u> about later. (BHM 93)

(22) 'Do you like gardening?' John Law asks, the unforeseen question catching her by surprise. She shrugs automatically.
'I like gardens.'
He laughs, perhaps at her expense, but not as if the joke is unkind. Later she <u>will regret</u> not having laughed with him. 'Not quite the same thing.' (HC 45)

This use of the present future forms *will hear* and *will regret* is parallel to the use of the past future *would* + infinitive, which I commented on at length in Section 5.1 above.

Turning now to past-tense narration, we find extensive use of the past perfect to 'look back' at earlier stages in the storyline:

(23) He was sitting beside his radio set which he <u>had</u> just <u>switched</u> off. It was late at night. He <u>had listened</u> to a symphony concert ... Now all was silent. (Bache and Davidsen-Nielsen 1997: 315)

(24) Harper paced for several seconds around the wide table on which sat a scale model of the PODS satellite – a cylindrical prism with multiple antennae and lenses behind reflective shields. Gabrielle

sat down, her dark eyes watching, waiting. The nausea in Harper's gut reminded him of how he <u>had felt</u> during the infamous press conference. He<u>'d put</u> on a lousy show that night, and everyone <u>had questioned</u> him about it. He<u>'d had</u> to lie again and say he was feeling ill that night and was not himself. His colleagues and the press shrugged off his lacklustre performance and quickly forgot about it.

Now the lie <u>had come</u> back to haunt him. (BDP 377—8)

However, as example (24) shows, given the right context also the simple past may be used to 'look back' from the narrative zero-point in past-tense narration: *shrugged* and *forgot* express reactions immediately following the event described by means of the past perfect and are thus clearly prior to the narrative zero-point. Interestingly, the last past perfect *had come* expresses a process which takes place after these past-tense processes but prior to, and in immediate relation to, the narrative zero-point. Note that while the simple present has three possible partners for the expression of anteriority (the present perfect, the simple past and the past perfect), the simple past has only one (the past perfect), and this accounts for the need to employ also the simple past itself to 'look back' at previous processes. In past-time narration we do not encounter examples of the present perfect. Note finally the interesting use of the circumstantial adjunct *now* in both (23) (*Now all was silent*) and (24) (*Now the lie had come back to haunt him*), which is further evidence of the nondeictic use of past tense forms in the narrative mode of communication. *Now* here expresses the narrative zeropoint, not the deictic zeropoint.

As we saw in our discussion of the inventory of the core system in Section 5.1, the past future *would* + infinitive is used, if not commonly at least unproblematically, in past-tense narration to look ahead to processes not yet reached in the storyline:

(25) Ready to weep he prepared himself for bed. He <u>would</u> not <u>sleep</u>. (Bache and Davidsen-Nielsen 1997: 315)

Having looked at some of the most important mechanisms for looking back and ahead relative to the narrative zero-point of the storyline in both present-tense and past-tense narration, we shall now briefly examine some of the peculiarities of the ±progressive distinction in these two realisations of the narrative mode. As argued in this section, the narrative mode of communication involves the 'mental presence' of the Addressee and a focus on the sequential relationship between processes rather than on the temporal orientation of each process relative to the moment of communication. This difference is cognitively significant. In the ordinary deictic mode of communicative interaction, the past tense will instruct the listener or Addressee to tag on to the world-before-now. When one views a past dynamic process from a present vantage point, one views it holistically, in its totality, unless otherwise instructed. However, when one is 'mentally present' at the 'occurrence' of a dynamic process, following the development of a storyline, the focus is much more neutral. There is in fact some emphasis on the ingression of the process (i.e. the initial stage) and there is room for elaboration of what happens in connection with the process. We get an impression of this difference by comparing once again the two modes of communication:

(26) 'I climbed the steep dune yesterday, now it's your turn.' (Bache and Davidsen-Nielsen 1997: 314, see also Bache 1985: 289 and Bache 1986)

(27) He climbed the steep dune before him hurriedly, not taking the time to remove his shoes and socks. His panting under the effort of running uphill seemed delicious to him; it was the taste of his renewed youth. (UMM 10)

In example (26) the past tense form *climbed* is used deictically to express a mentally and temporally distant, past process and it is obviously thought of in its totality, as a complete whole. By contrast, *climbed* in example (27) expresses a new process at the point reached in the storyline and the Addressee 'mentally witnesses' the climbing. Note that in its narrative context *climbed* could be replaced by the explicitly ingressive construction *began to climb* with little difference in meaning, and the author takes time to elaborate on the climbing: the description of the character not taking his time to remove shoes and socks, of his panting while climbing and of how he experiences the process serves to enrich the Addressee's mental experience and re-creation of what happens at this point in the storyline. In terms of aspectual value, I would like to suggest that *climbed* in (26) in addition to being past and telic is perfective whereas *climbed* in (27) in addition to being −TEMPORAL and telic is −ASPECTUAL (both perfectivity and non-aspectuality being possible meanings of the unmarked nonprogressive form). I would further like to suggest that it is the constellation of the features perfective and past that often complicates the 'transposition' of such constructions into the present tense in the deictic everyday mode of communicative interaction (as in e.g. *He climbed the steep dune* → **He climbs the steep dune*). As argued in Section 4.4.5 above, such transposition is only possible when the past tense construction is −ACTIONAL (thus blocking a perfective interpretation), as in *She knew the truth about him* → *She knows* *the truth about him*, or if a shift into the narrative mode of communication is accepted, as in e.g.:

> (28) 'Yesterday we all went to the beach. We had only just parked the car and got our boogie boards out when Jack <u>rushes</u> ahead of us and <u>climbs</u> this steep dune.

As noted in Bache (1986: 91ff) and Bache and Davidsen-Nielsen (1997: 314ff), the loss of temporal deixis and sometimes of positive perfective aspectual meaning in the narrative mode has important repercussions for the distinction between progressive and nonprogressive forms in English. More specifically we can say that the incompatibility relation:

> present ⇓ perfectivity

and its corresponding co-selection rule:

> present >> imperfective / –ASPECTUALITY

do not apply to the narrative mode of communication, simply because there is no present temporality in this mode. Thus, as we have established, in the deictic everyday mode of communicative interaction, we cannot use the present nonprogressive form to refer to a {present, +ACTIONAL} process but must use the present progressive:

> (29a) *'She can't come to the phone right now; she <u>showers</u>.'

> (29b) 'She can't come to the phone right now; she <u>is showering</u>.'

> (30a) *'Kathy is on duty this afternoon, and very busy until 3 p.m., I'm afraid; at this very moment she <u>drives</u> the Auditor General back to his hotel in South Kensington after lunch with the Treasurer.'

> (30b) 'Kathy is on duty this afternoon, and very busy until 3 p.m., I'm afraid; at this very moment she <u>is driving</u> the Auditor General back to his hotel in South Kensington after lunch with the Treasurer.'

However, in the narrative mode such clauses are completely unproblematical with the present nonprogressive:

> (31) She puts the book away and goes upstairs. In the bathroom she undresses as quickly as she can and then <u>showers</u> as slowly as she is able, letting the warmth settle into her. (HC 128)

> (32) She turns the radio down low, wraps two pies in a paper bag, takes them out with her to the car, and eats them as she <u>drives</u>, east to Westminster and onwards. (HC 208)

Outside the narrative mode, these constructions are only possible when interpreted as –ACTIONAL, e.g. as habitual:

(33) She <u>always showers</u> between construction site visits.

(34) She usually <u>drives</u> the Auditor General directly back to South Kensington after meetings in Soho.

This concludes my examination of some of the major differences between the two major modes of communication with respect to tense usage. Let me sum up the last part of the discussion by adding a few points to our list of characteristics of the narrative mode:

(k) For orientation of processes which do not coincide with the zero point of present-tense narration, the present future is used to instruct the Addressee to look ahead to a later point or stage in the storyline and the present perfect is used to instruct the Addressee to look back to a earlier point or stage in the storyline. The present perfect is here in competition with the simple past (which is often used in projection or to refer to processes located at specific 'past' points or in contrast to the narrative zero-point) and even to the past perfect (which explicitly instructs the Addressee to envisage a previous process as preceding another previous process).

(l) For orientation of processes which do not coincide with the zero point of past-tense narration, the past future is used to instruct the Addressee to look ahead in the storyline, and the past perfect is used to instruct the Addressee to look back. The past perfect is here in competition with the past, which however is used to look back only when the context supports such an interpretation (and thus prevents the Addressee from associating it with the zero-point of the storyline, which is of course more generally carried forward by the past).

(m) In past-tense narration the simple past is aspectually neutral rather than perfective, even when expressing +ACTIONAL processes. Instead of inviting the Addressee to view the process holistically, with an external focus, the simple past often has an association of ingression, i.e. of the process coming about at this point of the storyline, and it is compatible with situation-internal elaboration and detail.

(n) In the narrative mode of communication the simple present tense may be used regularly and unproblematically to express single

+ACTIONAL (including telic) processes because it here lacks temporal deixis and positive perfective meaning, and this obviously affects the distinction between progressive and nonprogressive forms; the choice relations involved in this part of the core tense system is thus sensitive to mode of communication too.

As already indicated, this presentation of the use of tense forms in the narrative mode of communication is not intended to provide a complete picture. Rather it serves to indicate that although it is possible to define the inventory of the core tense system and its realisations in a reasonably coherent manner so that each tense receives a distinct functional characterisation, the system is affected by higher-level communicative considerations. Projection and stipulation of conditions are two such special considerations and the narrative mode of communication is yet another. But there are others, some of which are closely related to specific genres (such as sports commentaries, headlines, performative utterances, etc.). All these functional considerations affect the choice relations between the formal members of the core tense system. Occasionally we may even get the sense that basic functional properties of the tenses are neutralised or fundamentally changed when subordinated to a special use. This, however, should not be considered damaging to the more genuinely functionalist approach to the core system proposed here, but rather as a challenge worthy of serious attention in a systemic functional framework. The kind of questions raised are precisely the kind of questions that can only be answered if you are prepared to adopt a both textually and contextually sensitive approach to the relevant data.

Notes

1. These phenomena are thoroughly described in the literature. One particularly interesting approach to conditional sentences is provided by Fauconnier (1994, 1997), who operates with mental spaces and treats conditional markers as space builders. His analysis could easily be extended to include also projection and, as we shall see, narration. For an interesting unified approach to tense within mental space theory, see Cutrer (1994).
2. Regarding the use of tense forms in dialogues in narration, such as the past tense form *survived* in the last line of the Fowles novel, see my discussion of example (12) below.

7 Conclusion

Halliday's Systemic Functional Grammar offers a very sound and attractive approach to language. It takes grammar seriously in a narrow sense but at the same time insists on viewing the systems of language in a much broader semantic, textual and social-semiotic framework. It brings grammar into direct contact with usage, discourse and pragmatics more generally (by associating grammatical systems with metafunctions and register variables, genre and eventually ideology). Along with Simon Dik's functional grammar (cf. e.g. Dik 1997a and 1997b), it is one of the few reasonably elaborate and comprehensive functional models available today. But what I especially like about SFL, and more specifically, *IFG* is its emphasis on paradigmatic relations, i.e. its description of language in terms of systems – a descriptive orientation which has been much neglected in both formal and functional theories, not least because of its obvious limitations in a narrow structuralist Saussurean context (see Bache 2002). Another advantage for which Halliday and his many followers deserve credit, especially in a pedagogical context, is the fact that SFL is not 'just' a theory but a practical way of working with language (and other modalities). Pupils and students can immediately put it to good use and scholars in all sorts of fields can find inspiration in the all-embracing SFL approach to expression. In short: SFL is worth taking seriously and it is certainly worth repairing and consolidating if one should occasionally encounter weaknesses, faulty arguments or mistakes. It is important constantly to ensure that the model not only specifies the meaning potential of language but also reflects actual usage and that it provides the best possible descriptions of usage from a functional perspective. Halliday's emphasis on application is very clearly expressed in the following quote:[1]

> the value of a theory lies in the use that can be made of it, and I have always considered a theory of language to be essentially consumer-oriented. In many instances, the theorist is himself also and at the same time a consumer, designing a theory for application to this own task. (Hallliday 1985b: 7)

Personally I must admit that I favour knowledge-orientation over 'consumer-orientation', or rather, a more even balance between knowledge-orientation and 'consumer-orientation'. However, even if you go along with Halliday here and consider application to be the ultimate goal of theorising, then one should think that at least you want to make sure that what you apply is the best possible theory. In the long run, application can only be successful if there is a basic concern for high quality. It is therefore perhaps slightly worrying when Halliday says:[2]

> A feature of systemic work is that it has tended to expand by moving into new spheres of activity, rather than reworking earlier positions. This reflects an ideological perspective in which language is seen not as unique or sui generis but as one aspect of the evolution of humans as sociocultural beings. (Halliday 1994b: 4507)

I for one fail to see a conflict between viewing language as an aspect of the evolution of humans as sociocultural beings and a concern for getting the fundamentals of one's description in the best possible shape by constantly reworking earlier positions and tuning the model according to both data and new findings in linguistics (inside as well as outside SFL). To pay attention to the former *at the expense* of the latter does not strike me as a sound ideological perspective at all. On the contrary, to ensure the best possible description of the evolution of humans as sociocultural beings we must continually strive to operate with the best theoretical and analytical apparatus. It is in this spirit that I have offered my suggestions for a more thorough revision of the *IFG* description of tense in English. From the very beginning I was bothered by the basic design of the *IFG* tense category in terms of a simple tripartite system generating a large number of tenses by means of recursion. This design strikes me as very similar to early transformational models with a too powerful generative component and a number of largely ad hoc constraints or filters (corresponding to Halliday's stop rules) – models long since abandoned, and with good reason. Another thing that really puzzled me was the large number of tense forms which I had never come across before, and which the native speakers I consulted found strange, unnatural or contrived. It was as if Halliday's category was designed more with a view to describing a very broad meaning potential to be realised by a very broad potential range of tense forms than with a view to capturing the essentials of actual tense usage. A final problem, in my view, was that although *IFG* grants paradigmatic relations a central place in SFL, in fact gives them a certain priority over syntax, the tense description seemed to be aimed more at devising a technical model for the derivation of an inventory of tense forms than at determining the exact nature of the choice relations involved as they present themselves to the Performer. There was too little focus on what motivates the Performer to select a given tense form in a particular context. To me, the *IFG* description of the English tense category simply lacked some of the attractiveness which characterises SFL more generally. In other words, I found that the *IFG* tense model needed functional tuning, both observationally, descriptively and explanatorily.

A closer examination in Chapter 3 of the mechanism of recursion confirmed my suspicion that to describe tense in English in terms of a basic tripartite system from which the Performer can choose recursively is problematic in a functional linguistic model. At any given point, the Performer's selection from a system will be based on previous choices (past systemic history), both in an immediate constructional sense and in a larger contextual sense. At the same time, any choice will to some extent anticipate and limit the range of possible subsequent choices. The communicative motivation for choosing the same value twice in a recursive process for the realisation of a complex expression (or a particular value at different points in the recursive process for the construction of different expressions) can therefore never be exactly the same. While this observation may have general validity, my concern was of course specifically for the tense system, and here I found that the values of the basic tripartite system simply do not remain constant in recursion. In one instance particularly, the difference is quite substantial: Halliday's primary present and his secondary present are virtually complementary with respect to experiential meaning. While the primary present is typically associated with non-actional processes and often incompatible with actional processes, the secondary present is typically associated with actional processes and is often incompatible with non-actional processes. This difference obviously affects choice relations. Moreover, I found the precise ordering of choices in recursion unclear (in both Halliday's general presentation and Matthiessen's more technical exposition).

A complex tense form does not seem to be the result of the Performer choosing once from the system (primary tense) and then considering the option of choosing again. On the contrary, there is a sense in which the Performer must choose (or at least prepare to choose) a secondary tense before entering the first recursive cycle, if only because the communicative effect of the first choice depends on whether it is the only choice or it is followed by subsequent choices. However, an even more serious problem is that the recursive system sets up unnatural immediate choice relations: in the *IFG* model, constructions like *had taken* (past in past), *was taking* (present in past) and *was going to take* (future in past) are presented as immediately choice-related (because they all realisations of values from two cycles in the recursive process and share the same primary choice, viz. past). These three constructions will in fact rarely, if ever, compete in a communicative context, but are communicatively much more closely related to other forms (for example, both *had taken* and *was taking* are much more closely related to *took* than to each other or to *was going to take*). By viewing the formal markers involved in the tense category as realisations of values from a single system with a recursive choice potential, the *IFG* model pays far too little attention to the their individual functional characteristics. The primary past –*ed* suffix and the secondary past HAVE + past participle are simply not functionally identical, and nor are the primary present Ø (or –*s*) suffix and the secondary present BE + present participle. The Performer's motivation for choosing the values realising these markers cannot be captured precisely enough by conflating them in a recursive process. To sum up, the descriptive adequacy of the *IFG* category of tense in English is highly questionable: there is too little in the way of insight into the functional nature of the tense markers, i.e. the nature of the values realising them, to justify what is essentially a too strong recursive component constrained by ad hoc stop rules.

The next step in my evaluation of the *IFG* approach to tense in English was to try to determine if the model was *observationally* adequate, i.e. if the 36 members in Halliday's System I were all regularly used tense forms. To that end, I decided to test their frequency in the British National Corpus and Collins Wordbanks*Online*, which when put together contain a total of 157,000,000 words, including a substantial 25,000,000-word subcorpus of spoken English). The result was even more disappointing than I had anticipated: 16 tenses appear to be non-existent in the two corpora, seven are very infrequent (with less than 250 hits, in some cases less than a handful), and only 13 are frequent (with thousands of examples). Naturally the lack or scarcity of certain forms in the two corpora should not be taken as proof that they do not, or could not, exist more generally, if only as a meaning potential to be realised in very special contexts. Nevertheless, the unavoidable conclusion of my investigation is that Halliday's tense model is far too powerful (even when constrained by stop rules) and that it is not observationally adequate in a *functional linguistic* sense (i.e. it does not adequately reflect actual usage). There is little evidence that after the first choice the Performer simply chooses 'again, and again and again' from the basic system (cf. Halliday 1976c: 147f; Matthiessen 1996: 438f). Interestingly enough, however, Halliday and Matthiessen's approach could be said to have a reasonable degree of observational adequacy in a *formal linguistic* sense: it defines a *potential* range of tenses irrespective of usage. In a functional grammar, however, it is important to strike a balance between sorting out the meaning potential of a category and reflecting actual usage.

Two other problems presented themselves in my empirical investigation, both concerning the expression of future meaning. The first problem was Halliday's secondary future BE *going to* + infinitive. Being a marker in 24 of the 36 tense forms in System I, it is in fact the second most important building block in the *IFG* tense model. But since it is included in all the non-existent and infrequent tenses (except one) and at the same time absent from all the frequent ones (except two), it is something of a liability to the model from the point of view of observational adequacy. The second problem was that *would* + infinitive is completely excluded from the *IFG* model. One good argument for including this construction as a past future form of Halliday's primary future *will* + infinitive is that it is a neutrally projected form of this primary future. That in itself qualifies it for membership of Halliday's System II (which comprises neutrally projected tense forms) and therefore, by definition, also System I (because System II is defined as a subset of System I). But there are also other reasons for including it in the core system. As a core tense it enables us to account not only for tense usage in projection as a *tense-internal mechanism* of 'backshifting', but also for tense usage in conditional sentences, again as a *tense-internal mechanism*, this time involving a kind of 'forward-shifting'. Both types of operation involve a range of tense forms but modify or neutralise their 'normal' functional content. Another, even more compelling reason to include *would* + infinitive in the core system is that in certain genres (such as narration and historical accounts) it is used to express aheadness in relation to a past time or the stage reached in a narrative storyline and thus forms part of a system of orientation with other tense forms. Although it is not a particularly frequent tense form, it is certainly there if you look for it in the right kind of context, and surely its temporal use must be accounted for.

On the basis of my critical review of *IFG's* recursive model of tense in English and of my search for Halliday's tenses in the BNC and CWO, I decided that a proposal for a revised SFL approach to tense in English must aim for a higher degree of overall adequacy: it must comply more clearly with genuinely functional linguistic standards and it must fare better in the kind of empirical investigation that I subjected the SFL model to (i.e. it must reflect actual usage more precisely). At the same time, it must of course be at least as compatible with the general SFL framework as the present models (preferably more compatible), for otherwise it would not qualify as a revision. One aspect of this last point is that a proposal should strive to take choice relations seriously: choice relations must be defined more precisely, and the Performer's communicative motivation for choosing a given tense form out of a number of options in a given context must be given closer attention. As a basis for the general functional tuning of the SFL model I chose the Cardiff school approach to tense (which offers a recursion-free description of tense and focuses more precisely on the functional nature of the individual tense markers) and Harder's instructional semantics (which offers an elegant, if too limited, functional description of the seriality of tense). In order to ensure an even stronger emphasis on choice relations I decided to formulate a number of principles of category description on the basis of my own research on verbal categories. These principles define the relevant parts of the metalanguage (and indeed, the role of this metalanguage in the description of the tense category), and thus enable us to set up categories for the description of paradigmatic relations. Verb forms are shown to be non-monadic, requiring description in terms of more than one functional category. To capture the complex, multifunctional nature of grammatical markers, the metalanguage operates with two related levels of description: the definition level (on which we find pure distinctions on the basis of minimal formal pairs) and the function level (on which such pure distinctions from different functional domains interact and merge in a 'categorial interplay' to form more complex meanings).

The result of the rather ambitious exercise of applying all these sources of inspiration to the task at hand was a proposal for a new SFL model of tense.[3] Like the *IFG* model, this model views tense as a logical resource for construing our experience of time, and formally complex tenses are defined in terms of serial time, where each additional value selected is seen in relation to the previous selection rather than in relation to a fixed point (such as the present moment of communication). The seriality of the new model is ensured by Harder's dynamic interaction of base times and function times (which not only represents an improvement of the old system of event time and reference time but also changes the focus of the model from traditional semantic representation to genuine functional construal), and tense is still viewed as a *compositional paradigm* rather than just a classical constructional one.

I suggest that the new core system should consist of four ordered choices where each choice has scope over subsequent choices (past/nonpast > future/nonfuture > perfect/nonperfect > progressive/nonprogressive). This system realises 16 core tenses. Each tense should be viewed as non-monadic, requiring description in terms of more than just one semantic or functional domain if choice relations are to be described adequately and exhaustively. The tenses realised by the core system are therefore to be thought of not just as tenses but also as realisations (members) of other categories, such as aspect, action and modality. To appropriately describe the choice relations that each form is a result of, it is necessary to sort out its expression of definition level meanings (the basic meanings of each category) and function level meanings (meanings arising from the categorial interplay). One important consequence of viewing tenses as non-monadic is that it is no longer possible to describe the structure of verbal expressions as simply univariate (i.e. a structure which exhibits the recurrence of the same fundamental function and a building up of a set of interdependent relations of the same kind): verbal expressions have both univariate and multivariate characteristics (where the elements carry both similar and distinct functions). In metafunctional terms, this means that the core tense system is not just a logical resource but also an experiential one (involving actional meanings), an interpersonal one (involving deixis) and a textual one (involving aspectual meanings). My claim is that these meanings not only characterise the individual tenses but often enter a dynamic categorial interplay, and that this fundamentally affects choice relations above and beyond the basic logical characteristics of the tense system.

As demonstrated also by the Cardiff grammarians, one advantage of not working with recursion as the governing principle of the tense category is that more attention can be paid to the individual characteristics of the four formal oppositions, or choices. Thus, while the old recursive *IFG* model naturally emphasised the similarities between primary and secondary tenses (i.e. between primary past and secondary past, between primary present and secondary present, and between primary future and secondary future), and sought to fit all the tenses into a univariate scheme, I suggest that the new SFL model should recognise the individual character of each tense and its choice relations and accept a combination of univariate and multivariate characteristics. Such a model can thus go much further in its description of the real choice relations involved in the tense category.

One major difference between the *IFG* model and the suggested alternative, as I envisage it, is that BE *going to* + infinitive is no longer recognised as a core tense but as an important supplementary one (along with a number of other periphrastic forms, such as BE *to* + infinitive, BE *about to* + infinitive and BE *on the point of* + present participle). Its exclusion is justified on both semantic and distributional grounds, and without this form, the core system gains considerable observational and descriptive adequacy. However, BE *going to* + infinitive must still receive adequate treatment in our overall tense description. Instead of regarding it as a recursively generated secondary tense, as in the *IFG* model, I propose to view its meaning and usage potential in terms of the possible combinations of the two variable parts making up this form: BE and the infinitive. More specifically, I argue that BE *going to* + infinitive is to be characterised in terms of the variability of BE in relation to the choices of the new SFL core tense system (except ±progressive, which is already chosen for BE *going*) and the variability of the infinitive in relation to those choices of the system that are relevant to nonfinite forms (±perfect and ±progressive), and which define a set of infinitives with a more general distribution. The result is a much simpler and more comprehensive description of the potential specific realisations of BE *going to* + infinitive which we get 'for free' in our new tense model. Instead of recursion, the two grammatically variable components of the form (BE and the infinitive) select separately from the core system.

In addition to a detailed description of both the univariate and multivariate characteristics of the core system, I finally discuss a number of special communicative functions which override the normal instructional-semantic content of the tenses. These special functions include projection of speech and thought, stipulation of conditions, and narration. One advantage of the new SFL tense model is that it offers a simpler and more adequate *category-internal* description of tense usage in both projected and conditional clauses and that it easily lends itself to a description of the use of tense in narration. In this mode of communication, the primary deictic distinction between past and nonpast is neutralised and this affects the instructional-semantic content of the whole system as well as markedness relations. In particular, the distinction between progressive and nonprogressive forms is changed in the present tense. The present nonprogressive form is much more compatible with +ACTIONAL processes in the narrative mode than in the ordinary real-time, deictic mode of communication. What my analysis of narration shows is that the new model copes with a broader range of textual functions and that it is generally more sensitive to choice relations.

Notes

1. I was reminded of this and the following quote by reading Harder's critical assessment of Systemic Functional Linguistics (Harder 2005: 32). While Harder ends up being fairly dismissive of SFL, I still believe in improving the model. Halliday's criterion on applicatibilty is also mentioned and critically commented on by Butler (2003a: 157; 2003b: 473–475).
2. Like me, Butler (2003a: 2002–2004) and Fawcett (2000a: 45) are very critical of Halliday's position on moving on rather than reworking theoretical issues.
3. By saying 'a proposal for a new SFL model of tense', I do not mean to imply that I have provided a fully formalised and computer-implemented model but rather that I have suggested a set of ideas and principles for such a model.

References

Aston, G. and Burnard, L. (1998) *The BNC Handbook: Exploring the British National Corpus with SARA*, Edinburgh: Edinburgh University Press.

Bache, C. (1982) Aspect and aktionsart: towards a semantic distinction. *Journal of Linguistics* 18: 57–72.

Bache, C. (1985) *Verbal Aspect: A General Theory and its Application to Present-Day English*. Odense: Odense University Press.

Bache, C. (1986) Tense and aspect in fiction. *Journal of Literary Semantics* 15: 82–97.

Bache, C. (1994) Verbal categories, form-meaning relationships and the perfect. In C. Bache, H. Basbøll and C. E. Lindberg (eds) *Tense, Aspect and Action: Empirical and Theoretical Contributions to Language Typology* 43–60. Berlin and New York: Mouton de Gruyter.

Bache, C. (1997) *The Study of Aspect, Tense and Action: Towards a Theory of the Semantics of Grammatical Categories*, 2nd revised edition. Frankfurt am Main, Berlin, Bern, New York, Paris and Vienna: Peter Lang.

Bache, C. (2000) *Essentials of Mastering English. A Concise Grammar*. Berlin and New York: Mouton de Gruyter.

Bache, C. (2002) On categories in linguistics. *Acta Linguistica Hafniensia* 34: 71–105.

Bache, C. (2007) *Would* as a tense marker in English. In M. H. Andersen, J. N. Jensen, M. Rathje and J. Schack (eds) *Ved Lejlighed: Festskrift til Niels Davidsen-Nielsen i anledning af 70-års-dagen. Dansk Sprognævns Skrifter 39*. 15–29. Copenhagen: Dansk Sprognævn

Bache, C. and Davidsen-Nielsen, N. (1997) *Mastering English Grammar*. Berlin and New York: Mouton de Gruyter.

Butler, C. S. (2003a) *Structure and Function: A guide to three major structural-functional theories. Part 1: Approaches to the simplex clause*. Amsterdam and Philadelphia: John Benjamins.

Butler, C. S. (2003b) *Structure and Function: A guide to three major structural-functional theories. Part 2: From clause to discourse and beyond*. Amsterdam and Philadelphia: John Benjamins.

Bybee, J. L., Perkins, R. and Pagliuca, W. (1994) *The Evolution of Grammar: Tense, Aspect, and Modality in the Languages of the World*. Chicago and London: University of Chicago Press.

Caffarel, A. (1992) Interacting between a generalized tense semantics and register-specific semantic tense systems: a bi-stratal exploration of the semantics of French tense. *Language Sciences* 14(4): 385–418.

Chomsky, N. (1957) *Syntactic Structures*. The Hague: Mouton.

Chomsky, N. (1965) *Aspects of the Theory of Syntax*. Cambridge, MA: MIT Press.

Chomsky, N. (1968) *Language and Mind*. New York: Harcourt, Brace and World.

Chomsky, N. (1986) *Knowledge of Language: Its Nature, Origin and Use*. New York: Praeger.

Comrie, B. (1976) *Aspect*. Cambridge: Cambridge University Press.

Comrie, B. (1985) *Tense*. Cambridge: Cambridge University Press.

Cutrer, L. M. (1994) Time and Tense in Narrative and in Everyday Language. Ph.D. Dissertation, University of California, San Diego, CA.

Davidsen-Nielsen, N. (1985) Has English a future. *Acta Linguistica Hafniensia* 21: 5–20.

Davidsen-Nielsen, N. (1990) *Tense and Mood in English: A Comparison with Danish*. Berlin and New York: Mouton de Gruyter.

Dik, S. (1997a) *The Theory of Functional Grammar. Part 1: The Structure of the Clause*. 2nd revised edition, (ed.) K. Hengeveld. Berlin and New York: Mouton de Gruyter.

Dik, S. (1997b) *The Theory of Functional Grammar. Part 2: Complex and Derived Constructions*. 2nd revised edition, (ed.) K. Hengeveld. Berlin and New York: Mouton de Gruyter.

Fauconnier, G. (1994) *Mental Spaces*. Cambridge: Cambridge University Press.

Fauconnier, G. (1997) *Mappings in Thought and Language*. Cambridge: Cambridge University Press.

Fawcett, R. P. (2000a) *A Theory of Syntax for Systemic Functional Linguistics*. Current Issues in Linguistic Theory 206. Amsterdam: John Benjamins.

Fawcett, R. P. (2000b) In place of Halliday's 'verbal group', Part 1: Evidence from the problems of Halliday's representations and the relative simplicity of the proposed alternative. *Word* 51.2: 157–203.

Fawcett, R. P. (2000c) In place of Halliday's 'verbal group', Part 2: Evidence from generation, semantics and interruptability. *Word* 51.3: 327–375.

Fawcett, R. P. (2004) *The GENESYS Lexicogrammar Version 5.4 (mini-grammar version) / GENESYS Version 5.5: The Clause (except Transitivity) + Transitivity*. Available through the Computational Linguistics Unit, Cardiff University.

Fawcett, R. P. (2008) *Invitation to Systemic Functional Linguistics through the Cardiff Grammar: an Extension and Simplification of Halliday's Systemic Functional Grammar*. London: Equinox.

Fawcett, R. P. (forthcoming) *The Functional Syntax Handbook: Analyzing English at the Level of Form*. London: Equinox.

Fawcett, R. P. (n.d.) From time concepts to time forms: towards an algorithm for generating time in a computer implementation of English, unpublished paper.

Fawcett, R. P., Tucker, G. H. and Lin, Yuen Q. (1993) How a systemic functional grammar works: the role of realization in realization. In H. Horacek and M. Zock (eds) *New Concepts in Natural Language Generation* 114–186. London: Pinter.

Forsyth, J. (1970) *A Grammar of Aspect: Usage and Meaning in the Russian Verb.* Cambridge: Cambridge University Press.

Halliday, M. A. K. (1976a) Chain and choice in language. In G. R. Kress (ed.) *System and Function in Language* 84–87. London: Oxford University Press.

Halliday, M. A. K. (1976b) Deep grammar: system as semantic choice. In G. R. Kress (ed.) *System and Function in Language* 88–98, London: Oxford University Press.

Halliday, M. A. K. (1976c) The English verbal group. In G. R. Kress (ed.) *System and Function in Language* 136–158. London: Oxford University Press.

Halliday, M. A. K. (1985a) *Introduction to Functional Grammar.* London: Edward Arnold.

Halliday, M. A. K. (1985b) Systemic background. In J. D. Benson and W. S. Greaves (eds) *Systemic Perspectives on Discourse, Volume 1: Selected Theoretical Papers from the 9th International Systemic Workshop (Advances in Discourse Processes Vol. XV)* 1–15. Norwood: N. J. Ablex Publishing Corporation.

Halliday, M. A. K. (1994a) *An Introduction to Functional Grammar*, 2nd edition. London, New York, Sydney and Auckland: Edward Arnold.

Halliday, M. A. K. (1994b) Systemic theory. In R. E. Asher and J. M. Y. Simpson (eds). *The Encyclopedia of Language and Linguistics* 4505–4508. Oxford: Pergamon Press.

Halliday, M. A. K. (2004) The spoken language corpus: a foundation for grammatical theory. In K. Aijmer and B. Altenberg (eds) *Advances in Corpus Linguistics. Papers from the 23rd International Conference on English Language Research on Computerized Corpora (ICAME 23)* 11–38. Amsterdam and New York: Rodopi.

Halliday, M. A. K. and James, Z. L. (1993) A quantitative study of polarity and primary tense in the English finite clause. In J. M. Sinclair, M. Hoey and G. Fox (eds) *Techniques of Description: Spoken and Written Discourse, A Festschrift for Malcolm Coulthard*, 32–66. London and New York: Routledge.

Halliday, M. A. K. and Matthiessen, C. M. I. M. (2004) *An Introduction to Functional Grammar*, 3rd edition. London, New York, Sydney and Auckland: Edward Arnold.

Harder, P. (1996) *Functional Semantics. A Theory of Meaning, Structure and Tense in English.* Berlin and New York: Mouton de Gruyter.

Harder, P. (2005) Dansk funktionel lingvistik: en introduktion. *Dansk Funktionel Lingvistik* 1–38. Copenhagen: The University of Copenhagen.

Huddleston, R. (1976) *An Introduction to English Transformational Syntax.* London: Longman.

Huddleston, R. D. and Pullum, G. K. (2002) *The Cambridge Grammar of the English Language.* Cambridge: Cambridge University Press.

Jakobson, R. (1932) Zur structur des russischen verbums. *Charisteria Guilelmo Mathesio Quinquagenario,* 74–83.

Jespersen, O. (1929) *The Philosophy of Grammar.* London: Allen and Unwin.

Kirsner, R. and Thompson, S. (1976) The role of inference in semantics: a study of sensory verb complements in English. *Glossa* 10: 200–240.

Matthiessen, C. M. I. M. (1983) Choosing primary tense in English. *Studies in Language* 7(3): 369–429.

Matthiessen, C. M. I. M. (1984) *Choosing Tense in English,* Information Sciences Institute Research Report, ISI/RR-84-143, University of Southern California.

Matthiessen, C. M. I. M. (1991) Resources in English for organizing and expressing time, unpublished manuscript. Department of Linguistics, University of Sydney.

Matthiessen, C. M. I. M. (1996) Tense in English seen through systemic-functional theory. In M. Berry, C. Butler, R. Fawcett and Guowen Huang (eds) *Meaning and Form: Systemic Functional Interpretations III,* 431–497. Norwood, NJ: Ablex Publishing Corporation.

Radford, A. (1981) *Transformational Syntax.* Cambridge: Cambridge University Press.

Reichenbach, H. (1947) *Elements of Symbolic Logic.* London: Macmillan.

List of the sources of the examples

The main empirical investigation was carried out on the basis of:

BNC   The British National Corpus (100,000,000 words)
SWO   Collins Wordbanks*Online* (57,000,000 words)

For further illustration, examples were used from the following sources:

Transcriptions of spoken language

BBCI   BBC Transcription Service: 'I was there': The Boxer Rebellion (interview with Mr Cousins) and The Sinking of the Titanic (interview with Mr Prentice).
BBCY   BBC Transcription Service: 'Your Every Day Drugs' (1. Tea and Coffee; 2. Another Little Drink).

Other sources

ALJ   Kingsley Amis, *Lucky Jim* (Penguin 14 00 1648 1).
BAD   Dan Brown, *Angels and Demons* (Corgi Books 0 552 15073 8).
BDP   Dan Brown, *Deception Point* (Pocket Books 0-671-02738-7).
BHM   Malcolm Bradbury, *The History Man* (Arrow 0 09 914910 9).
BSHE   Bill Bryson, *A Short History of Nearly Everything* (Black Swan 0 552 99704 8).
DSB   Margaret Drabble, *A Summer Bird-Cage* (Penguin 0 14 00.2634 7).
FET   John Fowles, *The Ebony Tower* (Signet 451-J6733).

FFLW   John Fowles, *The French Lieutenant's Woman* (Triad/Panther 568
         03403 X).
HC   Tobias Hill, *The Cryptographer* (Faber and Faber 0-571-21837-7).
IWOY   John Irving, *A Widow for One Year* (Ballatine Books 0-345-43479-X).
LMTW   Doris Lessing, *A Man and Two Women* (Panther 0 586 02552 9).
NEWS   Newsweek, 22 September 1980.
SCP   C. P. Snow, *Corridors of Power* (Penguin 0 14 00.2506 5).
SMD   John Steinbeck, *The Moon is Down* (Pan 0330 01188X).
SSR   C. P. Snow, *The Sleep of Reason* (Macmillan)
UMM   John Updike, *Marry Me* (Penguin 0 14 00.4643 7).
WSHP   Ronald Wright, *A Short History of Progress* (The Text Publishing
         Company 1 920885 79 X).

Appendix

Empirical investigation of the SFL tense system in BNC

1. **past : e.g. *took***
   query [*took*]: 37,218 hits

2. **present: e.g. *takes***
   query [*takes*]: 11,666 hits

3. **future: e.g. *will take***
   query [*will take*]: 3,379 hits

4. **past in past: e.g. *had taken***
   query [*had taken*]: 3,736 hits

5. **past in present: e.g. *has taken***
   query [*has taken*]: 1,956 hits

6. **past in future: e.g. *will have taken***
   query [*will have taken*]: 31 hits
   Supplementary queries. General [*will have*] query: 11,137 hits.
   The first 12 constructions with *will have* + past participle in random sets of 100 hits contained: *joined, been, become, changed, found, spent, learnt, forgotten, committed, shifted, hinged, survived.* Additional queries with the following frequent verbs: *done, made, had.*
   query [*will have joined*]: 2 hits
   query [*will have been*]: 637 hits (NB often passive constructions)
   query [*will have become*]: 35 hits
   query [*will have changed*]: 26 hits
   query [*will have found*]: 18 hits
   query [*will have spent*]: 15 hits
   query [*will have learnt*]: 10 hits
   query [*will have forgotten*]: 7 hits

query [*will have committed*]: 5 hits
query [*will have shifted*]: 4 hits
query [*will have hinged*]: 1 hit
query [*will have survived*]: 1 hit
query [*will have done*]: 45 hits
query [*will have made*]: 30 hits
query [*will have had*]: 78 hits
total: 914 hits
Total number of hits in 16 queries: 945 hits

7. **present in past: e.g. *was taking***
    query [*was taking*]: 951 hits (NB but this includes a few examples
    of the following kind: *It was taking a risk, when she thought about
    it, to go to the seaside in September*, in which the present participle
    is a predicator in a complement clause rather than head of the
    superordinate verbal construction).
    query [*were taking*]: 482 hits
    total: 1,443 hits

8. **present in present: e.g. *is taking***
    query [*is taking*]: 808 hits (NB: this includes a few examples of the
    following kind: *... and that is taking a hell of a risk*, in which the
    present participle is a predicator in a complement clause rather
    than head of the superordinate verbal construction).
    query [*are taking*]: 704 hits
    query [*am taking*]: 47 hits
    Total: 1,559 hits

9. **present in future: e.g. *will be taking***
    query [*will be taking*]: 143 hits
    Supplementary queries. General [*will be*] query: 69,734 hits. The
    first 12 constructions with *will be* + present participle *of any verb*
    in random sets of 100 hits contained: *implementing, running, help-
    ing, holding, climbing, hoping, thinking, launching, discussing, act-
    ing, receiving, arriving*. Additional queries with *doing, making,
    having*.
    query [*will be implementing*]: 2 hits
    query [*will be running*]: 56 hits
    query [*will be helping*]: 20 hits
    query [*will be holding*]: 54 hits
    query [*will be climbing*]: 2 hits
    query [*will be hoping*]: 83 hits

query [*will be thinking*]: 20 hits
query [*will be launching*]: 19 hits
query [*will be discussing*]: 32 hits
query [*will be acting*]: 10 hits
query [*will be receiving*]: 15 hits
query [*will be arriving*]: 20 hits
query [*will be doing*]: 107 hits
query [*will be making*]: 119 hits
query [*will be having*]: 31 hits
total: 590 hits
Total number of hits in 16 queries: 733

10. **future in past: e.g. *was going to take***
query [*was going to take*]: 98 hits
query [*were going to take*]: 21 hits
Supplementary queries. General [*was going to*] query: 4,515 hits.
The first 12 constructions with *was going to* + infinitive *of any verb*
in random sets of 100 hits contained: *live, save, be, catch, make,
reshuffle, have, shove, give, get, cope, restore.* Additional searches
with *do, make, happen.*
query [*was going to live*]: 20 hits
query [*was going to save*]: 8 hits
query [*was going to be*]: 903 hits (NB all sorts of subsequent constructions)
query [*was going to catch*]: 7 hits
query [*was going to make*]: 104 hits
query [*was going to reshuffle*]: 1 hit
query [*was going to have*]: 209 hits
query [*was going to shove*]: 1 hit
query [*was going to give*]: 36 hits
query [*was going to get*]: 123 hits
query [*was going to cope*]: 3 hits
query [*was going to restore*]: 2 hits
query [*was going to do*]: 191 hits
query [*was going to make*]: 104 hits
query [*was going to happen*]: 141 hits
total: 1,853 hits
Total number of hits in 17 queries: 1,972

11. **future in present: e.g. *is going to take***
query [*is going to take*]: 90 hits

query [*are going to take*]: 32 hits
query [*am going to take*]: 15 hits
Supplementary queries. General [*is going to*] query: 2,674 hits.
The first 12 constructions with *is going to* + infinitive *of any verb* in
random sets of 100 hits contained: *be, make, pack, leap-frog, take,
achieve, require, pay, cause, solve, buy, open.* Additional queries
with *do, have, happen.*
query [*is going to be*]: 947 hits (NB all sorts of subsequent
constructions)
query [*is going to make*]: 50 hits
query [*is going to pack*]: 1 hit
query [*is going to leap-frog*]: 1 hit
query [*is going to take*]: 91 hits
query [*is going to achieve*]: 2 hits
query [*is going to require*]: 2 hits
query [*is going to pay*]: 12 hits
query [*is going to cause*]: 10 hits
query [*is going to solve*]: 3 hits
query [*is going to buy*]: 11 hits
query [*is going to open*]: 4 hits
query [*is going to do*]: 62 hits
query [*is going to have*]: 108 hits
query [*is going to happen*]: 107 hits
total: 1,411 hits
Total number of hits in 18 queries: 1,548

12. **future in future: e.g. *will be going to take***
query [*will be going to take*]: no hits
query [*will be going to*] + infinitive *of any verb*: 3 hits (*help, see,
pay*)
wildcard query [*will _ be going to*] + infinitive of any verb: 2 hits
total: 5 hits

13. **past in future in past: e.g. *was going to have taken***
query [*were/was going to have taken*]: no hits
query [*were/was going to have*] + past participle *of any verb*: no hits
wildcard query [*were/was _ going to have*] + past participle *of any
verb*: no hits
non-finite query [*going to have*]: no relevant hits
total: no hits

14. **past in future in present: e.g.** *is going to have taken*
    query [*am/are/is going to have taken*]: no hits
    query [*am/are/is going to have*] + past participle *of any verb*: 1 hit
        most of them are going to have gone home for Easter
    wildcard query [*am/are/is _ going to have*] + past participle *of any verb*: no hits
    total: 1 hit

15. **past in future in future: e.g.** *will be going to have taken*
    query [*will be going to have taken*]: no hits
    query [*will be going to have*] + past participle *of any verb*: no hits
    wildcard query [*will _ be going to have*] + past participle *of any verb*: no hits
    non-finite query [*be going to have*]: no relevant hits
    total: no hits

16. **present in past in past: e.g.** *had been taking*
    query [*had been taking*]: 65 hits
    Supplementary queries. General [*had been*] query: 64,204 hits. The first 12 constructions with *had been* + present participle *of any verb* in random sets of 100 hits contained: *settling, watching, moving, meeting, painting, working, searching, practising, sitting, negotiating, meaning, singing.* Additional query with *doing, making, happening.*
    query [*had been settling*]: 2 hits
    query [*had been watching*]: 113 hits
    query [*had been moving*]: 19 hits
    query [*had been meeting*]: 4 hits
    query [*had been painting*]: 7 hits
    query [*had been working*]: 235 hits
    query [*had been searching*]: 22 hits
    query [*had been practising*]: 13 hits
    query [*had been sitting*]: 112 hits
    query [*had been negotiating*]: 9 hits
    query [*had been meaning*]: 3 hits
    query [*had been singing*]: 8 hits
    query [*had been doing*]: 135 hits
    query [*had been making*]: 68 hits
    query [*had been happening*]: 29 hits
    total: 779 hits
    Total number of hits in 16 queries: 844

17. **present in past in present: e.g. *has been taking***
    query [*has been taking*]: 54 hits
    query [*have been taking*]: 93 hits
    Supplementary queries. General [*has been*] query: 57,616 hits.
    The first 12 constructions with *has been* + present participle *of any*
    verb in random sets of 100 hits contained: *increasing, running,*
    doing, briefing, enjoying, going, arriving, practising, manufactur-
    ing, happening, turning, cashing. Additional query with *having,*
    making, trying.
    query [*has been increasing*]: 23 hits (NB only constructions with
    increasing as a verb)
    query [*has been running*]: 88 hits
    query [*has been doing*]: 68 hits
    query [*has been briefing*]: 1 hit
    query [*has been enjoying*]: 6 hits
    query [*has been going*]: 149 hits
    query [*has been arriving*]: 3 hits
    query [*has been practising*]: 8 hits
    query [*has been manufacturing*]: 3 hits
    query [*has been happening*]: 70 hits
    query [*has been turning*]: 10 hits
    query [*has been cashing*]: 1 hit
    query [*has been having*]: 41 hits
    query [*has been making*]: 58 hits
    query [*has been trying*]: 103 hits
    total: 632 hits
    Total number of hits in 16 queries: 779

18. **present in past in future: e.g. *will have been taking***
    query [*will have been taking*]: no hits
    query [*will have been*] + present participle *of any verb*: 20 hits
          Some readers will have been growing roses for years
    wildcard query [*will_ have been*] + present participle *of any verb*: 6
    hits
    total: 26 hits

19. **present in future in past: e.g. *was going to be taking***
    query [*was/were going to be taking*]: no hits
    query [*was/were going to be*] + present participle *of any verb*: 33 hits
          Someone said he was going to be doing engineering
          She never did tell people what they were going to be doing.

wildcard query [*was/were_ going to be*] + present participle *of any verb*: 10 hits
total: 43 hits

20.   **present in future in present: e.g.** *is going to be taking*
query [*am/are/is going to be taking*]: 4 hits
query [*am/are/is going to be*] + present participle *of any other verb*: 63 hits
> *I don't think he is going to be stepping back from the front line*
> *We are going to be seeing a great deal of him*
wildcard query [*am/are/is _ going to be*] + present participle *of any verb*: 20 hits
total: 87 hits

21.   **present in future in future: e.g.** *will be going to be taking*
query [*will be going to be taking*]: no hits
query [*will be going to be*] + present participle *of any verb*: no hits
wildcard query [*will _ be going to be*] + present participle *of any verb*: no hits
non-finite query [*be going to be*]: no relevant hits
total: no hits

22.   **future in past in past: e.g.** *had been going to take*
query [*had been going to take*]: 1 hit
query [*had been going to*] + infinitive *of any other verb*: 32 hits
> *She had been going to set it loose*
wildcard query [*had _ been going to*] + infinitive *of any verb*: 8 hits
total: 41 hits

23.   **future in past in present: e.g.** *has been going to take*
query [*has/have been going to take*]: no hits
query [*has/have been going to*] + infinitive *of any verb*: 1 hit
> *They have been going to stay with Jack regularly for years*
wildcard query [*has/have _ been going to*] + infinitive *of any verb*: no hits
total: 1 hit

24.   **future in past in future: e.g.** *will have been going to take*
query [*will have been going to take*]: no hits
query [*will have been going to* + infinitive *of any verb*]: no hits
wildcard query [*will _ have been going to*] + infinitive *of any verb*: no hits
non-finite query [*have been going to*]: no relevant hits
total: no hits

25. **past in future in past in past: e.g. *had been going to have taken***
query [*had been going to have taken*]: no hits
query [*had been going to have*] + past participle *of any verb*: no hits
wildcard query [*had _ been going to have*] + past participle *of any verb*: no hits
total: no hits

26. **past in future in past in present: e.g. *has been going to have taken***
query [*has/have been going to have taken*]: no hits
query [*has/have been going to have*] + past participle *of any verb*: no hits
wildcard query [*has/have _ been going to have*] + past participle *of any verb*: no hits
non-finite query [*been going to have*]: no hits
total: no hits

27. **past in future in past in future: e.g. *will have been going to have taken***
query [*will have been going to have taken*]: no hits
query [*will have been going to have*] + past participle *of any verb*: no hits
wildcard query [*will _ have been going to have*] + past participle *of any verb*: no hits
non-finite query [*have been going to have*]: no hits
total: no hits

28. **present in past in future in past: e.g. *was going to have been taking***
query [*was/were going to have been taking*]: no hits
query [*was/were going to have been*] + present participle *of any verb*: no hits
wildcard query [*was/were _ going to have been*] + present participle *of any verb*: no hits
non-finite query [*going to have been*]: no hits
total: no hits

29. **present in past in future in present: e.g. *is going to have been taking***
query [*am/are/is going to have been taking*]: no hits
query [*am/are/is going to have been*] + present participle *of any verb*: no hits

wildcard query [*am/are/is _ going to have been*] + present participle *of any verb*: no hits

non-finite query [*going to have been*]: no hits

total: no hits

30.   **present in past in future in future: e.g.** *will be going to have been taking*

query [*will be going to have been taking*]: no hits

query [*will be going to have been*] + present participle *of any verb*: no hits

wildcard query [*will _ be going to have been*] + present participle *of any verb*: no hits

non-finite query [*be going to have been*]: no hits

total: no hits

31.   **present in future in past in past: e.g.** *had been going to be taking*

query [*had been going to be taking*]: no hits

query [*had been going to be*] + present participle *of any verb*: no hits

wildcard query [*had _ been going to be*] + present participle *of any verb*: no hits

non-finite query [*been going to be*]: no hits

total: no hits

32.   **present in future in past in present: e.g.** *has been going to be taking*

query [*has/have been going to be taking*]: no hits

query [*has/have been going to be*] + present participle *of any verb*: no hits

wildcard query [*has/have _ been going to be*] + present participle *of any verb*: no hits

non-finite query [*been going to be*]: no hits

total: no hits

33.   **present in future in past in future: e.g.** *will have been going to be taking*

query [*will have been going to be taking*]: no hits

query [*will have been going to be*] + present participle *of any verb*: no hits

wildcard query [*will _ have been going to be*] + present participle *of any verb*: no hits

non-finite query [*have been going to be*]: no hits
total: no hits

34.   **present in past in future in past in past: e.g.** ***had been going to have been taking***
query [*had been going to have been taking*]: no hits
query [*had been going to have been*] + present participle *of any verb*: no hits
wildcard query [*had _ been going to have been*] + present participle *of any verb*: no hits
non-finite query [*been going to have been*]: no hits
total: no hits

35.   **present in past in future in past in present: e.g.** ***has been going to have been taking***
query [*has/have been going to have been taking*]: no hits
query [*has/have been going to have been*] + present participle *of any verb*: no hits
wildcard query [*has/have _ been going to have been*] + present participle *of any verb*: no hits
non-finite query [*been going to have been*]: no hits
total: no hits

36.   **present in past in future in past in future: e.g.** ***will have been going to have been taking***
query [*will have been going to have been taking*]: no hits
query [*will have been going to have been*] + present participle *of any verb*: no hits
wildcard query [*will _ have been going to have been*] + present participle *of any verb*: no hits
non-finite query [*have been going to have been*]: no hits
total: no hits

Index

Lightning Source UK Ltd.
Milton Keynes UK
27 August 2010

159054UK00002B/5/P